Spiritual Revolution

Spiritual Revolution

The Story of OM

Ian Randall

Authentic

MILTON KEYNES ● COLORADO SPRINGS ● HYDERABAD

14 13 12 11 10 09 08   7 6 5 4 3 2

First published 2008 by Authentic Media
9 Holdom Avenue, Bletchley, Milton Keynes, Bucks, MK1 1QR, UK
1820 Jet Stream Drive, Colorado Springs, CO 80921, USA
OM Authentic Media, Medchal Road, Jeedimetla Village,
Secunderabad 500 055, A.P., India
www.authenticmedia.co.uk

Authentic Media is a division of IBS-STL U.K., limited by guarantee,
with its Registered Office at Kingstown Broadway, Carlisle, Cumbria
CA3 0HA. Registered in England & Wales No. 1216232. Registered
charity 270162

British Library Cataloguing in Publication Data

A catalogue record for this book is available from the British Library

ISBN-13: 978-1-85078-766-2

Contents

Foreword

How do you capture fifty years of God's faithfulness in a relatively short volume? Fifty years of successes, failures, progress, regress. It's a tall order, but Ian Randall has done a brilliant job.

In a volume of this length we can only get the big picture. Thousands who have made a contribution to this ministry do not get a mention here. It is good to know that more complete records are kept in heaven!

Those of us in OM would want to say to all reading this, 'Give thanks and glory to God alone.' OM is a movement of ordinary people who have surrendered themselves, their gifts and their experience to God with the prayer – 'Lord, use us for your glory.'

In a quite remarkable way God has been pleased to answer that prayer and to a degree which constantly surprises and humbles us. As we have reached our fiftieth birthday, though we are thankful to God for what we have seen, the passion burns to see so much more. We will not rest until 'people from every tribe, tongue and nation' are ready to worship the Lamb with us eternally.

It is God who will bring this to pass, not OM, but we believe we have a continuing part to play in this great divine strategy. And so in our fiftieth year we find ourselves drawing towards the close of the largest project we have ever been involved in within OM Ships. We are struggling to adequately respond to all that God is doing in India. We have a renewed vision, born in the last few years, for the re-evangelisation of Europe. Opportunities in the Middle East, North Africa and West and Central Asia abound.

We could not, of course, be involved in all of this without our partners around the world – prayer and financial partners who are the backbone of this ministry. To you, and with thanks to God, we present this book, but also with the hope that this book will lead many others to partner with us.

Peter Maiden
International Director, Operation Mobilisation

Preface

When Peter Maiden, the International Director of Operation Mobilisation, asked if I would consider writing the history of OM to celebrate fifty years of the movement, I was delighted to say 'Yes.' I have known OM since the 1960s and have been an admirer of its founder, George Verwer, and of its highly enterprising approach to world mission.

Three people have worked closely with me as an editorial team on the project. The first is Peter Maiden. I have greatly valued Peter's wisdom and constant encouragement. The second is David Greenlee, OM's International Research Associate. Before taking that post, he served with OM Ships, completed doctoral studies at Trinity Evangelical Divinity School and was Field Leader of OM's ministries in a 'creative access' region. He and Vreni, his wife, currently live in Switzerland. As I have been writing, David has read and commented on my material with amazing rapidity and thoroughness, given me many contacts and suggested fruitful lines of enquiry. He also constructed the index. My third collaborator has been Peter Conlan, who, at my request, has written the final chapter of the OM story from his unique perspective. Peter has served with OM since the 1960s, first as an assistant ('gofer') to George Verwer, then helping to pioneer OM's Ship ministry. He continues to serve with the Ships' leadership team. Peter and Birgitta Conlan are my closest friends in OM and I am very grateful for their friendship. I have spent time with them researching Peter's splendid archive of OM documents – part of his much bigger collection of historical evangelical material.

Many other OMers and former OMers have kindly read through what I have written or have responded to queries. The list of names is too long for me to include here, but I am very thankful to each and have mentioned their names in the footnotes where appropriate. Three people I do wish to thank here by name, who have been with OM since its earliest days, are Jean Davey, Dale Rhoton and Jonathan McRostie. They have been unfailingly helpful as I have navigated my way through the story.

Parts of the OM story have been told already, and the bibliography includes a number of books written about aspects of OM and/or books by OMers or former OMers. Indeed, the purpose of the bibliography is to highlight these resources. I have relied on a number of these, most especially the splendid books by Elaine Rhoton on the *Logos* and the *Doulos*, OM's first two ships. I have also drawn from George Verwer's books, and have gained particular personal benefit from his *Out of the Comfort Zone*.[1] OM has had a huge influence on many people and on trends in mission in the twentieth century. The Appendix to this book contains an impressive list of ministries founded by former OMers. Despite this influence, the movement has been largely neglected in studies of world mission, including studies of short-term mission, which it helped to pioneer. The article on short-term missions in the *Evangelical Dictionary of World Missions*, for example, does not mention OM, and there is no entry on OM in the Dictionary.[2]

As well as a range of books from which I have drawn, a good deal of OM archive material exists in various places. I am very grateful to Vera Zabramski, George Verwer's PA for many years, who has given me access to documents held at the OM office in West Wickham, UK, and who has been an efficient facilitator of my research. Staff of OM India, particularly Alfy Franks and K. Lajja, kindly gave me valuable narratives relating to the Indian story and commented in detail on my drafts. I have also conducted a number of interviews, in person and by phone and e-mail. I am indebted to George Verwer for a most helpful interview with him, which gave me an excellent overall picture of the fifty years of the movement.

The book is enhanced by the photographs. These have come from many sources, and I am grateful to Birgitta and Peter Conlan and David Greenlee for their help in assembling them. Particular thanks go to Mike Wiltshire and Jean Davey for making their collections of photos available.

Of course there are many OMers who are not mentioned here – after all, well over one hundred thousand people have been with OM. In some cases, their work was sensitive and cannot be spoken about publicly. Many others did not find their way into the sources from which I have drawn. On this point, one reader wrote,

> your draft brought back memories ... What you have written is true. Incredible David and Goliath stories of God's sovereign power ... against such impossible odds. And stories of the 'unlikely individuals', 'jars of clay' that God threw into the mix, to show that 'this all-surpassing power is from Him and not from us' (2 Cor. 4:7). My joy is to remember all those that won't be mentioned, but that God used to do exploits.

Thank you also to Mark Finnie, Alison Hull, Kath Williams, Peter Little and all at Authentic Media for their contribution to the production of the book.

No doubt in trying to tell such a diverse story, set against a vast international backdrop, there are ways in which I have failed. For unintended misrepresentations or omissions, I apologise in advance. I hope, however, that I have managed to convey in these chapters something of the very significant place of OM within the history of mission and the remarkable vibrancy and quite astounding impact of this movement over the past fifty years.

During the time I have been researching OM's history and writing the book I have been working for two other remarkably vibrant institutions, the International Baptist Theological Seminary (IBTS) in Prague and Spurgeon's College in London. Over the years, my colleagues in these two creative centres of theological training have been an enormous encouragement to me. I was able to present some of my material on OM at post-graduate seminars at both IBTS and Spurgeon's. I am grateful to the coordinators of these events, Parush Parushev at IBTS and John Colwell at Spurgeon's, both of whom are valued friends, for these opportunities to engage in dialogue with students and teaching staff. I also want to pay warm tribute to the personal support I have received from Keith Jones, the Rector of IBTS, and Nigel Wright, the Principal of Spurgeon's.

Finally, I want to express my sincere thanks to my family. My cousin David, and my daughters Ailsa and Moragh, have been readers of, and commentators on, what I have written, and it has meant a great deal to me that they (completely unbiased as they are!) have enjoyed it so much. Janice, my wife, has helped me in many, many ways with the research, by carefully checking what I have written, and through keeping some balance to my life in the course of this project. Thank you to all!

I have tried to stress in this book what OM itself has stressed – that at the heart of all that has happened over the past fifty years has been a desire for authentic spirituality. I have felt the impact of this myself as I have written the book: I have been aware of the call to me always to seek to be an authentic disciple of Jesus Christ.

Ian Randall
International Baptist Theological Seminary
Prague
Czech Republic
Epiphany 2008

Chapter 1

Reckless Abandonment

Champagne corks popped, fireworks sparkled and midnight prayer vigils were held, as almost three billion people around the world welcomed the New Year – 1957. But that world was already changing. Half of Europe lay under the shadow of the Iron Curtain. In 1957, five Western European countries signed up to the Treaty of Rome, which led to the European Union. Mao Tse-tung, soon to implement his 'Great Leap Forward' in China, famously called for 'a hundred flowers' to bloom.[1] The USSR began the space race by launching Sputnik, the world's first artificial satellite. In the 'developing world', colonialism was collapsing as nations in Africa and elsewhere fought for independence. In America, Elvis Presley's *All Shook Up* was top of the charts.

Also that year, three unknown young students took a step of faith that would have consequences beyond their wildest dreams. Fifty years have passed since George Verwer, Dale Rhoton and Walter Borchard, then still in their teens, drove down Route 66 from Chicago towards Mexico City in a beat-up 1949 Dodge truck filled with Spanish gospels and tracts. This was the beginning of what was to become Operation Mobilisation (OM). An unlikely spiritual revolution had started.

This spiritual revolution was noted in a remarkable report written at the beginning of the 1960s to the Board of Emmaus Bible School, Illinois, USA, by William MacDonald, the evangelical school's respected President. He described 'a most welcome movement of the Holy Spirit among students mostly at Moody, Wheaton and Emmaus'. He noted how this had started in 1957 and how the group had grown and 'blanketed vast areas of Mexico with the gospel'. The young people from three colleges, all in the Chicago area – Moody Bible Institute, Wheaton College and Emmaus – had, he explained, banded together under the name 'Send the Light'. Some witnessing this movement, MacDonald continued, considered it a twentieth-century work of the Holy Spirit, with something of the power and fervour of Pentecost. He agreed. His summary of what he had seen in these students was dramatic: 'I must say that their reckless abandonment of everything for Christ is the most refreshing exhibition of New Testament Christianity I have ever seen.'[2]

We should go to Mexico

The leader of the group was George Verwer, who from 1958 to 1960 was a student at Moody. At the time William MacDonald was writing about the movement, George Verwer, as the director of Send the Light, was telling his own story. 'At the age of 14', he wrote, 'I was given a Gospel of St John in my high school and on the first page I signed a pledge promising to read it each day. I did this for three years before I was finally converted to the Lord.'[3] The gospel was given to him by Mrs Dorothea Clapp, an elderly lady who had prayed for eighteen years for the students in her local school, Ramsey High School – a school established in 1909 and regarded as one of the best in New Jersey. Mrs Clapp prayed that students would come to know Jesus Christ in a personal way; and daringly asked God that they would be witnesses for Christ in many parts of the world. In 1955, George Verwer made a personal commitment to Christ in Madison Square Garden, New York, at a rally organised by Jack Wyrtzen, the founder of an organisation called Word of Life. Billy Graham, who was to become the best-known evangelist in the world, was the speaker.[4]

It was obvious following his commitment to Christ that George Verwer was going to make a significant impact on others. He took advantage of his position as President of the Ramsey High School Student Council to connect with other students and distribute Gospels of John. Within a year, about two hundred of these fellow-students had made commitments to Christ. Already a budding entrepreneur, he went to the Grand Canyon on a fire extinguisher sales trip – and made what he later described as 'a deeper, more radical commitment to global missions and Christ'. For a time, Ramsey High School became a 'sending base': students who left it for further education continued to meet every day for prayer and to evangelise. George Verwer was struck that in the USA almost everyone owned *some* portion of the Bible, but this was far from the case in other countries. The first Gospel of John that George had received (through Mrs Clapp) had been made available by the Pocket Testament League (PTL) and he had started to raise money for the PTL even before his experience of personal faith.[5] By 1956, a vision was taking shape which George Verwer would carry forward with amazing results – a vision for the distribution of Christian literature on a massive scale.

In the autumn of 1956, George Verwer began studies at Maryville College, near Knoxville, Tennessee, and it was here that his convictions began to clarify. Maryville College, a private liberal arts college, was one of the fifty oldest colleges in the United States. George Verwer's parents, George and Eleanor, were connected with the Reformed Church of America, and Maryville's association with the Presbyterian Church (USA) made the college a natural choice.

At Maryville, George met two other students who were to launch out in mission with him: Walter Borchard, a fairly new Christian, and Dale Rhoton. Others soon became caught up in this work. Walter Borchard had never experienced the kind of vision and leadership he found in George Verwer. To be with George was to be caught up in a whirlwind of activity. Soon a small group was visiting schools, prisons and other places in the community. The emphasis was increasingly on books and literature. George's vision was expanded by attending a mission conference. The group also linked up with Youth for Christ (YFC) in Knoxville. YFC's verve and contemporary approach formed a key element in the growing strength of American evangelicalism.[6] Some Presbyterian leaders disliked the way the Maryville students carried out evangelism, but George was invited to speak in several local churches, especially Baptist churches. A number of students from this group went into full-time Christian ministry.[7]

Friendship with George Verwer altered the whole direction of Dale Rhoton's life. In 1960, in his report on Send the Light, George described how he had learned, while at Maryville, that 'south of the border, in Mexico, over 70 per cent of the people had not one portion of the Scriptures'. On reading this, he felt 'that God wanted me to dedicate my summers to distributing Gospels there instead of the United States'. Always a team-builder, he immediately presented the challenge to Dale and, as he put it, 'we bowed in prayer to commit the entire matter to the Lord'.[8]

Dale Rhoton's version has more colour. He wrote: 'After one of George's typically fiery passionate loud prayers I began a rather phlegmatic prayer. I was stunned when in the middle of my prayer he suddenly stood up and shouted, "I got it!"' Not surprisingly, Dale asked what he had got.

> His [George's] answer: 'We should go to Mexico in the summer.' That was the first he had mentioned Mexico to me and he wanted an immediate positive response. I said I would have to pray about it. We were quickly back on our knees and a few minutes later he again put the question to me, 'Well, are you ready to go?' 'George, it takes longer than that.' I'll never forget the pained look on his face as he lamented, 'Why does it take people so long to see it?'[9]

The incident is revealing. George Verwer had an amazing assurance, even in his late teens, that he was in touch with God's will and that others should follow his lead. He questioned himself frequently but there were also many very significant moments when he simply felt that he had grasped what had to be done and expected others to 'see it'. Dale Rhoton's experience was often to be repeated. He wrote: 'I did "see it" and I did go.' Yet, as with many of the developments associated with George Verwer, at the time there was no longer-term strategy. In 1957 Dale saw the trip to Mexico as a strictly one-off trip – a short-term mission outreach.[10] But a number of those who were involved, including him, also had long-term aims in mission. Although Operation Mobilisation, which developed out of these events in 1957, has been perceived as essentially 'short-term', many of its earliest members were in fact committed to career Christian service from the start.

It is also worth noting that others in the USA had been involved in short-term mission before, including mission in Mexico. Jim Elliot, a student at Wheaton College, whose missionary service led to his death, worked in Mexico for six weeks in 1947, learning from a local missionary family.[11] Another example is Loren Cunningham, who in the summer of 1954, aged eighteen, joined a group of Christians on a short-term mission trip to Mexico. In 1960, after Bible school and university, he started a mission aimed at sending out large numbers of young people for shorter and longer periods – Youth With a Mission (YWAM).[12] In the 1960s, a meeting between George Verwer and Loren Cunningham began a friendship that would impact both movements, OM and YWAM, in years to come.

Moving one step at a time

In 1957, George Verwer believed he was being led to pioneer rather than copy others. He, Dale Rhoton and Walter Borchard, all students without financial resources, sold some of their possessions to raise money for a mission trip. George was later to see 1957 as one of the most important years in his life, both because of Mexico and because in the early part of the summer vacation he began to evangelise door-to-door and in other ways in New Jersey.

The door-to-door evangelism included what was to become a long-term hallmark of OM – selling Christian books. Often these sales financed the outreach. At this early stage in his missional thinking, George Verwer took steps to set up Send the Light (STL), which was formally established as a publishing and literature distribution company in 1958. His mother did most of the administration for several years. Among the books being sold in 1957 was the recently published *Through Gates of Splendor* by

Jim Elliot's widow, Elisabeth.[13] Also in 1957, the huge Billy Graham Crusade was underway in Madison Square Garden – by June 1957 the total attendance had passed the half-million mark and the closing service attracted one hundred thousand people to Yankee Stadium.[14] George Verwer seized the opportunity this afforded to organise buses to take people to hear Billy Graham.

The weeks spent in New Jersey in the summer of 1957 also provided the young students with further important contacts. For example, they met the sister of John Beekman, a Wycliffe Bible translator in Mexico. A number of New Jersey businessmen gave financial support to George Verwer's proposals. In 1958, when a Board of Trustees for Send the Light was set up, several became Board members. Another crucial contact was Kenneth Taylor, then at Moody Bible Institute and later to become internationally famous through his production of *The Living Bible*.[15] Moody had been established in 1886 by the great American evangelist, D.L. Moody, and in 1894 Moody Publishers had been founded. In the 1950s those working at Moody were still committed to the vision of publishing books to reach a large audience, including non-Christians. George Verwer was able to tap into this strategic resource, and Taylor helped to provide ten thousand Gospels of John in Spanish for the Mexican outreach. Filled with anticipation, George, Walter and Dale set off for Mexico in 1957 in what was to become their legendary 1949 Dodge truck, having managed to add twenty thousand tracts to the ten thousand Gospels.[16]

George Verwer later described what happened on that first trip to Mexico:

> Within seven days, almost all of our literature was gone. We saw people fight to get a Gospel of St. John. We saw people run across fields to pick up a Gospel tract. As we travelled along the roads, we saw and talked with hundreds of people who had never even seen a portion of God's Word. After that first summer in Mexico, I knew that God wanted me on the mission field as soon as possible.[17]

In the meantime, there were further short-term mission ventures that could be pursued. George Verwer immediately began to make plans to return to Mexico, in the summer of 1958. 'At that stage,' he said fifty years later, 'I didn't have a global dream; I was moving one step at a time, thinking especially of those parts of the world where people had never received a gospel.' Although there was a spirit of 'reckless abandonment', there was also realism. The 'step at a time' approach has been characteristic of OM. Although the dream George had in 1957 was not a clear one, as he himself explained, it was a dream that the Scriptures, the word of God for all people, should be made as widely available as possible.[18]

Maryville College was now too restrictive for George Verwer. In January 1958 he transferred to Moody Bible Institute. Dale Rhoton had already transferred to Wheaton College and Walter Borchard, whose career was to be in social work, followed suit. They were now close to a whole network of evangelical connections in the Chicago area. Walter has described George as being 'in heaven at Moody'.[19] As part of the new generation of evangelical leaders emerging in America,[20] George Verwer shared their confidence that the evangelical message was utterly relevant to the contemporary world.[21]

Among the influences on the group at Moody was Oswald J. Smith, of the People's Church, Toronto, whose book, *Passion for Souls*,[22] had a powerful impact. The Navigators, founded by Dawson Trotman, with their stress on Bible study, memorisation of Scripture and discipleship, were growing significantly in the 1950s. Their emphases and their booklet *Born to Reproduce* also helped to shape OM. In addition, in the late 1950s the Wheaton College community in particular was feeling the enormous impact and challenge of the death of Jim Elliot and his four colleagues, who in the course of their mission to reach the Waorani (Auca), an indigenous people of Ecuador, had all been killed in 1956. Many who joined OM, and especially early OMers, were familiar with Jim Elliot's words, 'He is no fool who gives what he cannot keep to gain that which he cannot lose.'[23] Elisabeth Elliot was later to become a friend of OM and a speaker at OM conferences.

As well as absorbing these influences, George Verwer began to exert his own remarkable influence on a circle of students and

others whom he met. From time to time, he was given the opportunity to speak for a few minutes in the Moody Chapel.[24] In the
summer of 1958, three Moody students went with him to Mexico
and met Baldemar Aguilar, a young Mexican, who agreed to
work with them. This step was to lead to a crucial element marking OM's international development – the early recognition,
affirmation and support of local leadership. Baldemar Aguilar
became the Mexican director of the STL work. The Bible Medita-
tion League of Columbus, Ohio, donated over twenty-five thousand pieces of literature, including one thousand Gospels of John,
for distribution. During this summer mission a modern Christian
bookstore was opened in Saltillo, the capital of the state of
Coahuila. Other Mexican evangelical bookstores were to follow.
A prayer letter issued in 1958 by STL, from New Jersey and
Mexico, described how the team found one bookstore containing
literature that attracted their attention. 'We were greatly
impressed', said the letter, 'with the fine quality printing we
found.' Then the team realised that it was communist literature.[25]

The need to reach out in the countries where communism was a
significant force, and especially in countries that were dominated
by communist governments, became a major theme in OM.
George Verwer highlighted not only the need for witness but also
the global threat of communism. The *New Jersey Paterson Evening News* of 16 November 1961 reported: 'Verwer says, Reds
plan to dominate world!' This was in line with much of the anti-
communist rhetoric that marked North America in this period. At
OM events, examples of the tremendous dedication of communists to their cause were used to challenge evangelical believers to
even greater dedication to Christ and to mission. The printed page
was a major way of communicating in this period, used internationally by both communists and evangelical Christians, with
OM being at the forefront of the global evangelical literature
campaign.

Two other new Mexican STL initiatives in the summer of 1958
were a free Bible correspondence course and a broadcasting venture. These were patterned on the Emmaus Bible School method.
In 1949, William MacDonald saw the potential of study courses

not only for Christians but also for use in evangelism, and so the course *What the Bible Teaches* was launched. Following this, sections of the material were broadcast over the radio. Moody Bible Institute had also pioneered Christian radio (as early as 1926). The STL correspondence course started in a small way but the number of students grew rapidly, among them a group of inmates from the Monterrey prison.[26] The radio programmes were, like the opening of the first bookstore, regarded as something humanly impossible. It was commonly believed that the Mexican government did not permit religious broadcasting anywhere in the country. This broadcast was allowed, however, because it advertised the items on sale in the bookstore and was regarded as commercial broadcasting.[27]

Believe God

The Mexican connections now began to expand. Initially very few evangelical churches in Mexico were involved, but the number grew rapidly. Links were made with Methodist, Baptist and Pentecostal congregations. George Verwer found it especially encouraging to preach in Pentecostal churches, where despite his broken Spanish his messages were received with great enthusiasm.[28] Transdenominationally, Youth for Christ was expanding internationally – Billy Graham had been YFC's first and very effective field representative – and at a Youth for Christ Congress in Mexico City, George Verwer's team was asked to handle the literature.[29] The desire to cooperate with a range of churches and other agencies was to be another feature of OM.

In the autumn of 1958, back at Moody and Wheaton in particular, the students who had been to Mexico met together daily for prayer. Crucial themes now began to emerge in the area of spirituality, such as 'forsaking all' to follow Christ, as the early disciples did, and spiritual 'victory'. In this context, the truly committed life was contrasted with the life of the 'chocolate soldier' – the title of an uncompromising booklet by a missionary hero, C.T. Studd. At the same time, there was an insistence on 'esteeming others'

better than oneself and on 'believing the best' about others.
Young people who were interested in becoming part of the emerging movement had to listen to several hours of 'orientation tapes'
on OM themes.[30] Among the subjects covered were prayer and the
word of God, love for Christ, the importance of unity and good
relationships, and the necessity of self-discipline in the work of
the Lord. William MacDonald referred to this orientation in positive terms as something 'that leaves one humbled, inspired and
invigorated'.[31]   The orientation was intended to foster an
approach to spirituality that was owned by the whole group.

The vision espoused by the student group was attractive. Jean
Hall (later Davey), a student at Moody, found George Verwer
'loud (and) dominant' when she first met him in 1958, but she was
inspired by his weekly meetings at Moody – in particular by the
stress on spiritual struggle, prayer and love as motives for mission. She saw in the meetings a combination of humour, joy and
fervour. Since she could speak some Spanish, she expressed interest in the next Mexican mission, but initially girls were not
invited. However, it was decided a carload of girls could become
part of the Christmas 1958 mission. Jean was not included at first,
but one girl dropped out and Jean asked George what she would
need in order to go. The reply was: 'Believe God for $90.' This
was a considerable sum, but two days later a cheque for precisely
this amount arrived.[32] The principle adopted in OM was that each
person joining the movement should find their own finances, 'believing God' for provision and not telling others about their
needs.

The language of 'believe God' was to become common, sometimes in the form of a question: 'What are you believing God for?'
At one OM summer conference George said: 'This work is so
geared that even one day of unbelief can set us back weeks.'[33] Jean
wrote a letter in early December 1958 which captures the excited,
faith-filled atmosphere of the first Christmas outreach: 'Not long
ago I met a group of fellows who had been doing missionary work
in Mexico during their vacations. I was amazed to hear how God
had wonderfully blessed their work…They are going into Mexico
again over Christmas and I feel definitely that God is leading me

to go with them. This is a big step of faith for me.' Taking the 'step of faith' was crucial. She asked for prayer for the three Mexican STL full-time workers, other Mexican part-time workers, the bookstore and the radio broadcasts.[34]

STL letters stressed the support coming from Protestant pastors.[35] Working with local churches in seeking to fulfil the vision was to be another theme of OM. The movement sometimes spoke of itself as an 'outreach agency of the local church'. However, financial needs were not shared with churches – unless the churches enquired.

Greg Livingstone, a student at Wheaton who was intent on becoming a lawyer, was another person who was challenged by George about 'believing God'. In 1959 Dale Rhoton invited Greg Livingstone to an all-night prayer meeting at Moody. Such a thing had not been part of Greg's experience at his little Baptist church in Aspen, Colorado, but he decided to attend. The focus was on 'The Muslim world'. When he arrived, he found a group of young men, on their knees on hard wooden floors, praying over maps of various countries. He reached out to shake hands with George Verwer, who immediately demanded, 'What country are you claiming, brother?' Not wanting to be perceived as less spiritual than the others, Greg asked, 'What's left?' 'Libya ... you got Libya,' was the reply. Libya was pointed out on the map, and Greg spent the next several hours in a prayer circle asking God to send workers there. 'That night in October 1959', Greg Livingstone said later, 'God opened my eyes that my ambitions were too small.'[36]

The first Christmas STL mission in Mexico saw Dick Griffin, a student at Moody, also joining the movement. George Verwer challenged Dick: 'Pray about going down to Mexico.' As Dick Griffin recounts the story, he replied by asking what it would cost. In typical style, he was told by George: 'It'll cost you your life.'[37] Dick and his wife Helen were to remain in Mexico for the whole of their ministry. In total, twenty-eight people were involved by the end of 1958. Someone in Chicago who had recently become a Christian donated a two and a half ton truck to carry the large amounts of literature being transported to Mexico. George

Verwer later wrote: 'One mechanic said [the truck] would not make it out of Chicago, but by the power of God it went to Mexico City and back with a quarter-million pieces of literature and ten young men.'[38]

The use of unlikely and unpromising vehicles such as the Dodge truck was to be a continuing – indeed central – theme in Operation Mobilisation. Jean Hall wrote in her diary (20 December 1958) in typical terms about her transport to Mexico – in an 'old dusty car'. This stress on the basic nature of the transport was in line with the overall vision of simple living and, in addition, the unlikely vehicles in some ways mirrored the idea of using inexperienced people who would not have found a place in other missions. Jean also noted the place of the women on the team she joined. 'The five of us girls', she wrote, 'are packed neatly into the car under coats, blankets and sandwiches.' She stressed that the truck came 'as a direct answer to prayer'.[39] A later report described seven girls 'crushed into a Chevrolet sedan' on the way to Mexico. The boot (trunk) was filled and there were blankets and packages of literature taking up every bit of space.[40] Much longer journeys would characterise OM teams in the future, and sleeping in vans and trucks would became a common feature.

The emphasis on prayer has to be taken fully into account in order to understand the spirituality of OM. At Moody a classroom was made available to the STL group and daily prayer meetings were held. Prayer was the heartbeat. George Verwer suggested people get into little groups to pray, which was a new style of praying. Maps were used to direct intercession for countries. There was also confession: the group used the New Testament language of 'walking in the light'. George Verwer was always ready to acknowledge his mistakes, and this had a powerful impact on the group. All-night prayer meetings were held, and George asked Alan Redpath, a British Baptist minister who was pastor of the Moody Memorial Church in Chicago, if all-night prayer could take place in the church. Alan Redpath not only permitted this, but participated, and was later to be an OM conference speaker. William MacDonald commented: 'When these young people get on their knees before God, it is a sheer privilege to be present. The prayers are short, fervent and specific. Some are punctuated by a cry from the heart, "Lord, break me."' There were 'faith-filled' prayers for the world. 'To them', he added, 'it is faithless to speak of countries being closed to the gospel. Such an attitude, they feel, degrades God as being powerless. When one of them finished praying for Russia at an all-night prayer meeting, Krushchev looked like a midget, according to a visitor.'[41]

As this new movement was beginning to grow within the student community in North America, in other parts of the Western world there was a decline in traditional missionary activity. In wider Western society, especially from the early 1960s, secularism was advancing. There were also significant moves towards independence among national churches in what had been traditional missionary locations.[42] The gradual decline of Christianity in Europe meant that there was something of a crisis in the West – could Europe still be a mission-sending area? The 'mission base' seemed increasingly to be a 'mission field'.[43] By contrast, it was with a feeling of confidence – 'believing God' – that George Verwer and his young associates launched out. Western decline in world mission commitment does not appear to have been a major factor motivating them.[44] Rather they saw a general need, and their response helped to change the face of world mission. The decline of Christianity in Europe was, however, important in one respect: it presented George Verwer with a challenge, and was to lead to his departure from the USA to set up mission bases in Spain, Britain and Belgium.[45]

Spiritual Pied Pipers

The Christmas 1958 mission to Mexico was a turning point. Instead of George Verwer travelling south with two or three other students, nineteen mission members from outside Mexico participated. A similar number returned in June 1959. Over the summer the Mexican correspondence course enrolment rose to three thousand and the Mexican staff of Send the Light increased to ten. By the end of the summer, 150 churches across the country were co-operating in the STL mission.[46] A modern bookshop was opened in the centre of Mexico City (The Bookstore of the Abundant Life) and in the course of seven months, over half a million evangelical books and tracts were sold or given away. Supporting missions included Moody Bible Literature, Back to the Bible Broadcast and Christian Literature Crusade. Increasing numbers of students linked up with George Verwer at Moody, and a number of these were to stay long-term with OM. The closest links beyond Moody, Wheaton and Emmaus were with other well-known American evangelical schools such as Taylor College, Houghton College and Asbury College.[47]

Christmas 1959 saw forty-nine students going to Mexico, including Jonathan McRostie, who had studied at Moody and Wheaton and who would become a central OM leader, based in Europe. Among the other STL leaders were Bob Cook, George Verwer's Spanish teacher at Moody, and Jean Hall. Other girls on the 1959 campaign included Betty Snavely (later Holt), Barbara Bowker, who later married Mainard Tom, and Helen Scantling, who married Dick Griffin and remained in Mexico. A few months after the mission, Jean and Betty graduated from Moody: they were among the considerable number of Moody graduates who would serve with OM. In the Christmas 1959 outreach, seven thousand Gospels of John were sold, along with several thousand books, all in the space of ten days. A bookstore opened in Guadalajara, the second largest city in Mexico.[48] William Mac-Donald wrote: 'These young people are spiritual Pied Pipers. There is something alluring and winsome about lives that are so sold out to Jesus Christ, and everywhere they go, they find some others to face up to the claims of Jesus Christ.'[49]

To be 'sold out to Jesus Christ' was to take very seriously what it meant to be a disciple. It meant acting on what Jesus said. If his instructions were to give away your coat to someone in need (Mt. 5:40), then there was no alternative to giving away the coat. Dale Rhoton offered an example of how George Verwer implemented this teaching:

While preaching in a small church in greater Mexico City, [George Verwer] was overwhelmed by the generosity of a collection that was taken. It was not so much money but he knew the people had given sacrificially. The pastor accompanied George to his van to say good-bye. George asked the pastor if he had a suit. 'No', he replied. George responded, 'I have plenty of clothes.' It was night and the pastor could not see what was going on. George took his suit off, handed it to him and drove off. It was quite a sight to see a young, skinny George Verwer in his underwear around midnight knocking on the door of the Christian bookshop where the team was staying.[50]

This incident was typical of George, and he drew around him others who embraced the same revolutionary and sacrificial outlook.[51] 'Don't try to get the biggest apple' was a common saying. A key verse used in thinking about discipleship was Luke 14:33. The one who wanted to be a disciple of Jesus had to 'forsake all'.[52]

Disciples were also in the business of training more disciples. The radical nature of the discipleship in the STL group constantly drew others. From the very beginning, the movement that became OM was characterised not only by mission work but also by equipping leaders. Often new Christians – usually young people – were given demanding responsibility very quickly. Reporting on the Christmas 1959 mission, George Verwer stated: 'A young man named Daniel accepted Christ in the streets of Guadalajara and became a full time worker.' His report also talked about a Mexican, Fortunato, who 'after reading the Gospel, asked Dick Griffin (who will take over my work in Mexico) how he could find Christ as his Savior. He, too, received Christ and is now working full time in our correspondence school.'[53] Perhaps in an unconscious way, what was happening through some of these students in the 1950s was an outworking of D.L. Moody's original vision – but in new forms. D.L. Moody wanted to train Christian workers – 'gap-men' (although they included women) – who would, as he put it, function 'in the gap' between the laity and ministers. Relatively few of those who gathered around George

Verwer became ordained ministers, but several became pioneers in world mission.

Perhaps it was precisely this 'fast track' into active ministry that had special attraction for young people in the post-war period. Entry into ordained ministry in one of the major denominations, and indeed into quite a number of missionary societies, was often possible only after more extended theological training. Students at Moody, Wheaton and Emmaus were clearly not against training, but as they recruited others into their movement, there appears to have been no particular emphasis on formal theological study. This was in line with the thinking of the 'faith missions' and was also influenced by the Brethren movement. At the core of Brethren thinking was the desire to connect directly with and seek to restore the pattern of the New Testament church.[54] The Brethren saw no distinction between clergy and laity and believed passionately in local churches – usually termed assemblies – encouraging members (usually male) into ministry.[55] George Verwer's own instincts were transdenominational, but he was baptised (by Dale Rhoton) in a Brethren assembly. William MacDonald, who was a leading Brethren figure, wrote that several of the student group (perhaps not all) 'seek to labour with a view to gathering converts together according to the teachings of the New Testament'.[56]

Another feature that attracted the young people who went to Mexico was the idea of 'living by faith', an idea closely associated with nineteenth-century Brethren leaders such as George Müller and Anthony Norris Groves, or faith mission 'father-figures' such as Hudson Taylor of the China Inland Mission (CIM) – who was influenced by the Brethren.[57] It was commonly believed that Müller never made known the financial needs of his massive orphanage work, although in fact his way of operating was quite complex.[58] However, in the early days of OM, questions about finances would probably be answered by a statement like: 'Our great need is for prayer.' This was later to change, as we will see, and indeed from the beginning of OM, people in business contributed significantly to the work. But there was a radical challenge in the early period to abandon all securities, especially guaranteed income, and to rely on God. Compared to the Iron Curtain or Bamboo Curtain, the 'luxury curtain' of the USA was seen as a bigger barrier to mission. The lure of luxury had to be resisted: in Mexico, for example, many team members were living on one dollar per day.

This idea of living by faith and in very simple ways was initially being worked out in the 1950s among single students. In January 1960, however, George Verwer and Drena Knecht were married. The background was that one day in autumn 1958 George went to the Moody Science Films office, met the very attractive secretary, Drena, from Wisconsin, and was smitten. By the summer of 1959, they were engaged and Drena joined the STL group going to Mexico City. Drena longed to be on the mission field and she was not put off, even when George impressed upon her that if she married him, she might find herself doing mission among 'cannibals in New Guinea'.[59] That was the kind of mission she was expecting to do.[60] Dale Rhoton was a speaker at George and Drena's wedding reception, and his prediction that George would give away the wedding gifts was to be proved correct.[61]

Where others have not gone

By autumn 1959 the work in Mexico was taking root. Indigenous fellowship groups were emerging. For example, in Monterrey a group was meeting at the *basurero* – the city's garbage dump – to learn to read and to receive the message that 'God so loved the world'. Reports from the team – Dick Griffin, Dick Stevenson, Ruth Ford (later Nuscher) and Jean Hall – spoke of local people like Perfecta Ivarra, a mother of ten, being taught to read. STL letters noted that the stress on the love of God and practical living was resulting in personal commitments to Christ.[62] By 1960 there were more than four thousand students enrolled in STL's Bible correspondence course and students wishing to go further were encouraged to think about 'Concentrated Bible Study' through Emmaus. The combination of social and evangelistic ministry was associated by many evangelicals in the 1950s with a 'social gospel' which they rejected, but the combination was to become characteristic of OM and other evangelical agencies.[63] Mainard Tom, whose roots were in Hawaii, became leader of the STL group at Moody. By this time George Verwer wanted to move beyond Mexico. He wrote: 'We definitely feel God is leading us to go to places where others have not gone and to pray for things that others have not prayed for.'[64]

After their marriage in January 1960, George and Drena Verwer spent a few months living in Mexico City before moving to Spain. *Moody Memo* reported (on 18 March 1960) on events in this period that became legendary: 'George Verwer, a January graduate, and Drena Knecht, former Film Department secretary, were married in January and immediately set off in an old International truck (which mechanics said would never get out of Chicago) to continue the mission in Mexico.' Having no money and running low in petrol, they stopped at a filling station. George explained to the proprietor about their wedding and their mission and asked if they could exchange the wedding cake (in fact this was one of their two wedding cakes) for petrol. The proprietor said: 'I'm a Christian. I'll fill your tank and you keep the cake.' The same thing happened a second time. The report concluded: 'But the third time the proprietor was not a Christian so he took the wedding cake.'[65]

George Verwer had set his sights on work in Europe and in the Middle East, and in October 1960 Jean Hall received a letter from Mainard Tom, written on a Moody Bible Institute table napkin. It read: 'George says you and Betty Snavely should go to Spain as soon as you see your money come in. PS: Benjamin Baldemar Verwer born.'[66] The features of this early period are marked: people were being mobilised for global mission; money was being saved – hence the napkin; and the birth of a young Verwer was certainly important, but for Mainard Tom it was (as suggested by the 'PS') secondary.

If the aim was to 'go to places where others have not gone' then Mexico and Spain were not obvious destinations. There was a history of Protestant mission in Spain. However, like Mexico, Spain was a Roman Catholic country in which the Protestant evangelical presence was relatively weak. Also, those who had learned Spanish in order to engage in the mission in Mexico could transfer that skill to Spain. The STL reports from Mexico highlighted the issues that came up in Catholic settings. For example: 'In one area the priest sent notices threatening the people with excommunication if they so much as retained literature from the "extensive Protestant crusade".' One woman was interested in buying a book by Billy Graham, *The Secret of Happiness*,[67] and commented: 'Is there such a thing as happiness?' She was apologetic when she turned down the book: 'I'm sorry. I am a Catholic and we aren't permitted to read your books.' At times a more ecumenical note might be sounded. In western Mexico 'the Mother Superior of a Catholic Convent in San Pedro bought our books for all the priests to read'. One lay person said: 'I bought this book several months ago and have recommended it to the Padre Superior.'[68] On the whole, there was very limited recognition (if any) among either Catholics or Protestants of a common Christian heritage. Spain was viewed as 'closed' to active missionary work. For STL this made it a magnet.

Spain was not, however, the only country in view. There was an awareness of the massive challenges for Christianity posed by Islam and communism. Two Wheaton students began to plan to move to Turkey. One was Dale Rhoton, who was a member of a Brethren assembly that met near the Wheaton College campus. He had originally imagined he would become a Wycliffe Bible translator and had gone through their summer programme. The other was Roger Malstead, also in the Brethren. Roger had already been involved in YFC activities and work among migrants in southern California and Mexico before coming to Wheaton in 1959. He became involved in George's meetings. By 1961 both Dale and Roger were in Turkey, and they are rightly regarded as helping to pioneer a new stage in the growth of the evangelical presence in that country. In 2005 the Brethren magazine *Uplook* commented that 'in 1961 at age 19, Roger Malstead and Dale Rhoton (Wheaton students, sent from assemblies in the US and working with OM) began the modern era of outreach in Turkey'.[69]

Roger Malstead achieved fame, or notoriety, during his presidency of the freshman class at Wheaton in 1959–60. He resigned from this office in protest over the way money was being spent, money that could have been given away. He then transferred, in 1960, to Biola College, California, to continue his studies before joining George Verwer in Europe and going to the Middle East.

Conclusion

Richard Tiplady, in *World of Difference*, speaks about three waves in Protestant mission.[70] The first, in the eighteenth century, is associated especially with William Carey and the Baptist Missionary Society (BMS), although Carey himself drew from the earlier Moravian movement in central Europe.[71] The mid-nineteenth century saw the rise of the second wave, the faith missions, most notably the China Inland Mission (later the Overseas Missionary Fellowship).[72] Tiplady sees the third wave as coming in the 1950s and 1960s, with mission organisations such as YWAM, Operation Mobilisation, Frontiers and World Horizons, all of which have combined training, mission and discipleship within their programmes. He draws attention to whole generations of students being trained through these movements.[73] There have been other waves: for example, in America in the later nineteenth century Arthur T. Pierson and the Student Volunteers were very important, with their motto 'The evangelisation of the world in this generation.' [74]

There is no doubt, however, that something new and dynamic developed in the 1950s. From small beginnings, George Verwer and others pioneered the idea of short-term mission projects utilising large numbers of young people, many of them students. Some of the ideas were drawn from elsewhere and in the late 1950s there were no fully worked-out plans. Nor was it the case that 'short-term' was seen as an end in itself. An important goal was that from among the short-termers there would be those who would make mission their life's work. In terms of practicalities, the availability of faster modes of transport was a crucial factor in enabling short-term mission to take place, and transport was to figure largely in OM's story. But woven through all of this was a fresh spiritual energy, and the energy generated among the young people who came together around George Verwer was to contribute to a spiritual revolution in world mission. 'Some Christians', commented William MacDonald, 'call them fanatics'. His view was: 'They are – in every good sense in which the word can be used of humble, energetic, dedicated believers.'[75] The impact of the members of this group, and of the many others who subsequently joined OM, was to be of great significance for the direction of world mission.

Chapter 2

A Revolution of Love

Amid much talk of social and political revolution in the 1960s, OM used the language of the 'revolution of love'. This period saw the birth of Operation Mobilisation as a movement. Within a few years, the small numbers of students involved in mission to Mexico had spawned OM, a movement that drew in and mobilised thousands of young people. From the autumn of 1960, Americans began to arrive in Spain, forming a small group by autumn 1961, and in the summer of 1962 the first Operation Mobilisation summer campaign across Europe took place, with two hundred young people participating. A year later, 1963 saw outreach taking place on a much larger scale, attracting young people from thirty countries, and a mission strategy was put together. A statement produced after this outreach explained: 'Operation Mobilization believes that the Christian Church needs a revolution – a revolution of love!' It also echoed the nineteenth-century idea of 'evangelising the world in this generation', asserting: 'We are convinced that the proclaiming of Jesus Christ throughout the world will become a reality in this generation. The strategy was then set out. 'We encourage believers to take out a summer, several months, or a year from their work or studies.' OM also wanted to work with local churches. 'We are not a new denomination or mission board but attempt to work as servants with the established, local churches wherever we go.'[1] Many of the early emphases, such as literature distribution, continued.[2] This chapter looks at how these goals were achieved in Europe and the Middle East in the 1960s.

An open door

In autumn 1960, George, who was by then living with Drena and their son Benjamin in Madrid, wrote that there was an 'open door' for the gospel in Spain. This was a very different perspective to the one usually presented by evangelicals about Spain during Franco's regime. The 'open door' in Spain did not exist, George said, because the government had allowed evangelical literature to be printed and distributed (it had not), but because some Roman Catholics had written good books and there had been recent, modern translations of the Bible which could be sold and distributed legally in Spain. He referred to several books, such as *A Dios por La Ciencia* ('To God through Science'),[3] a Catholic book which he considered 'one of the best Christian books I have seen', and the new Bible translations – such as a translation of the gospels which 'has a text that seems to be the best I have read in Spanish'. He added that it would be worth opening a store just to sell this Good News version.[4]

The small team around the Verwers comprised Jean Hall, Betty Snavely and Mike and Diana McKinley (with their two small children). The team members were connected with each other through Moody. Betty Snavely, who was surprised to find herself in Madrid, wrote: 'All my life, up until this point, I had believed that only rich people and missionaries traveled overseas.' She spoke of herself as 'a nobody from an unknown family, with no personal wealth'. Yet despite this she had the goal of 'somehow penetrating the Iron Curtain'.[5]

The team members distributed evangelical literature and printed tracts and newsletters in a home outside Madrid. One major method of distribution was by mail. Taking addresses from the Spanish telephone directory (a five-volume book), letters were sent offering a free Gospel of John and a correspondence course. A Portuguese return address was used. Four Spanish young people were engaged full-time on this project, and during the first two years over twenty thousand people replied.[6]

As in Mexico, a rented bookstore was soon opened in Madrid, with living quarters at the back. The bookshop emphasised that it sold books that were acceptable to the Catholic Church and it also stocked postage stamps. George Verwer was interested in philately and his supporters sent stamps, sometimes whole collections, to be sold. He had found out that there were thousands of stamp collectors in Madrid. This stamp dealership brought people into the shop and helped to raise money. Advertising space was bought at Metro stops and through the advertising, including a competition and prizes, people were introduced to biblical texts.[7] In the light of this, there were unusual prayer requests. A November 1960 letter urged readers: 'Pray that many stamp collectors will get the vision to sell all – and that soon stamps will be here to sell and be used in the Lord's work.'[8] The theme in these prayer letters was 'believing prayer' for enterprises on a much larger scale. Doing a mail-out to a million people in Spain would, it was noted, cost $24,000. The Verwers were 'trusting God' to bring this in. 'We must enter into more believing prayer.' This hymn by Charles Wesley was often sung and quoted:

Faith, mighty faith
The promise sees,
And looks to God alone.
Laughs at impossibilities,
And cries, 'It shall be done.'[9]

Looking 'to God alone' was important, but so too was creative initiative.

By the summer of 1961 a Spanish director, Federico Aparisi, was in place, working from 7 am to 11 pm, sleeping and eating in the office where mailings of literature were organised. The team members worshipped at the large Brethren assembly in Madrid on the Calle de Trafalgar – where George Verwer had recruited Federico. The Madrid authorities tried to stop the team's mailings, but their efforts were thwarted because mail was sent from many different locations. In addition to posting hundreds of thousands of letters, the team drove around putting them into mailboxes and doorways, sometimes all day and night, covering entire towns. 'In a sense', George commented, 'it is a battle of wits.'[10]

The initial group was joined by fifteen more Americans who arrived in Algeciras, southern Spain, by ship in September 1961. Most were graduates of Moody, Wheaton or Emmaus, and had taken part in outreach in Mexico. Following a month-long conference in Madrid, they spent a year in France, Belgium, Switzerland, Austria, Germany and Spain, recruiting European young people for the 1962 summer outreach. Distribution of literature in Spain increased. There were also crucial personal contacts. In October 1961, Christa Fischer (later Eicher), an East German, approached the Madrid team about work. Although they could not help, George Verwer gave her a copy in German of *Peace with God*, by Billy Graham,[11] and within a few days she committed her life to Christ, turned down a high paying job and joined the team.[12]

Mike McKinley and Federico Aparisi were the same age (24), friends from the Brethren; but the Spaniard was the leader. He became, said Mike McKinley, 'my mentor', 'his knowledge and wisdom were beyond me at the time'. This fitted well with the OM vision for local, indigenous leadership operating in a multi-cultural team setting.

These team members were often arrested and questioned. One lady who took books showed them to her husband who was in the secret police, and the team was rounded up.[13] There were also some light-hearted moments, as different cultural attitudes were highlighted.[14] Divergence within the team over a range of cultural issues was a foretaste of what would happen on many future occasions in the history of OM. Team members in Spain had to adapt in various ways. They initially lived and worked out of one crowded flat, the centre for the Spanish team, although later more spacious accommodation in a building near the Plaza de Castilla Metro station was found.[15] Cooking was done on simple stoves. Gradually they obtained furniture. Surplus clothing was donated and kept for those who might need it – this system was later known in OM as 'Charlie'.

Many methods used by the Spanish team were revolutionary. There were other Protestant missionaries working in more traditional fashion in Spain and Portugal, notably the Evangelical

Alliance Mission (TEAM). Some TEAM missionaries in this period also had links with both Wheaton College and Moody Bible Institute.[16] All the Protestant missionaries in Madrid knew each other and met up for prayer and fellowship. George Verwer was wary, however, of using the label 'Protestant'. He told the team in August 1961 that in witnessing they should remember that they were not 'Protestants' but rather 'a group of Christians of all different faiths' who were interested in bringing 'the Good News of the Gospel to everyone'.[17] OM contributed to the growth of a strand of church life which would tend to use the designation 'evangelical' rather than 'Protestant'.

This approach was not intended to downplay Christian heritage. In Spain, as elsewhere, the support of Brethren assemblies and other evangelical churches was seen as crucial. Federico Aparisi recruited Daniel González, also in the Brethren, who became a significant OM leader. In Portugal Estinio Herreros, a young pastor, was recruited.[18] As we will see, some pastors and leaders became critical of George Verwer, including some Brethren leaders, but in other Brethren assemblies support was strong. In 1967 George reported: 'I spoke in both of the new [Brethren] assemblies in the Barcelona area, as well as the large assembly with whom we work.' He added that almost four hundred were at the 'breaking of bread' (the Brethren term for Holy Communion) that Sunday morning – 'and because of that morning and because of that meeting a great volume of prayer will be going up on our behalf'.[19] It is not that George Verwer's own vision was in any way limited to Brethren life – Drena was Baptist, and later the family would settle in Bromley Baptist church in Kent, England. Rather his pragmatism meant that he looked for church contacts wherever these were to be found.[20]

Christ was a revolutionist

George Verwer longed to bring the gospel 'into closed countries'.[21] Spain was regarded as closed, but there were some 'open doors'. However, the communist countries presented few such openings. Hence it was natural, especially in the political context of the Cold War, to seek to address this challenge. In August 1961, Roger Malstead (now in Europe) and George Verwer, crossed through the Iron Curtain into Czechoslovakia, en route to Russia. George wrote to supporters describing how they had obtained a visa for Russia and stowed in their vehicle (an Opel station wagon) rubber stamps that would be used for printing Russian tracts and 1,700 gospels in Russian and Slovak. He explained that a letter which would soon follow (he was a prolific letter writer) would be from Russia – in code.[22] The excitement was palpable.

At first all went well. At the Czechoslovak border, the car was checked carefully but the literature and equipment were not found. After a successful crossing into the USSR, they started printing tracts in a hotel room. The plan, as in Spain, was to look up addresses in phone books and then to mail tracts. A seemingly insignificant incident, however, was to prove disastrous. 'Because some margarine had melted on a Gospel of John', George Verwer reported a month later, 'I decided to throw it out of the window when no one was looking.'[23]

This was a mistake. Someone saw the Gospel, and the two were confronted, near Lvov, by armed police, and arrested as spies.[24] George Verwer described what followed as 'one of the greatest experiences of our life', as they had two days to witness to their interrogators. They were then deported. George was hopeful that the confiscated literature would be distributed because of its curiosity value.[25] Roger Malstead, in his account, was not as upbeat. He suggested that up to twenty Gospels were distributed and that the guards probably burned the rest. He described the escort out of Czechoslovakia with one motorcycle in front and one behind. As they were ready to drive into Austria, George said, 'Roger, drive away really slowly,' and got into the back, flipped up the rear door of the station wagon and started taking pictures of the communist guards. Roger called out, 'Verwer, you're nuts,' put his foot on the accelerator and drove across.[26]

George Verwer, however, knew the value of publicity. As a result of this drama, he was able to address public meetings in the

USA about 'My experiences behind the iron curtain', 'Russia ... their plan to win the world' and 'Arrest – Interrogation'. His addresses included slides of the photographs he had taken, all designed to foster American support. Even *Pravda* and the *International Herald Tribune* reported on two Americans, 'Thurber and Malsted', expelled from the Soviet Union for distributing anti-Soviet literature.[27]

The name 'Operation Mobilisation' came to George Verwer in Vienna, Austria, just after his unexpected return from the USSR. He had climbed a huge tree to pray. From this vantage point, watching a group of young people boarding a holiday bus, he shouted to Roger Malstead, 'Operation Mobilisation!' The idea was to mobilise busloads of Christian young people for mission.[28] As a result, George asked leaders in Spain about the name Operation Mobilisation, and after a prayer retreat – at which they agreed – this name was used for the next summer outreach. Operation Mobilisation was never intended to be the permanent name of the organisation, though that is what it became.[29] In autumn 1961, George Verwer was invited to speak to national Spanish leaders and pastors in Madrid, and at this meeting the intention was to present OM and to introduce Federico Aparisi as the leader of the work in Spain.

The publicity over the Russian episode was well received in America, but Spanish evangelical leaders did not want the incident mentioned because of political sensitivities. Serious disagreements over this and other issues became evident at the meeting with the Spanish leaders. George Verwer gave them something of a lecture about their lack of vision for furthering the gospel in Spain and the wider world. Tempers flared. Later that evening a delegation of Spanish pastors came to the Verwers' flat and there was a confrontation. From the standpoint of these evangelicals, they had suffered for years under a harsh dictatorship and had done all they could to serve the Lord in very adverse circumstances. Now someone from the USA, who knew nothing of their sacrifice and suffering, had arrived to tell them what to do. George apologised, but damage done in this encounter took time to repair.[30] Despite the difficulties, Federico Aparisi succeeded in recruiting 30–35 Spanish young people to work with OM outside Spain in 1962. One of the teams in Italy included five Spanish girls. The reaction of the Spanish pastors illustrates two different perspectives on mission. One, in line with certain wider societal aspirations of the time, stressed revolution. In November 1961, the OM team produced what became known as the 'Madrid Manifesto'. Drafted by Jean Hall and signed by twenty-five students, it began, very daringly, with the claim: 'The Lord Jesus Christ was a revolutionist!' Then followed a series of sayings of Jesus, culminating in: 'Except a man forsake all that he hath, he cannot be my disciple.' The manifesto continued: 'Do you suppose that all these ideas fell in with the cultural pattern of Christ's day? Of course not! . . . Literal adherence to the principles laid down by Jesus Christ would, without doubt, result in worldwide revolution ... Outside this sphere of total abandonment is the nauseating, insipid Christianity of our day. We have committed ourselves in reckless abandonment to the legitimate claims of Christ on our blood-bought lives ... we must forsake all! Christ must have absolute control of our time and money ... We must yield possessions, comforts, food and sleep ... we will press forward until every creature has heard the Gospel.'[31] By contrast with this optimistic stress on 'worldwide revolution', evangelicals in Spain were struggling in a hostile society – and some were now being blamed for the activities of OM. Yet it does seem, from the evidence of the very large numbers asking for OM Bible correspondence courses, that OM was reaching people in Spain who were engaged in a spiritual search.[32]

In February 1962, the Verwers left Spain and moved to London. STL was set up in the UK. At this point there were thirty-seven people in the OM teams, based in five countries – Spain, France, Austria, Turkey and England. The crucial contact in England was Bill Bathman, an American who had a vision for mission in Eastern Europe. He had urged George Verwer to come to England and arranged for him to speak at an annual 'Network' (National Evangelistic Teams) conference, which about 250 young people usually attended. The other speakers in 1962 were well-known British evangelicals – Paul Tucker, a Baptist pastor in London, and A. Lindsay Glegg, an enterprising and influential lay leader who became a supporter of OM. The report on the event in *The Christian* was entitled 'Revolutionists for Jesus Christ', taking up George Verwer's theme. Many at the conference showed keen interest in George's plan to mobilise students across Europe.[33] His messages had a magnetic power.

George Verwer anticipated meetings 'in many different assemblies and churches' in Britain and hoped that as a result many young people would join OM.[34] Recruiting became a major emphasis. By March 1962, he was 'booked solid for meetings all over the country'.[35] Contacts were also made in this period across Europe: George had the opportunity to speak at an Italian Brethren conference, for example, and Giovanni Definis was appointed OM leader in Italy.

In Britain, George spoke at as many Bible colleges as possible: at one, Moorlands Bible College, in Devon, about a quarter of the students were motivated to come on mission with OM.[36] The roots of Moorlands were in the Brethren, and British Brethren contacts were crucial in OM's early period.[37] But OM's denominational connections were varied. Carey Baptist, a large church in Preston, north-west England, was represented at the Network conference and one-third of the young people from this congregation later joined OM summer teams. Its contribution to OM was outstanding. In Bolton, also in the north-west of England, major support came from the Methodist Church.[38]

As a result of the connections made across Europe, young people were mobilised for summer mission. Americans were also involved, including Hoise Birks, an African American student at Moody who later served in India and Iran. At that time, African Americans were not welcomed into most American missionary societies. During the summer of 1962, nearly two hundred young people from twenty-five countries – including ninety from Britain, sixty from elsewhere in Western Europe (principally Germany, Austria, France, Belgium, Switzerland and the Netherlands) and ten from the Middle East – gathered for a week-long conference near Paris. Conferences would become a feature of

OM. The addresses given were taped,[39] and these messages on cassette – especially those by George Verwer – had a widespread influence in many student prayer cells.

Jonathan McRostie, a gifted organiser, coordinated teams going to different destinations. In 1962 team members roughed it across Europe, often sleeping in their vehicles or on church floors, and distributed no less than 25 million pieces of Christian literature in many major cities in Italy, Austria, Belgium, the Netherlands, Germany and France. The literature contained offers of a correspondence course or a Gospel and, by the end of the summer, there were eight thousand replies from Italy, five thousand from France, four thousand from Austria and Germany, and smaller numbers from elsewhere.[40] Mobilisation across several countries in Europe had begun, with literature distribution taking place on a quite unprecedented scale. Nor was this 'hit-and-run': OM's work in each of these countries would continue.

Even higher goals

More extensive mission was planned for 1963 and George Verwer appealed for those who would serve and lead OM teams.[41] A history of this period in the OM story recorded that 'even higher goals were set' for the summer of 1963. The plan was to visit approximately one hundred thousand small villages and towns in South-Western Europe and distribute evangelistic books and Bibles.[42] At this early stage in OM's life, a remarkable amount of organisation was evident. 'If you accept this challenge,' said George to potential team leaders, 'there will be certain books that you will be required to read and exams will be given on these books. You also will have to listen to certain tape recordings that present principles of leadership and discipleship. Also we will send you a forty-seven page leadership manual which you will have to study and be examined on.' This 'manual' was an evolving and growing document, initially covering topics ranging from 'lining up and organising a meeting' to 'social relationships' within teams (for example, there was to be no dating during the first year with OM) and later included issues such as 'handling doctrinal differences'. It warned against OM becoming 'another one of those sickly, watered-down "Christian" organisations'; instead OM wanted to 'see God do the impossible'.[43] George Verwer often played down or rejected the idea of 'joining a movement'. 'You are the movement' was a favourite phrase.[44]

In many ways the 1963 summer outreach was OM's turning point. The operation was on a remarkable scale. For three months, close to two thousand young people from thirty countries (seven hundred of them from Britain) were involved. The teams that went across Europe were coordinated from two bases. The UK base was a former army barracks in Chigwell, Essex, and the Netherlands base was at Gulpen, near Maastricht. Jonathan McRostie was coordinator at Chigwell, and Steve Hart, also from America, who was later to become well known as OM's chief accountant, was at Gulpen. Jonathan subsequently organised many of OM's summer campaigns.

A conference at Lamorlaye, near Paris, launched the 1963 mission and more than four hundred different local churches and twenty-five different missionary organisations played a part. Teams visited more than 80 per cent of all the villages in Italy, Spain, Austria, Belgium and France. They had innumerable personal conversations, held about one thousand open-air meetings, took hundreds of church services, showed many films (this was an emphasis taken from Moody) and distributed millions of pieces of literature. Nearly two hundred cars and lorries were utilised and they covered almost one million miles. Many vehicles had been purchased at scrapyards, but most travelled up to ten thousand miles.[45] OM was now strongly vehicle-orientated. 'Tiny' Snell (a huge man) of Los Angeles, co-founder of the International Hot Rod Club, came over to Europe to supervise vehicle repairs.[46] Participants brought many different gifts. By 1963, OM was speaking of itself as 'a student movement serving in twenty-two countries' and 'a spontaneous movement spreading throughout the world'.[47]

Although most of the two thousand participants in 1963 were Europeans, from several different countries and representing a mix of cultures, the American connection was also very important. Greg Livingstone had outstanding gifts as a recruiter and George Verwer had instructed him to hire a charter aeroplane to bring Americans to Europe. Having asked his wife, Sally, to attend his classes at Wheaton Graduate School, he travelled round visiting Bible schools and colleges across the USA, and as a result 103 students – including ten (uninvited) women – gathered at John F. Kennedy airport, New York, and flew to Paris.[48] Mainard Tom, who had led the student STL team at Moody, coordinated the French-speaking team in Paris. Among the Americans involved in 1963 was Loren Cunningham, the founder of YWAM. George Verwer had been at a small meeting hosted by Jack McAlister of World Literature Crusade (later Every Home for Christ) in southern California, at which he had met Loren Cunningham and Bill Bright, the founder of Campus Crusade.[49] These three would go on to have a remarkable impact on world evangelism.

Reports in this period indicated some of the ways in which OM teams sought to be at the leading edge of mission. From 1961, teams had begun to work in Turkey, followed by North Africa, Jordan, Lebanon, Syria and Iran – where thousands wrote in for Bible correspondence courses. In October 1962, a team composed of some early OMers set off from Madrid in an old truck loaded with literature, went over to Morocco, and then drove through a number of countries including Algeria, Tunisia, Libya, Egypt and Jordan, eventually returning to Spain. This took about nine months. In Algeria, over a half a million tracts were given out. This was soon after the Algerian War of Independence and, with a new government in place, there was a unique opportunity.[50] Little could be written about such ventures at the time, but in winter 1963 George Verwer asked for young people who would work with OM for at least a year, seeking 'open doors' in communist countries and ways into the Muslim world.[51] Lebanon became a base for OM's work in parts of the Arab world: teams went out from Beirut with Arabic, French, Armenian and English literature.[52] In the period 1962 to 1967, teams in the Middle East sponsored or published over nineteen thousand copies of books, seventeen thousand Bible courses and hundreds of thousands of tracts.[53]

Although communist and Islamic countries presented particular challenges, all OM outreach was demanding. One women's team in Spain in 1963 was arrested on thirteen separate occasions.[54] Jean Walker, who married Paul White, an STL student leader at Moody, wrote in 1963 about the opportunities a women's team had for witness in Spain, as well as about the reality of assaults, imprisonment, exhaustion and illness.[55] She had some 'wonderful' days, but she also noted how awful it was at night to have four team members trying to sleep in one car.[56] It may be that some of the hardships contributed to lower numbers on OM summer missions following 1963, but on the other hand 1963–4 saw the first OM 'year teams' in action. This was highly significant. Four weeks of teaching took place at a conference in Atherton, near Bolton, England, as preparation for those taking part in 'a year-long training programme' – in Europe, Turkey, Iran, Lebanon, Israel or India. About two hundred were involved. As well as giving teaching on subjects like discipleship, these OM training conferences included an emphasis on human psychology and on how to work together.[57]

As OM's operations expanded, regional centres were established. By 1964, OM had an office and a bookshop operating in a converted pub in Bolton. An OM Central Accounting Office was set up and a UK Board of Directors for OM was formed, with members from a range of churches, especially Anglican. Several came from Manchester, and OM's UK office later moved there. William Dalley, who became involved in the early period, was to become the longest-serving Board member. The Board was crucial in providing accountability and a financial framework, and OM Boards, many containing experienced business people, were later set up in many countries, making a crucial contribution to OM. The UK arm of OM and the UK Board did not direct wider OM operations: the emphasis was on decentralisation and flexibility. OM's European headquarters, a former paper factory in Zaventem, on the outskirts of Brussels, was obtained through the generosity of Bob Cook, an OM backer. The 'old miracle trucks' that moved in and out of Zaventem became symbolic of OM. Zaventem operated as a conference centre and as the logistical hub of an increasingly complex network under the leadership of Jonathan McRostie.[58] In Sweden, a group of young people, inspired by the early OM summer campaigns, formed a small Christian publishing house called 'Proclama' in order to spread the OM message throughout Scandinavia. Living like an OM team, 'by faith', they translated and distributed key OM discipleship literature and evangelistic material. The 'official' OM Swedish office operated out of Zaventem, but when Hans and Ruth Ström returned from India to Sweden in 1970, they set up an OM office in Smålandstenar in the south of Sweden. The recruiting and sending out of hundreds of young people from Scandinavia as a whole was routed through Sweden until national offices were established in Norway and Denmark. Due to a favourable international attitude to Scandinavian passport holders, the Middle East and Turkey saw a particular growth in the numbers of Nordic OM workers.[59]

Long-term OM work of various kinds began to take shape across Europe. In southern Europe, OM became involved in planting congregations in towns with no known evangelical church. Church planting was a new direction for OM, and would gradually increase in importance, but OM's primary vision was to work with existing church networks, not create new ones. Eastern Europe remained a priority, and a conference in Poland in 1965 attracted seventy people. Details of activities in Russia and other communist countries were deliberately withheld, and although the smuggling of Christian literature began from 1964, there were only oblique references – for example to 'literature heading toward Siberia'.[60] The Verwers, now with three children, Benjamin, Daniel and Christa, exemplified the way in which OM was becoming a movement with a global reach, even at this early stage. Europe and India were key centres and for three years from 1965, the Verwers spent half the year in India and half in Europe.

OM leaders recognised early on that it was not possible to enter some countries as a missionary. Roger and Yvonne Malstead and Dale and Elaine Rhoton were able to enter Turkey

as English teachers and students. Others followed in their footsteps in the Middle East, a number of recent university graduates
subsequently taking academic posts in Turkey. This kind of
'tentmaking', as it was later commonly called (in 1 Corinthians 9,
Paul spoke of supporting himself – and his trade was tentmaking),
was a long-established way of undertaking witness and became
much more prominent within OM, particularly in the Arab
world, Iran and Afghanistan. The American evangelical thinker,
Francis Schaeffer, was also significant for OM, encouraging
OMers to see all of life as under the Lordship of Christ, with
no dichotomy between the sacred and the secular. A positive
theology of work was another crucial element in thinking about
tentmaking. Dale Rhoton also had an enormous influence on OM
work in this area, especially through his exploration of how
witness should be sensitive to culture.[61]

The Holy Spirit is moving

In December 1966, John Watts, who was in charge of STL in the
UK, with its focus on literature, reported on developments within
OM: the move of STL's headquarters from Lancashire to property in Bromley, Kent, made available through the generosity of
Christian businessman, Kenneth Frampton; the work of one
thousand young people from twenty countries in OM summer
teams; the distribution of over fifteen million pieces of literature;
the growth of One and Two Year OM teams to four hundred
people; and the participation of larger groups from Britain,
Sweden and Finland in OM teams. George Verwer, Greg
Livingstone and Dale Rhoton had recruited a significant group of
students from Cambridge University, including Peter Wales,
Nigel Lee, John Hymus, Jon Neal, Peter Balaam, John Lennox
and Anthony Gilbert. Against this background, John Watts who
was from the Brethren, concluded his 1966 report: 'It does seem
that in all societies and Christian circles the Holy Spirit is moving
with greater power and effect, and there is more response than for
many years.'[62] He had a business background and believed in

'good management principles' in OM,[63] but for him organisation and openness to the Spirit did not need to conflict.

In the same month, December 1966, Keith Beckwith, who led the part of OM's work in the UK that was not within the STL literature arm, also reported on significant new ventures. He was from Hebron Hall (Brethren) in Carlisle, in the north of England, had studied at London University and Moorlands Bible College, and joined OM in 1963. Having studied languages, including Polish, he spoke enthusiastically about conferences being held with Polish young people.[64] Just before Christmas, Jonathan McRostie, as part of his ministry of coordinating OM's European enterprises, sent John Watts and Keith Beckwith off from Zaventem on a visit to Poland with prayer for God's blessing. Hopes were high. But Jonathan heard tragic news a few days later – both John and Keith had died in a head-on collision with a lorry near Poznan.[65]

George Verwer spoke of the death of John Watts and Keith Beckwith as 'the greatest test of my faith I have ever had', describing them as 'two of my closest friends on earth'. He came over from India to the UK and spoke at the funerals.[66] At a subsequent memorial service for Keith, at All Souls Church, Langham Place, London, Greg Livingstone spoke in tribute.[67] OM had lost its British leadership in one blow, and other leaders had to be found. Derek Virgin took over as coordinator for the UK, along with Peter Wales and Phil Vogel (later director of British YFC). Gerry and Jean Davey, who had been in Spain (Jean Hall had married Gerry Davey) moved to the UK to take responsibility for STL. Gerry had been introduced to OM through his brother Ted, a student at the Bible Training Institute in Glasgow, who had joined OM. Gerry's participation in OM's summer 1963 outreach led to his turning down doctoral studies in the USA and becoming a long-term OMer.[68] He was to be central to OM's literature ministry.

George Verwer did not want the deaths of his two friends to be seen as a defeat; he saw them as urging the work forward. OM's key leaders at this point – Dale Rhoton, Jonathan McRostie and Greg Livingstone – similarly stressed commitment to seeing a greater spiritual 'advance for Christ', as they put it, happening 'around the world in our generation'.[69]

The sense that the Holy Spirit was moving did not mean that OM was naïve about the challenges the Christian faith faced, not least – in an increasingly post-Christian Europe – serious intellectual challenges. Dale Rhoton was particularly important as a thinker, and addressed existentialist philosophy. He also wrote a booklet, *Christian Strategy*. The 1960s saw a huge rise in the number of university students in Europe, with student ideas taking revolutionary forms. OM sought to mobilise Christian students and, in 1966, a new branch of OM started under the name Operation University. As well as the OM group at Cambridge, students were recruited from Oxford University, such as John Clark, who was to hold significant mission posts within the Church of England, including Secretary of Partnership for World Mission.

Greg Livingstone took major responsibility for OM's student work and some students spent time with Francis Schaeffer in his L'Abri community in Switzerland. OM teams worked among students in the Netherlands, Austria, Germany and France. George Verwer challenged American students to join the one-year OM programme.[70] Jack Rendel and Mickey Walker, both at Moody, joined OM in this period and stayed long-term. Greg Livingstone argued in favour of short-term action alongside long-term mission.[71] As examples of such cooperation, in Paris Mike Evans and an OM team helped to start student groups, and in Vienna a year-team was involved in student work in conjunction with local churches.[72]

The awareness within OM of the intellectual struggles that many students and others had regarding Christian faith was matched by recognition of the reality of inner spiritual struggles among committed young Christians. Jonathan McRostie describes how he led OM work in 1963 'in the midst of many doubts and struggles', and how George Verwer, instead of sending him home, stood with him. Along with OM's stress on commitment was a desire to convey the message of God's mercy and grace. In his time of personal spiritual weakness, Jonathan saw no less than seven hundred recruits joining OM. He valued the care George showed him and recognised also that God was graciously intent on 'furthering his purposes through weak people'.[73] Another example was Peter Conlan, who completed his studies at Birmingham Bible Institute and joined OM in 1967. During his first meeting with George, Peter 'admitted to so many spiritual struggles and questions that any normal mission agency would have rejected me outright'. In fact, George handed over a few books 'to read overnight', and invited Peter to join him 'starting from tomorrow'. OM was willing to take risks with young people. Within six weeks, Peter Conlan was 'typing [George Verwer's] letters in a humid, cockroach-infested flat in Bombay'.[74]

OM was also realistic in facing up to the cost involved in discipleship. William MacDonald's book, *True Discipleship*, published in 1963 and made widely available by Send the Light, became (apart from the Bible) the most-read book in OM. Early on in his hard-hitting work, William MacDonald quoted the Brethren author, C.A. Coates, that the pathway of the true disciple is 'a path which so far as the world goes is one of dishonour and reproach'.[75] One of the books written by George Verwer, a forthright call for reality in the Christian life, was entitled *Pseudo Discipleship*. At the same time, OM did not want its team members to incur unnecessary reproach. George encouraged those thinking about joining an OM team to talk the matter over with their parents and their pastor, to gain sensible advice from them. There were a number of very false stories going around about OM's work, he explained, but he urged: 'Don't let these keep you from God's will.'[76]

For some, God's will was hard to follow. The OM report for 1966 referred to four of those working in Turkey being imprisoned. It had been 'another hard year' in Turkey, with many arrests. Dale Rhoton's wife, Elaine, had been refused entry, and the Malsteads had been forced to leave. At the same time, conversations had taken place with university students, who were 'quite open to the Gospel'. Across the Arab world, in Lebanon, Jordan, Syria, Iraq and Kuwait, John Ferwerda, initially wary of OM, was now coordinating OM's work; 'laying the groundwork' for the future. An Operation University team was able to work in Beirut. In Israel, although some team leaders such as Hanna Zack had been refused entry, others had (they believed) seen 'foundations laid for greater things'.[77] Faith in the ongoing work of the Holy Spirit was sustained in the midst of setbacks.

Be filled with the Spirit

In the 1960s, however, the doctrine of the Holy Spirit became controversial within evangelical circles. In 1960 Dennis Bennett, an Episcopalian clergyman in California, described how he had received 'the fullness of the Spirit' (often termed the baptism of the Spirit) and spoken in tongues.[78] This event was significant for what became the 'charismatic' or 'neo-Pentecostal' movement. In October 1964, when this movement was only a year old in the UK, George Verwer spoke on the subject of the Spirit's work at an OM conference in Bolton. His message became a booklet, *Extremism*. The title might suggest advocacy of extreme commitment, and many evangelicals saw OM as extreme, but in fact it was an argument against extremism. 'The Holy Spirit', he began, 'was given to the Church that we might be one, that we might love one another, that we might have a Comforter, a Teacher, a Counsellor, a Guide. Yet today the Church is more divided over the doctrine of the Holy Spirit than one would dare imagine.' George wanted to avoid an unnecessary clash over this issue. Having worked with Pentecostal pastors in the USA and Mexico, he had known the empowering of the Spirit in his own life, and was in touch with emerging leaders within the British charismatic movement such as Arthur Wallis. Moody Bible Institute had been anti-Pentecostal, and George was aware of the diverse viewpoints in OM, but his emphasis was on accepting one another.[79] In later messages he was to refer to this as being 'big-hearted'.

Extremism showed that George Verwer had given considerable thought to key areas of evangelical spirituality. He delineated first the Calvinistic strand of theology and spirituality – to be found, he suggested, among Baptists, Brethren, Presbyterian and

Reformed churches. Their emphasis was on the sovereignty of God and a distinction was made between the baptism of the Holy Spirit, seen as simultaneous with conversion, and the subsequent daily filling of the Spirit. The second group of evangelicals comprised those sympathetic to Arminian theology: e.g. Methodists, Nazarenes and Pentecostals. For some of them, the 'second blessing' or 'baptism of the Spirit' was a means to receiving power for service.[80] George referred to outstanding figures from both camps, including George Whitefield (Calvinist), John Wesley and Charles Finney (Arminian), and emphasised that although he inclined towards Calvinism, OM distributed literature from *both* camps. The priority should be the fruit of the Spirit, although he also affirmed gifts. He pleaded for serious study rather than superficial dogmatism. There was an unfortunate tendency in OM, he admitted, to 'look down' on theologians; but theology, he insisted, was 'the study of God'. He had heard some young people say 'I don't *need* any theology.' His response was: 'How ridiculous!'[81]

Although there was room for diversity in OM, and different denominational perspectives were present, a 'Discipleship Manual' which was produced by OM emphasised that where young people were 'riding on a particular denominational hobby-horse' and seeking to persuade others, this would be stopped. Meetings under the auspices of OM should not include 'shouting and excessive display of emotions'.[82] OM did not have a place for extreme Calvinists who saw no need for evangelism, nor Exclusive Brethren, who had degenerated into a sect, nor ultra-Pentecostals who pushed their own teachings on the baptism of the Spirit, casting out demons and healing. George Verwer cautioned those in OM who equated 'real revival' with the baptism of the Spirit and spiritual gifts. On healing, he had seen sick people healed after prayer, but he opposed the idea that 'all sickness is of the devil'.[83] Many Christians, he commented, were saying 'We are in the latter days', or 'We need a revival', or 'The Lord is sovereign' – slogans that in some respects reflected their theology – but what was needed, he argued, was to 'deny self and take up our cross and follow Him'.[84]

This statement about 'taking up the cross' – one of many in a similar vein – summed up the heart of OM's spirituality. Christ-centred discipleship was crucial in thinking about the Spirit-filled life. The theme was taken up in OM's 'Discipleship Manual', in which the first chapter was 'Followers of Jesus'. On the grounds of commitment to the simple lifestyle, coffee had to be 'eliminated from the diet of OM', since tea was less expensive and healthier, and OMers had to 'avoid completely eating in restaurants'. At this stage in OM's history, the call to follow Jesus involved demands that at times seemed to resemble the legalism that Jesus condemned. William MacDonald's book, *True Discipleship*, was often quoted. This book, as well as being an enormous influence on OM, was also in part a product of what was being expressed in OM's life in the 1960s. Thus William MacDonald wrote in his foreword that although he had been among Christians who knew the principles of 'New Testament discipleship' he had 'somehow concluded that they were too extreme and impracticable'. Then he had met a group of young believers (OMers) 'who set out to demonstrate that the Saviour's terms of discipleship are not only highly practicable but that they are the only terms which will ever result in the evangelization of the world'.[85] It was little wonder that *True Discipleship* was so highly prized.

There were many other books, however, which were recommended within OM. Indeed the focus on reading helpful literature became a marked feature of the movement. George Verwer became famous for the number of books he would recommend when speaking at conference events. He spoke about the impact of the writings of people such as Thomas à Kempis, Martin Luther, John Bunyan, E.M. Bounds, William Booth and other Salvation Army leaders, Madam Guyon, Billy Graham, Watchman Nee and Roy Hession. Examinations took place for those wishing to join OM teams, and part of the testing involved questions about set books.

One highly valued writer was A.W. Tozer, a pastor in the Christian and Missionary Alliance, who wrote in prophetic terms about subjects like worship, knowing God and the filling of the Spirit. George Verwer described Tozer's writings as 'all tremendous' and Tozer himself, who died in 1963, as a 'great, brilliant scholar, a man of God', commenting: 'There are very few men who have made as much impact on evangelical thinking in past years as A.W. Tozer.'[86] STL promoted many of Tozer's writings. It is a mistake to think of the spirituality of OM as marked by unthinking zeal. The admiration shown for someone who was regarded as a 'brilliant scholar' and a 'man of God' sums up the integrated approach that was being sought.

The Calvary Road, by Roy Hession, a book born in the East African Revival of the years before and after the Second World War, stressed repentance and brokenness and was particularly praised by George Verwer.[87] Other writers commended within OM, such as Stanley Voke, were part of this Revival movement. But repentance and brokenness, which became part of the DNA of OM, although rightly focusing on the cross, could at times produce a 'worm theology' in which people felt they had nothing good to offer.[88] OM's rules could also be repressive. However, alongside these strands – and sometimes in tension with them – was a strong emphasis within OM on the 'revolution of love' (the title of one of George Verwer's books), an emphasis on love that was drawn in part from the writings of Theodore Epp of 'Back to the Bible' broadcasts, and later Paul Billheimer, who tried to find common ground within various streams of evangelical spirituality.

George Verwer illustrated this 'revolution of love' as it worked out in practice by citing an occasion when he spoke at the famous Hyde Park Corner in London. After he had spoken, his OM colleague, Virgil Amos, who was an African American, gave a message. The Hyde Park Corner crowd had watched race riots in America on TV and had been told that all white Americans hated black Americans. Yet here were two people standing together in public, united across the racial divide. 'They could see', said George, 'that we loved each other, that we respected each other. They could see that there was something real binding us together, and they heard that reason was Jesus Christ.'[89] The revolution of love was not simply something inward: it had implications that challenged prevailing cultures.

Conclusion

The 1960s was an amazing decade for OM, as the movement spread from the USA and Mexico into Spain and then into country after country in Europe and further East. The next chapter will examine its remarkable growth in India. By the end of the 1960s, OM's annual summer outreach in Europe was well established. The huge numbers of 1963 were not repeated again in the 1960s but in 1967, a typical year, over eight hundred young people participated in forty teams across Europe. Tapes of George Verwer's preaching were circulating across the student world, with Bible school, college and university prayer cells listening with excitement. New OM leadership, drawn from these students, was continually emerging. There were setbacks, the most significant loss being the death of John Watts and Keith Beckwith, both outstanding young leaders. Of the new developments, several were crucial. The first was the emergence of the 'year programme'. By the later 1960s, over four hundred young people were involved in year teams, the majority coming from North America – the USA and Canada – and the UK, but a growing number, reaching almost half of those involved, from other parts of Europe and from the Middle and Far East. The year programme became, for many who participated, a pathway into longer term work with OM. Another crucial development was entry into the Islamic world, a focus that would become increasingly important. George Verwer saw that witness in Islamic countries needed long-term commitment, and envisaged work being done by nationals.[90] Finally, a distinctive OM spirituality developed in this period. At its core was discipleship and spiritual revolution.

Chapter 3

Go East

The 1960s saw a stream of Westerners heading to the Far East to seek spiritual enlightenment, perhaps the most famous being the Beatles. OMers also took this path, although for very different reasons. In 1963 Dale Rhoton reported to supporters: 'We are taking the opportunity to inform you of our initiative and plans ... Lord-willing, the team shall leave around November 5th or 7th, 1963 from Manchester, England. At present 20 to 50 youths feel His leading to join the work.'[1] One of the members of that initial team, Greg Livingstone, later recalled: 'When I told George Verwer I didn't even know where India was, he said, "Go East – you can't miss it!"'[2] The plans were in fact more carefully laid than that recollection might suggest. George's attention, as a history of OM India written by Regina Alexander puts it, 'went beyond the Middle East to India, a land with a church history as old as the church itself, a land that could boast of having had the father of modern missions, William Carey, and others'. A particular concern was for the Muslims of India.[3] Accordingly, George asked Dale to include India in an exploratory visit he was making to Afghanistan. The outcome of this visit and other meetings was the beginning of OM's work in India, which would lead over time to India playing a key part in re-shaping the global identity of OM. This chapter looks at OM in India in the 1960s.

Send him to India

It was far from the case that all the OM initiatives in the 1960s came from the West. Thomas Samuel, who had committed his life to Christ at a Billy Graham crusade in India in 1956 and who, in 1963, had recently finished seminary studies, heard about OM's European summer outreach.[4] Travelling to Europe seemed impossible: he could not afford the fare and had no passport. But, as Thomas Samuel later recounted, two friends of his, Mrs Lal, 'a lady of affluence', and Mr Venugopal, 'a senior officer in the Railways', supplied his fare, and the passport was 'easily sorted out by a police officer who used to enjoy my game of football'. Thomas sailed from Bombay (now Mumbai) and after three weeks arrived in France, to attend the OM conference in Lamorlaye. He was deeply impressed by 'the zeal, enthusiasm and dedication' he witnessed, and by the passion of George Verwer – this 'thin, wiry, energetic man who was jumping around' – and he prayed that God would 'put India on George's heart and send him to India'. Within a few days, conversations about this were taking place and Thomas gave George the contact addresses of Christian leaders he knew in Delhi. Thomas stayed on for six months in Europe, studying at Capernwray Bible School in England, under the leadership of Major Ian Thomas.[5]

During his visit to India, Dale Rhoton had met missionaries who said that India was not yet ready for OM since the churches had not learned to give support to Christian work: therefore the 'life of faith' would be an impossibility. But two people belonging to Gospel Literature Service (GLS), Bill Thompson, who had links with the Honor Oak Fellowship in London (where OM was to hold conferences), and Mrs Christine Durham, thought otherwise, and offered assistance to OM.[6] The connection with GLS was to be strategic in OM's massive literature enterprises in India. Thomas Samuel was also busy publicising OM. In a report published by the Evangelical Literature Fellowship of India (founded in 1954), he wrote that what he had seen in Europe was one of the largest Christian literature outreaches imaginable and 'was not Operation Mobilisation but faith in operation – I saw God at work!' He also noted that there was a possibility of a small OM group travelling overland (a two-month, hazardous journey) from Europe to northern India.[7]

This vision became a reality. The first OM teams bound for India took shape during a month-long conference in Atherton, England, which followed OM's 1963 summer mission. There were substantial bills to be paid from OM's summer activities and none of the team members left until this happened: it was a principle to be free of debt. As the money came in, most of the teams that were planning to spend the coming year in Europe, the Middle East or India, left the UK and moved to a picturesque little village in Switzerland, Les Cullayes, located just outside Lausanne. Konrad Sonderegger, the OM Coordinator for Europe (especially the German-speaking and French-speaking parts), had found – unusually for OM at that stage – a very pleasant small hotel for the teams, Pension de Signal.[8] In the same period, George Verwer flew to India in order to connect with the India team when it arrived in the country, and he played a crucial role in helping OM to take root in India in this early period. He travelled across the country, taking meetings and sharing his vision. His initial contacts, as well as with GLS, included Indian Methodist leaders, for example those in Madras and Bangalore.[9]

Greg Livingstone was given the task of being the initial overall OM team leader for the outreach to India. He and his wife Sally, together with Ron Penny, who had studied at Moorlands Bible College, were among those in the first of the two OM groups to start the long overland journey from Europe. Frank Dietz and Gordon Magney, both from the USA – Frank had recruited for OM in the Chicago area and Gordon had been at Wheaton – who had worked together in Spain were members of the other group to leave Europe. They travelled in a Volkswagen to Turkey and then picked up a large truck. These OM vehicles needed to cope with ten thousand kilometres of roads through Europe, Turkey, Iran, Afghanistan and Pakistan.[10]

The first leg of the journey was through Yugoslavia and into Bulgaria. In Sofia, Frank's group was welcomed by members of the Baptist Church, despite the fact that the team was unknown and communist reprisals could follow in the wake of contacts with the West. He comments: 'The believers in Bulgaria did two things that stand out in my mind and helped us on our way to

India. First, after the service, where the team had the opportunity to share their testimony ... the members of the church came and shook hands with the team and left wads of Bulgarian money in their hands. It wasn't any good outside of Bulgaria, but inside of the country it bought fuel. The second thing that the believers did in Bulgaria was to take us to their homes at their own peril where we could get warm, rest and have some good home cooked food ... It was through their generosity that we got through Bulgaria into Turkey.'[11]

The challenges grew as the team members moved across Turkey's rocky terrain, the vast, desert space of Iran and the rugged mountain ways of Afghanistan. Snowstorms were severe, even life-threatening.[12] In the Iranian desert the axle of one of the vehicles broke.[13] Some members were arrested for distributing literature in eastern Turkey and after being freed (after twenty-four hours) drove on quickly, but stuck in snow and had to seek help. Men from the village dug them out and then demanded payment. Agreement was reached for them to have some old fur coats that the OMers were using as warm bedding. The Turkish men were willing to pay for them and this helped finance the journey. In Tehran, the team was assisted by Bob Rutz, a businessman-missionary. The team also encountered young people on the 'hippie trail'; two of them, Ray and Bill Mayhew (brothers), unexpectedly joined the OM convoy. The team stipulated that the two should cut their hair and join in devotions. Later both became Christians and served with OM.[14]

On New Year's Day 1964, the OM vehicles arrived at the border of India. Ron Penny and Greg Livingstone had gone ahead. For the others, entry was not straightforward. One vehicle was confiscated because of a discrepancy in the engine number. The main achievement, however – and it was remarkable – was that they had arrived. Driving slowly, avoiding bullock carts and children fascinated by the 'strange, pale-faced people in the ancient truck', they reached Delhi.[15] New and very different ministries, in city slums and remote villages, awaited them.

Coming to India was, George Verwer explained, a life-changing experience for him. On 2 April 1964, in a letter addressed to Christians in India, he wrote: 'Never has any of the 23 countries that I have preached in affected me quite like India. And by God's grace I hope to return in October.' In his report, familiar notes were sounded. The teams in India had 'been seeing the blessing of the Lord' in the distribution of 'thousands of portions of the Word' and in personal conversations. He continued:

> These teams will be visiting major cities, staying two weeks or so in each place with a desire to see distribution and evangelism while at the same time establishing local groups in each place that will carry on the work after they leave. This of course is the burden of all those of us who are not Indians . . . that is seeing Indians doing the job.[16]

The primary concerns were to distribute literature in massive quantities and mobilise churches. It is highly significant that many of OM's closest links in India were with national Indian leaders rather than with foreign missionaries, although there were foreigners, such as those with GLS, with the Oriental Missionary Society (OMS) – Wesley Duewel for example – and with the Christian and Missionary Alliance (CMA) who saw the potential contribution OM could make in India.[17]

No fancy table

Links quickly developed in India between OM and the Bakht Singh assemblies. Bakht Singh, who was born to Hindu parents in the Punjab and brought up as a Sikh, became a Christian in 1929, while studying in the West. He returned to India and became a highly effective evangelist. From 1950, his work was centred in Hyderabad, in the south-eastern state of Andhra Pradesh, under the name 'Hebron'.[18] From the 1950s to the 1970s, the local assemblies (these were Indian assemblies but had similarities to the assemblies of the wider Brethren movement) which Bakht Singh and his co-workers planted were probably the fastest growing evangelical churches in India. From the later 1940s, Bakht Singh became more widely known in Europe, the USA and

Canada. He spoke at the InterVarsity Student Mission Convention (later Urbana) in Toronto, Canada, and in Chicago. Norman Grubb, the radically-minded secretary of the missionary society WEC, visited Bakht Singh's churches and considered them the nearest thing he had seen to a replica of the early church.[19] Bakht Singh also encouraged Thomas Samuel, and it is therefore not surprising that OM gravitated to the Hebron Fellowship. Greg Livingstone's team spent their first few weeks with the Bakht Singh assembly in Delhi. George Verwer spoke of how Bakht Singh 'extended his love and acceptance' to OM.[20]

When Thomas Samuel returned to India from England, he met Bakht Singh at the railway station in Bombay, and together they 'knelt on the dirty railway station platform' while Bakht Singh prayed for the younger man. Thomas, his wife Marykutty, and their three children moved to Bangalore, Karnataka state (at that time Mysore), where they lived in two rooms. Thomas began to coordinate the work of OM India: recruiting nationals, setting up a training centre and giving leadership. The style of leadership was, as he commented, 'pretty radical', and contrasted with 'the existing styles prevalent then'. He had, as OM National Coordinator, 'no fancy table or office'; indeed for a time his office table was a crate of books. His income came largely through book-selling, with an occasional allowance sent from the OM office in Bombay.[21]

OM's transparently simple lifestyle was attractive to Indians and the OM team expanded. In Bereilly, in Uttar Pradesh state, S.C. Prasad Tyagi, who was from a Hindu background and had become a Methodist, joined the team. Greg and Sally Livingstone were involved in recruiting men and women to OM India. However, after seeing misunderstandings occur when mixed teams of single women and men travelled together, they realised that it was better to have women and men in separate teams.[22] In both men's and women's teams, Indians and foreigners shared the same working conditions. Many established missionaries, by contrast, worked from missionary compounds.[23]

A further OM team came overland from England to Bombay in autumn 1964; among the members were Ray Eicher, Christa

Fischer (who had joined OM in Madrid), Grace Carlson, and Mike and Audrey Wiltshire. Unfortunately, having an Indian passport, Ray was not allowed into Pakistan. He had to leave the trucks and stayed back in the small desert town of Zahedan. He had only $10. But, remarkably, a previously unknown Indian businessman he met bought him an air-ticket to Karachi, where a friend bought him a deck-class ticket on a ship into Bombay.[24]

Christa Fischer, who studied at Hindustan Bible Institute (HBI), had outstanding leadership abilities and initially coordinated a women's team in Andhra Pradesh. The women's teams were to be a very important part of OM's early ministry in India. For Indian women, OM offering them leadership was revolutionary. Christa's ministry in 1965–6 took her, with others such as Sosakutty and K.V. Saramma (two adventurous fellow-students at HBI), to various parts of India. Some of the team also worked with Karin Ahlen from Sweden. They served in Kerala state, in the south, and in Delhi. Christa Fischer married Ray Eicher in 1967 and they moved to Rajasthan; Nocha Mares (later Myers), a Hispanic American, took over Christa's work. Manjula Shah made a significant contribution, together with two British women, Joan Beesley (later Clark), who had a vision for training, and Linda Cowley, who was a highly effective leader. In 1969, with the outreach still growing, Valerie Freese Green and Saramma George were joined by Enid Massey, from the Punjab, and significant women's ministry began in that northern region.[25] OM offered women from varied backgrounds opportunities to develop in Christian service.

OM's experiences in north and south India showed (as was well known to church leaders in India) that Christians were concentrated in the south but rare in the north. OM aimed to mobilise Christians in the south to work in the north, for example in Rajasthan and Bihar states.[26] Thus George Verwer sent Frank Dietz to Kerala state, in the far south, to challenge the churches there. Another 'sending' area was Andhra Pradesh. Here the relationship with the Hebron Fellowship was crucial; OM, with its expertise in transport, provided trucks, drivers and mechanics for teams (Hebron owned no vehicles), and Bakht Singh provided young people from his assemblies. One team, including Keith Lock and Dave Armstrong, went as far as West Bengal. Another worked its way in 1965 through western India to Jammu and Kashmir, a predominantly Muslim area. This was the time of the Indo-Pakistani war: churches were being burned and the team members were chased by an angry mob, but soldiers arrived and escorted them to safety. There was little to show for their efforts, but they discovered later that a Muslim shopkeeper in Srinagar had bought and read a Gospel and became convinced that Jesus is Lord. He began to attend church, his shop became an outlet for Gospels and Bibles and, over subsequent years, his literature work connected with thousands of people.[27]

As part of OM's strategic development in India, various bases were established. An OM training centre was established in Kerala state, with its strong Christian presence. According to tradition, the apostle Thomas arrived on the shores of Kerala in AD 52, and churches there, such as the Mar Thoma Church, associate themselves with this tradition. Bishop Mar Athanasius of the Mar Thoma Church, both a bishop and a missionary leader, took an interest in OM's work,[28] and George Verwer was invited to speak at the huge Maramon Convention of the Mar Thoma Church. He shared meetings with E. Stanley Jones, the highly respected author of *The Christ of the Indian Road*, and Harold Ockenga, who was the first President of the National Association of Evangelicals in the USA and a seminal evangelical thinker. It is striking that the young and relatively unknown George Verwer should be accepted and given these opportunities by Christians in Kerala with such different traditions.[29]

The OM recruits trained in Kerala often went north to neighbouring Karnataka state, where there would be an orientation conference, and then would move on. Teams went east from Kerala to Tamil Nadu (then Madras state). Some met considerable opposition, with rocks thrown at the windscreens of the trucks. Bombay developed as a strategic OM centre, with Ron George, who had been one of George Verwer's first contacts in England, leading the work there. GLS gave OM office premises in Worli, Bombay, and literature storage space, and with the help of

GLS and the Bible Society, huge quantities of literature were produced. Mike Wiltshire, a journalist in the UK, oversaw this highly complex logistical operation. George Verwer spent six months of every year in India, speaking widely. Premila Franks was his secretary. An important part of the work of the teams in the 1960s was literature distribution, which involved considerable travel. OM had a centre in Delhi at which the twenty to thirty OM vehicles were serviced and repaired. Finding accommodation for teams was difficult and in the first twelve years, OM teams used no less than twenty-three different premises in Bombay. In the early years, the men's teams lived and slept in the warehouse, between the books. There was certainly 'no fancy table'. One Indian OM recruit commented on how 'daring discipleship' and the 'revolution of love' preached and practised by George and other OMers motivated many new recruits into mission.[30]

A sense of strong unity

Thomas Samuel emphasised the 'sense of strong unity' felt in the OM teams. There were Indians and foreigners, participants from different denominations and castes, all working together. This unity proved attractive. Although in the early days Thomas found it difficult to recruit nationals to OM, as he travelled around on his bicycle and spoke about the movement, individuals joined and some took on wider responsibility. Among the first recruits were Puttaraj, from Karnataka; K. Thampy, who became head of the OM Accounts Department and served until 1989; and K.P. Yohanan from Kerala, who would develop a significant ministry of his own. Others included Chacko Thomas, K. Rajendran, T.I. Thomas, T. Divakaran, P.P. Daniel and N.J. Varghese, who went on to plant churches in Bihar.

Some gave up promising careers. Thomas Samuel had been employed by American Express, and in OM the contrast with his previous way of life was marked. Others who made similar moves included Alfy Franks, who had worked in the office of a machine factory and who later became joint OM India leader with Ray

Eicher; Ebenezer Sunder Raj, an engineer; David Burder, who was gifted in marketing; Enoch Antony, whose gifts were used in leading the Delhi base; and Thomas Mathai, a college lecturer who followed A.G. Philip in leading the OM work in Kerala. For all these significant Indian leaders of OM, their way of life could have been very different. As National Coordinator of OM India, Thomas Samuel occasionally could not afford to hire a bicycle for a day. There were temptations to work for established missionary organisations, especially in the light of OM's 'oft repeated and true refrain: no money, no money, no money', but these workers wanted to be trained in 'the school of faith'.[31]

OM's profile was raised through personal contacts and through a magazine that Thomas Samuel launched, *Spiritual Revolution*. This magazine, the first of its kind produced within OM, highlighted the wider needs of India as well as developments in OM. In 1966 there was an article about the huge food crisis in India. At the same time the spiritual needs of the nation were stressed: 'But as serious as the threat of famine is for us, there are many who believe that India faces today yet another type of need – a deep SPIRITUAL HUNGER!'[32] A year later *Spiritual Revolution* quoted a report of the United Bible Societies which said that OM in India was becoming 'one of the important allies of the Bible Societies in the cause of the wider dissemination of the Scriptures'.[33] This was a remarkable statement, considering that OM had been in India for only three years. The international dimension of OM was also emphasised in the magazine. It was noted in 1968 that the Rajasthan OM team had been able to speak to the Maharishi Yogi, famous for his association with the Beatles.[34] Reports were included of OM events outside India, such as a gathering in a concert auditorium in Stockholm which attracted three thousand Swedes, Finns, Norwegians and Danes.[35]

By 1967, there were around fifty longer-term OMers in India, including foreigners, and about seven vehicles that kept the teams moving. Each year trucks transported thirty to forty Westerners overland to India from Europe. Team members engaged in varied

forms of ministry. For example, from 1967 to 1970 Dave
Armstrong studied at Allahabad University, gaining a Bachelor's
degree and witnessing frequently. Most teams concentrated on
personal witness and distributing literature, which advertised
radio programmes and a correspondence course. Spirituality was
also given high value. OM India conferences were important
times of spiritual renewal for the teams. Alfy Franks describes
this: 'Besides evangelism, great emphasis was laid on a personal
walk with God and living together on the teams, daily quiet time,
Bible study, devotions, weekly half nights of prayers, memory
verses ...'[36]

On the question of unity among the Christians, articles in
Spiritual Revolution played down any idea that OM, in India or
elsewhere, was seeking to operate apart from the churches. In
1969 Thomas Samuel wrote: 'I am sure that we all agree that
God's instrument in evangelising India will not be Operation
Mobilisation or any other group, but rather the entire body of
Christ, the Church.'[37] Co-operation continued between OM
teams and the Bakht Singh 'Hebron' assemblies. The Hebron
Messenger of April 1965, reporting on joint Hebron-OM action,
hoped for 'more co-workers',[38] and in 1969 Spiritual Revolution
spoke about teams consisting of 'brothers from assemblies, especially those in training at Hebron, with an OM truck driver'.[39]

Bakht Singh's trust in George Verwer was evidenced in a number of ways. At the massive Hebron conferences – these 'Holy
Convocations', as they were called, attracted up to twenty-five
thousand people – and within local Hebron assemblies the
addresses were normally given by those belonging to the movement, but Bakht Singh asked George to speak at the Convocations
and in the assemblies. His messages were translated into Telugu
(the main language of Andhra Pradesh state), Tamil and Hindi.
OM was also allowed to set up book exhibitions. Some assembly
leaders were unhappy about some of these developments, but
Bakht Singh was open to new spiritual challenges. While some of
the Hebron leaders were unwilling to reach out to mainline
denominations, Bakht Singh did not condemn George for preaching wherever he was invited.

At the same time, OM allowed Bakht Singh to reshape aspects of their operations. Normally the composition of OM teams was an OM matter, one aim being to have a mix of denominational backgrounds, but while working with Hebron, George allowed Bakht Singh to select teams. Bakht Singh's influence directed OM towards church planting.[40] There was a great deal of synergy between OM and Hebron, but differences in philosophy led to a break in the close relationship. OM was a cross-denominational movement, with missional rather than ecclesial matters as its priority.[41]

In any case, by the end of the 1960s, OM was establishing its own identity in India and thus less interested in being an adjunct to another movement. Larger-scale OM training conferences were by now held across India. In 1967, a twenty-eight day OM All-India Training Conference took place, helping to deepen unity and give greater strength to OM. These events had an excitement of their own, not least because of their cross-cultural nature. An 'OM HAPPENING' (as it was billed) in 1969 was described as 'living, eating, sleeping, praying, preaching, studying with young people from Calcutta, Bihar, Orissa, Assam, Kerala, Madras, Gujarat, England, America, Africa and Europe'. The 'HAPPENING' was for two weeks in May, in Calcutta. Among the 'attractions' were 'sleeping on the floor' and 'eating off a banana leaf'.[42] This was classic OM terminology.

As OM's work grew, it was decided that OM India should be registered as a charitable society, with Indian office bearers. By 1970 this had been achieved. OM India became a public trust registered with the government of Maharashtra in Bombay. The first trustees were Thomas Samuel, Thomas Mathai, Enoch Antony, Ray Eicher, David Burder and Alfy Franks. By this time OM India had spread to seven states, with bases in Bangalore (Karnataka), Cochin (Kerala), Madras (Tamil Nadu), Ahmedabad (Gujarat), Lucknow (Uttar Pradesh), Ranchi (Bihar) and Calcutta (West Bengal).[43] The growth and development over the six years of OM's work in India was unparalleled in any other country in which OM served.

A training-study-cultural-educational programme

The growth of OM in India, as in other countries, owed much to the personal inspirational leadership of George Verwer, with support from key associates such as Greg Livingstone. For Greg and others involved in OM India in the early period, George was 'hearing from the Lord' in an unusual way and was clearly 'anointed'.[44] Thomas Samuel, similarly, 'greatly admired Bro. George Verwer', while also noting that OM's leader was 'a real radical with whom I did not always see eye to eye'. The disagreements, as will be seen later, became significant. For Thomas, however, one of the crucial and enduring influences within OM India was George's life; he was 'a leader who set the example', and it was this which gave weight to his challenges to many on OM teams to 'sacrifice our all for the Lord'.[45]

K.P. Yohannan, who was to lead OM's work in the Punjab, attended the annual OM training conference in Bangalore in 1966 and heard George Verwer speak at a session. This address, says Yohannan, 'challenged me as never before to commit myself to a life of breathtaking, radical discipleship. I was impressed with how Verwer put the will of God for the lost world before career, family and self. Alone that night in my bed, I argued with both God and my own conscience ... Suddenly, I felt I was not alone in the room ... I felt the presence of God and fell on my knees beside the bed.' K.P. Yohannan's widely read book, *Revolution in World Mission*, is dedicated to George Verwer, 'whose life and example have influenced me more than any other single individual's'.[46]

This year (1966) also saw a major crisis for OM India. In view of the pressing need for finance, George Verwer suggested that OMers coming from the West to India could bring in goods, such as cassette players and transistor radios, and then sell them. In 1965, he sent money to Frank Dietz in Kuwait to buy a large quantity of such goods.[47] Each person coming into India could bring a quota of goods – up to about two hundred dollars' worth. The OMers declared these goods, papers were filled in, and they were kept in Mike Wiltshire's flat in Bombay. There was no thought in the minds of OMers that this was against the law. But customs authorities became suspicious, especially when they found a leaflet about a possible OM ship. In their minds, this meant smuggling.[48]

The OM premises were searched on 7 December 1966, and Mike Wiltshire and George (who had to rush back to Bombay from Andhra Pradesh) were arrested. Oscar Brown, the chief magistrate of Bombay for many years, defended them. The police soon realised that the OMers were not smugglers, but they were accused of selling personal belongings, which was illegal. They made clear that they had not realised this was the case.[49]

The situation was, nonetheless, serious. OM was described in newspapers as 'a fellowship of international smugglers'. In an attempt to clarify OM's work, a statement was produced by Send the Light on 13 December 1966. It quoted from Gandhi – 'I shall say to the Hindus, you are not complete until you have reverently studied the teachings of Jesus' – and explained that 'we don't go around baptizing people and getting them to change their name, etc., but rather help the Indian Church to understand the true Christian message of love, and to distribute literature about Jesus Christ so that what Gandhi has requested might become a reality. We are also helping some needy families in terms of food and shelter, etc.'[50] In the early months of 1967, there was anxiety over what would happen to the OM team and their confiscated files, typewriters and other equipment. OM had backers in India with Western links, such as GLS, but in the Indian context the movement was vulnerable.

In order to address the continuing suspicions that OM members were financing evangelism by dubious, covert means, George Verwer stated that the aim of OM was not primarily evangelisation but training and preparation. Those entering India were coming as 'learners' and the short-term programme was described as a 'training-study-cultural-educational programme'. He insisted again that OM did not 'proselytize and baptise people'.[51] The case against OM was brought on 24 April 1967 and was over in ten minutes, the OMers being 'admonished' and ordered to pay two thousand rupees for having unknowingly broken the law.[52] This was not, however, the end of the story.

In 1968, 'the whole of the OM India family was shaken by the news that George had been stopped at Bombay airport and deported'.[53] Peter Conlan, at the airport to meet George, watched in alarm as armed police marched him back to the plane. Hours later he received a call from George, 'I'm in Bangkok, come and join me as soon as you can.'[54] This was a testing time for OM, but George Verwer found a way to continue his close connection with India. He set up his base in Kathmandu, Nepal, and during the next two years leaders from India went there to see him. The developing leadership of OM India benefited from leadership seminars and other training opportunities offered in Kathmandu.[55]

Although George Verwer had to leave India, the role of Westerners within OM India continued to be significant for some years. There was a strong commitment to fostering healthy relationships between Westerners and Indians, and to Westerners following Indian leadership. In fact there was mutual learning. Mike Wakely, who had studied at Trinity College, Dublin, before joining OM, recalled his early experiences:

> I went to India thirty-five years ago with Operation Mobilisation and spent my first three years in daily street evangelism with a team of young Indian Christians. Our routine was to drive into a town, open up the back of our four-ton delivery van and preach the gospel message from the tailgate. We would then mingle with the crowd and sell gospel packets and other evangelistic books. We were enthusiastic, full of faith and zeal, and convinced that the gospel was the answer to India's problems. We expected people to respond and turn to Christ, though few actually did. They were heady and exciting years.[56]

Alfy Franks applauded those 'foreigners who came to India, came with a mandate – just to serve'. Among those he highlighted were Philip Morris, who developed OM Books India from 1967 and gave himself to fund-raising for crucial projects. Rosemary Morris, his wife, was also fully involved in leadership.[57] Ron Penny and Gordon Magney worked in Bihar, often known as 'the graveyard of missionaries', and invested particularly in Christian literature. Gordon married Grace Carlson and they remained in

Asia, giving dedicated service over four decades. Ron Penny gave consistent leadership in Bihar until he went to Calcutta to continue his ministry there, eventually becoming the only one of the original OMers from the West to undertake the whole of his service in India. He handed over in Bihar to George Miley, an American who had come over to Europe and then to India. He had been assisting George Verwer and his later influence in OM would be highly significant.[58]

A new idea that took shape in India was selling educational books. In 1965 an OM team going overland to India stopped in Turkey and loaded up books from an OM bookstore that was closing. Many were educational books. When the team reached Iraq, it was decided to hold a book exhibition and this was put on at Basra University in southern Iraq. Large quantities of books were sold. On arrival in India, the rest of the books were sold.[59] Peter Hill and Victor Gledhill, working in Bombay, developed the idea of selling Christian literature alongside good secular educational books. They approached a large bookshop in the city and persuaded the manager to give them books on a 'sale or return' basis. A book exhibition in a local Roman Catholic school was an immediate success. Often the Bombay team had only managed to bring in thirty rupees after a day of selling Christian books, but this exhibition resulted in sales totalling hundreds of rupees. Further possibilities were explored. Several schools were visited and truckloads of educational and Christians books were sold on the pavements. Sales amounted to thousands of rupees. On one visit to Kathmandu, a very successful book exhibition was held in one of the largest hotels in the city. These experiences were crucial in forming the vision for the Educational Book Exhibits – which would subsequently become such a vital part of OM's international ministry.[60]

Reach the poor

Despite the contribution to OM's work that could be and was made from the West, it was always George Verwer's ideal that, wherever possible, missional leadership in any country should be local, not foreign. A classic example was K.P. Yohannan, who – at the age of sixteen – heard a team from OM, which included Ron George and Frank Dietz, presenting the challenge of north India at his church in Kerala. In their presentation the team 'told of stonings and beatings they received while preaching Christ in the non-Christian villages of Rajasthan and Bihar on the hot, arid plains of North India'. As K.P. Yohannan put it: 'Sheltered from contact with the rest of India by the high peaks of the Western Ghats, the lush jungles of Kerala on the Malabar Coast were all I knew ... The rest of India seemed an ocean away.' This was not an unusual outlook for those living in Kerala. What was unusual was how this sixteen-year-old responded. 'As the Gospel team portrayed the desperately lost condition of the rest of the country – 500,000 villages without a Gospel witness – I felt a strange sorrow for the lost ... At the challenge to "forsake all and follow Christ," I somewhat rashly took the leap, agreeing to join the student group for a short summer crusade in unreached parts of North India.'[61] The message of 'forsaking all' was bearing fruit across the globe.

For the next seven years, K.P. Yohannan was one of those serving with OM teams all over north India. Marcus Chacko notes that these teams followed what he calls an 'intuition-oriented strategy'. They were 'constantly on the move and they almost functioned like survey teams exploring new possibilities and new fields'. They spoke to large numbers of people. The motivation of these teams was the deeply felt desire to reach out to those who had not known any relevant Christian witness. A great deal of effort, Marcus Chacko notes, was concentrated on distribution of tracts and gospel literature while doing open air preaching.[62] This was precisely K.P. Yohannan's experience. The teams would preach and visit, deliver literature and then move on.[63]

Yet not all of those who took the path of Christian discipleship as a result of OM's work were from the poor within Indian society. In northern Kerala, a devout high-caste Hindu family suffered a business failure and the youngest son, Divakaran, went on a pilgrimage to Sabari Malai, where the deity Iyyappa is worshipped.

Angered by the sight of hundreds of people inflicting different forms of penance on themselves, yet failing to find peace, he returned disillusioned. He left in 1966 for Delhi, where he had a cousin, but the cousin was not there and, feeling very depressed, Divakaran contemplated suicide. He had planned to study medicine, but life no longer held meaning.

Travelling on a bus to the jungle, intent on killing himself, he felt a voice telling him to get off, and on doing so he met two young men, OMers, who spoke to him about Jesus Christ. He bought a Bible, but still followed through his plan to commit suicide. Later that day he drank two bottles of poison. At the same time he thought, 'Jesus, if you are real, then save me.' Three days later he woke in a hospital ward. He had been found, had received emergency hospital treatment, and the OM members had been tracked down. They led him to commitment to Christ. He then joined OM, later went to the South India Biblical Seminary, Bangarapet, and ultimately became associate executive director of OM India.[64]

Rudy Gomez had also been disillusioned. Having left the Roman Catholic Church in which he had been brought up, he became involved in street gangs in the early 1960s. By 1968 he was aware of his need and he met Danny Smith, who was setting up an OM experiment in Calcutta, 'The Ideal Book Shop'. Rudy offered to paint the shop and, through the influence of the Christian community, committed himself to Christ. He spoke to his gang about what had happened, but his conversion was treated as a joke. His friends called him 'Rev. Rudy the Moody'. It was clear that the influence of the gang was a problem and so Rudy was offered a place on an OM team. The initial commitment extended to twenty years. He spent time in Orissa, Bihar and Bombay, where his gifts were used in heading up the OM Audio Visual Department; he developed new and innovative film projection technology that was widely used. In his personality and reactions Rudy Gomez was volatile, and there were times of tension in his teams, but he was one of many examples of people who found a place in the OM community and whose lives were changed as a result.[65]

Many other stories have not been written down in such detail and some that have been recorded do not mention the names of individuals who were brought to Christian faith through OM. In most cases, those whose lives were changed continued to witness in their own localities. In 1968, for example, a team visited the Kashmir Valley. One person from an Islamic background, Ghulam Rasool Bhatt, was deeply affected and wrote this vivid report:

> They came as a whirlwind, held open air preaching, distributed tracts, sold gospel literature while doing shop to shop visitation in Srinagar. One of my servants bought a packet of books. Out of curiosity I started reading *Youhanna ka Injil* (John's Gospel). Though John 3:16 was blasphemous I kept on reading ... I was attracted by the sacrifice of Christ on the cross. During that time I was also in contact with a Western missionary who was also a teacher in Srinagar. It was in one of those several conversations I received Jesus Christ as my personal Lord and Saviour. See! Today I am Christian even though all my relatives are followers of Islam.[66]

Marcus Chacko, who recorded this account, suggests that this story is typical of many others. Often the OM teams did not know the effect of what they did.[67]

Conclusion

OM in India goes back to 1963 when, as David Lundy (who was with OM India) describes it in *We are the World*, 'a truckful of bedraggled Westerners arrived overland from Belgium, not knowing the local language or culture, and not being connected with the Indian church in any way, only sure of their radical brand of discipleship and the message that "Jesus saves"'.[68] There were in fact some contacts with the Indian Church, but it is certainly true that OM began its work in India in a highly unusual way. One history, commenting on the arrival of the two vehicles at the Indian border on New Year's Day 1964, describes how the OM group from Europe 'unheralded and virtually unnoticed ... entered the great land of India'.[69]

Cities like Delhi or Bombay, with their huge slums, presented an enormous challenge. OM India rightly developed its own identity, but it was also integral to wider OM work. Within three years, OM had distributed thirty million pieces of Christian literature in India, much of it produced within the country itself; teams were operating in or had visited most Indian states; and Indians were leading the OM movement. India became OM's most significant region. It became a badge of honour in OM to have served in India. In the decades after the 1960s, OM in India would continue to develop, in ways that would impact not only the spiritual but also the political life of the nation.

Chapter 4

A Lot of Ship

Following the early Indian experience, regular long-distance travel soon became a feature of OM. This was in tune with the greater ability to travel that characterised Western society. Several months after the first team went to India, George Verwer was talking to some OM leaders in England and someone mentioned the idea of using a ship for evangelism and challenging Christians to fresh commitment. Looking at a world map, some of the young OMers pointed out how many countries had sea coasts.[1] George considered the possibilities: 'Think of the money that could be saved in travel alone!'[2] He had been thinking about sea travel since an early voyage from the USA to Europe. OM also had to ship a large number of vehicles, at considerable cost, across the English Channel for the summer mission in Europe. In 1965, on an overland journey to India in a large truck with a Volkswagen van in the back, the only way the OM team could reach their destination was by going to Kuwait and sending the vehicles by ship to Bombay. Cholera had broken out in Pakistan and the border between Iran and Pakistan was closed.[3] The idea of an OM ship took shape.

Gradually George Verwer became convinced, through prayer and discussions within OM, that it was right to obtain a ship. At an informal meeting in 1964 in Bolton (held during an OM conference), Alf Ridpath, who had experience in the merchant navy, was particularly enthusiastic.[4] George encountered very mixed reactions from OMers, not surprisingly: the cost would be huge and hardly anyone he spoke to in the shipping world showed interest. He calculated that about 80 per cent of the reaction he received was negative.[5] In 1966, however, the first professional crew member, Graham Scott, a young British merchant naval officer qualified to sail as captain of a ship, decided to leave his promising career and join the project.[6] He and George Verwer produced a booklet with forty reasons in favour of obtaining a ship.[7] Four years later, the ship became a reality. It would become OM's best-known ministry.

Now is the hour

There were two main challenges in making the dream about the ship a reality. The first was finding crew members. In fact, many of the eventual crew members were not yet Christians when the idea of the ship was first discussed. Slowly people felt drawn to the vision. One was Björn Kristiansen from Norway, who had commanded an oil tanker in Indonesia. He experienced a dramatic conversion in 1967 after a serious illness and began to think in terms of a ship that would carry the message of Jesus Christ to the thirteen thousand Indonesian islands. In 1970 he returned to Norway to find a ship. He then heard, through Christians working in Lloyd's of London (the shipping insurers), about OM. He met with Graham Scott, who offered him the position of first officer. However, there was no ship.

Another person involved at an early stage was Bernhard (Hardy) Erne, with his wife, Trudy, and their small child, from Switzerland. He heard about the ship, and as someone with considerable experience at sea who had then become a Christian, felt he should become involved. His church in Switzerland was doubtful, but he and his wife decided to drive to Belgium for the 1968 OM conference in Zaventem.[8]

In that year a number of people connected with OM were saying that the project was unrealistic and impracticable. Faith was being tested.[9] Bernhard Erne's experience illustrates the challenges. He wrote about arriving at Zaventem: 'From the letter we had received from OM beforehand we expected to find a ship's team meeting together and learning from each other ... A man came in, a typical Englishman. It was the British captain. Later I met another man, but he left again. That was the entire ship's team!' Bernhard was then shown where he would stay, which to his amazement was 'an empty room – absolutely barren, just four walls, the floor and the ceiling'. Matters only grew worse when the bedding turned out to be a roll of corrugated cardboard. This was the typical OM conference scenario at that time. 'If I hadn't sold everything', Bernhard Erne commented, 'I think I would have returned home. But I believed God would provide the ship. That's why I stayed.'[10]

In 1969 it seemed clear, with George Verwer no longer able to live in India, that a new direction was opening up for OM. As part of this new direction, a leaflet with a photo of a ship was circulated, entitled *Now is the hour for the Ship*.[11] By August 1970 fifteen officers and crew had joined, including John Yarr, a chief engineer from Australia who left a well-paid job to come to England with his wife and four children; Rashad Babukhan, a young Arab deck officer from Aden; Alfred Boschbach, a German cook who had just completed Bible college; Dave Thomas, a British engineer who was to become intimately involved with many aspects of the ship ministry and OM's wider work over many years; and Decio de Carvalho, who left his job with an international airline.[12]

The second challenge was to find a suitable ship. A ship called the *Zambesi* was considered in 1969, but then sold to other buyers. George Verwer asked two of his entrepreneurial colleagues to try to find suitable ships. Peter Conlan, who had worked closely with George in India, was sent to Athens to see if the shipping magnate Aristotle Onassis might have a suitable ship, but was told bluntly: 'If we gave you, free, the smallest ship we have on the market, you couldn't cope with it.' Meanwhile Mike Wiltshire, also previously in India, was asked by George to make investigations about the *Umanak*, a 2,300 ton Danish liner used between Copenhagen and Greenland. It had been thought that a ship with a ventilation system built for Greenland's climate could not be adapted, nor did it have a large auditorium, but members of the 'ship team' became increasingly convinced that this could be the vessel. George and Björn Kristiansen accordingly made a visit to Copenhagen.[13] A major problem was that a French and a Nigerian shipping company were negotiating for its purchase, but in a dramatic turn of events the French company was unable to complete negotiations and the Nigerians could not take money out of Nigeria.[14]

The news that the *Umanak* was free for negotiations came through on 8 September 1970 during the OM European conference, which that year was held in a disused factory in London. OM's international conferences were for teaching purposes (messages were translated simultaneously into seven languages), team preparation and prayer – and with this news, spontaneous excited thanksgiving broke out. George Verwer, Björn Kristiansen and John Yarr left that evening for a meeting with the ship's owners, the Royal Greenland Trading Company, and the following day OM leaders received this recorded message by telephone: 'This is George in Copenhagen. We've again inspected the UMANAK and have spoken at length with the owners ... We have had a technical inspection this afternoon. This particular Marine Engineer said that this ship is in very good condition and we are getting a "lot of ship" for our money.' The surveyor estimated that the ship would be functional for at least ten years.[15]

There was unanimous affirmation by those involved that the purchase should go ahead, and so the contract was signed. At that point OM had only about 70 per cent of the money needed, but the remaining 30 per cent came in by the deadline of 15 October 1970. Various suggestions were received for a name and eventually the *Logos*, 'the Word', was agreed – from a word used in the Greek New Testament for Christ. The official owners of the ship were now Educational Book Exhibits, an arm of OM's work that had developed in India. Val Grieve, a lawyer in Manchester, UK, and a strong supporter of OM from its early days, was chairman of this company. The *Logos* was taken to Rotterdam, remaining there for major repairs, refurbishment and internal adjustment. Through offers of expertise and through favourable terms, this work was done for much less than the normal cost.[16]

The Board of Directors of Educational Book Exhibits decided that the ship should be registered in a neutral country: Singapore was chosen. On 24 December 1970, Peter Conlan flew to Singapore to conduct negotiations. There he was faced with the major problem that the *Logos* did not fit into a sea-going classification. Having apparently achieved nothing, he moved on to take meetings in Pakistan, but then decided to send a telegram to Russell Self in Singapore (the head of the Bible Society there), with whom he had stayed, asking if it was worth another attempt. Russell Self's telegram said 'Advise Coming' and in further discussions with the marine department, a classification was found. The *Logos* was duly registered, and in Rotterdam the crew welded the name onto the side of the ship.[17]

It is significant that by this time, as OM became more global, there was more willingness within OM to fly. Although some North Americans took cheap flights to Europe for summer missions,[18] the emphasis in OM in the 1960s was on more austere travelling methods. OMers mainly used – and often slept in – vans and trucks, as in the overland journeys to India. In 1969, George Verwer wrote a lengthy letter to OM leaders to justify Peter Conlan flying to the USA. He explained that Peter was very effective in giving his testimony and singing, had insights that were important in screening young people wanting to join OM (this was a reference to an interest in psychology that characterised OM), had worked with George and understood him and that, as a Brit, brought a different perspective.[19] With the acquisition of the ship, Peter and others were to be used much more fully as diplomats-at-large, often needing to reach places quickly, which meant frequent air travel.

The good ship *Logos*

The first leg of the first voyage of the *Logos* took her to London. On the Saturday that she was opened to the public, 1,600 people came aboard. A large meeting was held in the Metropolitan Tabernacle at the Elephant and Castle. News about the ship spread, but it was evident that more publicity was needed and Mike Wiltshire, using his journalistic expertise, produced a glossy brochure, *Educational Book Exhibit: Great Discoveries*, which announced the ship provided an 'international Educational Book Exhibit programme of training, learning and education'. At this point, Philip Morris, who was fully involved in the Educational Book Exhibits in India, received a message from George Verwer asking him to come and buy books for the *Logos*. He did not want to, but the request became an order and he found himself in London where, amazingly, he obtained large numbers of books at very low prices.

The ship project received generally favourable coverage in the Christian press, one newspaper finding it refreshing to hear about 'a Christian project which, by its sheer audacity, takes one's breath away', although in the widely read *Crusade* magazine the editor, David Winter, was initially rather scathing. When he later visited the ship, however, he appreciated the way 'the crew of the good ship *Logos* summoned up all their reserves of Christian grace' and instead of making him walk the plank gave him an excellent lunch and showed him 'this beautifully equipped vessel'.[20]

George Verwer did not want to claim more than was warranted for the *Logos*. He pointed to other Christian organisations that had responded practically to the problems of transporting people, for example the Missionary Aviation Fellowship (MAF).[21] Also he noted other ships dedicated to the purposes of mission: George Whitefield, the great eighteenth-century transatlantic evangelist, had one; the London (Congregational) Missionary Society had a ship in the South Seas; and a ship called the *Ebenezer*, owned by a Finnish man, operated in Indonesia. Other examples could have been added: George Grenfell, a pioneer missionary with the Baptist Missionary Society in the Congo, had a river steamer built, the *Peace*. But George Verwer argued that the *Logos* was 'the first Christian ship ever launched of this size', that is an ocean-going vessel. Compared to many vessels at sea, the *Logos* was small, but in places like Indonesia, when alongside normal coasters, it was large.[22] More important than size was the potential range of activities. Educational book exhibits, conferences and seminars, on-shore meetings, taking literature for distribution, training, vehicle transportation and emergency relief – these were some of the possibilities being explored in 1971.[23]

On 26 February 1971 the *Logos*, with 130 people on board, set sail for India, understandably amid great excitement. This major voyage, to a country that represented a top priority for OM, was the fulfilment of a dream. The ship called at Le Havre, France, and then Vigo, Spain, where a hundred evangelical leaders came on board for a three-day conference. George Verwer spoke about the 'four great needs of the church': quiet listening to God, prayer and worship, unity and love, and reality. These messages were well received by Spanish evangelicals. The next stop was Las Palmas in the Canary Islands, where fuel was cheap, and the ship team found people on the quayside waiting for them: the *Logos* had been featured prominently on Spanish radio. The ship waited there for eight days until all the European bills were paid – a rather depressing eight days after a heady start.

Mike Wiltshire flew to Lagos, Nigeria, the next stop, to deal with port affairs. This kind of preparatory work – always referred to as 'line-up' – would happen many hundreds of times in the future.[24] Lagos saw the first educational book exhibition set up on board and it attracted great interest over the course of two weeks. The next port was Cape Town, South Africa, a visit that produced important contacts which led to a recruiting base for OM in South Africa. In Mombasa, Kenya, George Miley, who had been in India, joined the ship. George Verwer was ship director, but he was often not on board and he made George Miley his assistant. Two years later, George Miley took permanent leadership of the *Logos*.[25]

For George Verwer, the developments in 1971 meant that this was an especially stretching and exciting period. As the ship arrived off the shore of Kerala, India, in May 1971, and sailed into Cochin Harbour, and as OMers came out in small boats to meet the ship, he was overwhelmed. On shore, he kissed the ground and wept for joy.[26] In Cochin, a new first engineer joined the ship – Mike Poynor, with his wife Carol Ann and two small daughters. Mike Poynor was a quiet Texan (some on *Logos* had previously thought this was not possible) and a brilliant engineer. In Madras, a brochure had been prepared, *The Miracle Ship*, and this had been picked up by the media. Thousands came expecting to see healings. Later the description 'Educational Ship' was preferred.[27] Ebbo Buurma from the Netherlands, welder and then chief steward on the ship, recalled Madras: 'The miracle was that we survived at all! I remember one day we counted up to fifteen thousand people coming to the *Logos*.' Soon a way was found to ensure that visitors who were serious could have space on board: a small entrance fee was charged, and put towards the purchase of books. A staggering one hundred thousand people boarded the *Logos* during six weeks in Madras.[28] In line with George Verwer's vision for training, about fifty Indian volunteers worked on the ship, joining Europeans and North Americans. To have young Indians such as Chacko Thomas involved (he later became an international OM leader) was highly significant for the internationalisation of OM in the 1970s.[29]

Much of the second half of 1971 was spent in Southeast Asia and the Gulf. Björn Kristiansen had a particular interest in and knowledge of Indonesia, and a visit to the port of Surabaya on Java showed OM the potential for the ship's ministry outside India. Leadership conferences were held on board and on shore. There was a huge response, with meetings on shore attracting as many as eight thousand people. It became clear that there was considerable scope for teaching and for Bible distribution.

After the overthrow of communism in this region, when any suspected communists could be killed, many people had become Christians so that they would not be suspected of being communists, but had little personal commitment to Christianity. Also it was clear that there was a great need for Christian unity in the region. The Reformed Church was the largest Protestant body, followed by the Pentecostals, and the OM team – in line with OM's concern for unity – sought to bring pastors together, to preach in many churches, and to deal with what was seen as a 'divisive spirit' among Christian bodies. Literature distribution took place on a massive scale, and in its customary fashion OM offered correspondence courses. About five thousand people signed up.[30]

After dry dock in Singapore, the last task in what had been a dramatic year was to go to Dubai and Kuwait to off-load personnel who were returning to Europe. In Dubai there was an unexpected cash windfall: a very rich man decided he wanted a rare tooth (from a narwhal) which was on the ship – the tooth had been donated by the Faroese seamen's mission – and he was willing to part with a considerable sum for it.[31] Frank and Anneli Dietz, who had been with the ship in Rotterdam, rejoined at this point, and Frank was given responsibility for what was called the Intensive Training (IT) programme. This was based on the rigorous 'Outward Bound' training, whose motto was 'To serve, to strive, and not to yield.'[32] George Verwer's idea was to have a spiritual Outward Bound course lasting for six months. For Frank, there were two important things about the programme: it was character building and encouraged a biblical world-view.[33] A number of significant leaders, in India and elsewhere, were developed in the IT programme.

The true OM vision

Writing in 1973, George Verwer suggested that in many cases 'team life on the ship is more conducive to giving the true OM vision and principles of total operation, than many teams which are based on shore'.[34] Part of the *Logos* training involved learning to work closely with people of different outlooks, temperaments and backgrounds. Tensions were exacerbated because of the type of people the ship attracted. As Elaine Rhoton put it: 'The OM ship's project by its very nature tended to attract the bold, individualistic, adventurous types, so the OM ship had a superabundance of forceful, bigger-than-life personalities – the kind of people who have the vision and drive necessary to pioneer a project but who also, unfortunately, often produce a trail of sparks as they run against others in the process.'[35]

Tensions were not continuous; indeed, some of the closest and most long-lasting friendships within OM were formed on board.

One aspect of this (and for many the most significant), was that within the limits of the 'social policy', in which permission to date had to be approved, many romances flourished – as they did in OM as a whole. In this early period, for example, Björn Kristiansen married Ann Rossiter, an English midwife whom he met on the *Logos*. One of the early OMers working in the Middle East, Hanna Zack, who became the women's leader on the *Logos*, married George Miley. But there were always some difficult – sometimes very difficult – relationships on board, and occasionally the problems loomed large. George Miley wrote: 'There are indeed many black days when we wonder if this ministry can, or even should, continue.'[36]

One such 'black day', in 1972, occurred as an unforeseen consequence of the visit of President Marcos, the President of the Philippines. This was the incident of the expensive cigars. It became the ship's practice to invite a high-ranking official to a reception at each port and in the Philippines, much to the surprise of the team, the President agreed to come. Gifts were given and received in the traditional way at the official reception, but resentment among the engineers on board boiled up because they received medallions while the deck officers received beautifully wrapped gifts – expensive cigars. The issue was not the cigars themselves, since noone on board smoked. Rather, when the *Logos* had been asked to provide a list of ship's officers, the engineers had not been included. The engineers showed their strong displeasure. Action evidently had to be taken.

George Miley and Frank Dietz felt intimidated because they were not professional seamen and there were fears that 'the project might go under simply because of the antagonism ... on board'. George Miley, partly because he had joined the ship reluctantly, had stood back from the problems. The 'battle of the cigars' convinced him that he had to be proactive: people were brought together and a new spiritual direction for the ship team was set.[37]

As well as tensions caused by rank, George Verwer was aware of tensions caused by varied cultural contexts. 'We cannot come', he insisted, 'as a brazen group of Westerners transporting

European culture. This ship is becoming more Asian every day. One fourth of the adults on the ship are Asians.'[38] In Sri Lanka, George Barathan joined the ship and was one of the first Asians to take major responsibility in this area, becoming *Logos* programme director, doing extensive line-up, and later becoming OM's Singapore field director. K. Rajendran, from India, was another significant Asian leader, serving as *Logos* personnel director.[39] The ship ministry has been another important dimension of the huge part that Asia has played in the story of OM.

For George Verwer, the variety of cultures present on the ship, with people from over twenty nations, offered a great educational and spiritual experience, one that was richer even than being with OM in India. Indeed the ideal mix of experience for an OM leader became both India and the ship. This served to bond the wider OM leadership together over this period in the movement's history. George Verwer made it clear that those who had spent two years in India would be challenged to spend a year on the *Logos*. As he developed the theme of cross-cultural sensitivity, George suggested that taking personal transistor radios and tape-recorders on board could represent a problem, a 'stumbling-block', for those who could not afford such things. He encouraged everyone on board to 'unite in terms of living on the barest essentials', although at the same time he hoped that people would not 'judge one another'.[40]

A further pressure was the amount and complexity of the work to be done on the ship. The daily routine started between 5.00 am and 6.30 am. Work was carried out on deck, in the engine room, in the school, the galley, the pantry, the radio room, the print room, the office, the clinic, the laundry and the library. Other tasks included mechanical work on vehicles – thirty vehicles could be transported at once – as well as plumbing, painting, cleaning and electrical work. Other ministries emerged: for example a singing group, the 'Logos Singers'. When in port the pressures increased. After the very busy programme in 1972 in the Philippines, for example, many on board were drained. 'The crew was understaffed and overworked, fighting constantly to keep old equipment working, especially the generators.'[41] The team needed rest, but instead they were soon in Indonesia, facing a demanding range of activities: Christian Literature Crusade (CLC) provided a huge amount of literature for distribution; teams travelled in Volkswagen vans into the villages; meetings on shore attracted twenty thousand people; 120 Indonesian volunteers worked on the ship; over three thousand copies of an Indonesian edition of George Verwer's book, *Revolution of Love*, were sold; and up to ten thousand people per night attended the showing of Gospel films.[42] An enormous amount of work was needed to deliver and oversee all this.

The larger scale of the *Logos'* journeys attracted many more people into OM. In 1973 John Yarr and his family returned to Australia, leading to the development there of an OM prayer and recruiting base. In Sudan, in the same year, a young Sudanese Christian, Kamal Fahmi, walked into Peter and Birgitta Conlan's *Logos* line-up office in Khartoum and announced that God was calling him to join the ship. But when he later spoke to someone else he was told 'how complicated it is to join and that I needed personal [financial] support'. Kamal Fahmi asked advice from a missionary in charge of the youth group in his church, and although the missionary did not discourage him, he commented that 'these people [OM] are not organized'. A conversation took place with George Miley and Frank Dietz, who initially told Kamal that he was too young, but the next day they changed their minds, accepting him on a trial basis.[43] He was later to become a leader in the region and one of the significant international leaders of OM.

In the USA, there were important developments within STL. Harley and Debi Rollins from the USA left the management of the bookstore on the *Logos* in 1974, when Harley took up the position of sales director for STL in Bromley, Kent. A US publisher gave some free books to the *Logos* and as a result STL USA, as it was then known, was begun in 1975 by Harley Rollins' father. It was located in a garage in Waynesboro, Georgia, USA. In what was a major step forward for OM's literature work, Harley returned to his native Georgia in 1977 to develop the STL USA operation (later renamed OM Literature). The first major donation launching this ministry to a new level was fifty thousand *Living Bibles*, given by Kenneth Taylor. As the STL ministry expanded, new premises were found. Huge quantities of books were shipped abroad, especially to India and the ships. Among these were many 'bookazines' (books in magazine format) which were distributed by OM teams around the world. In 1990, Harley Rollins set up a Christian literature business named 'Rollins Associates' and served as chairman of a charity, 'Great Commission Foundation', as well as being on the board of The Wilson Foundation, which gave significant help to OM.[44]

Such new developments often emerged step by step, rather than being carefully planned. But was 'the true OM vision' one that necessarily involved the kind of rapid expansion that was taking place in the 1970s? George Verwer, who placed a very high value on relationships, was concerned that OM's programme was beginning to involve too many people, which could lead to the movement becoming impersonal. 'In many ways', he mused in the mid-1970s, 'I want to stop ... having new projects, and just dig in with all intensity where we are.' Yet he had a passion for genuine 'special projects' in mission, partly influenced by the thinking of the significant Spanish evangelical author and publisher, Samuel Vila. George's 'burden for spiritual life and reality' was central to all that he did, but he was convinced that alongside the priority of 'spiritual life, reality, worship' there needed to be a vision for 'new avenues of outreach' in many lands.[45]

Operation World

The *Logos* opened up many new countries to OM. Over the course of eighteen years, the ship visited 103 countries. Destinations in the 1970s, in addition to those already mentioned, included Bangladesh, Thailand, the United Arab Emirates, Iran, Qatar, Malaysia, the Maldives, Djibouti, Oman, Bahrain, Brunei, Taiwan, South Korea, Japan, Italy, Turkey, Egypt, Malta, Tunisia, Portugal, Ireland, Germany, Norway, Sweden, Belgium, Senegal, Sierra Leone, Liberia, Ivory Coast, Ghana, Nigeria,

Cameroon, Mauritius, Reunion, Comoros, Tanzania, France, Jordan, Saudi Arabia, Pakistan, Papua New Guinea, Australia, New Zealand, Tonga, Western Samoa, Fiji, New Caledonia and the New Hebrides. Many countries in Asia were visited on a regular basis.

The last few months of 1972 and the first part of 1973 are indicative of the *Logos*' patterns at other times. In November 1972 the ship berthed in Abadan, Iran, with an oil company providing the berth free of charge. A reporter from Iran's leading weekly newspaper came on board, was greatly impressed, and wrote a four-page feature. Des Harper, later assistant director of the *Logos*, joined the ship.[46] The early part of 1973 saw what was termed 'break-throughs in Bombay'. Reports noted that 750,000 pieces of literature went out during the month-long stay. Television crews made a documentary about the ship. Schools were particularly open: the Vice-Principal of one Roman Catholic school in the city read a book by George Verwer ten times.[47] By March 1973 the ship had been in Madras, where five thousand people came on board each day; in Goa, where many *Living Bibles* were sold; and in Sri Lanka, where ministry and cheap refuelling took place.[48] Much of this pattern of activity would be repeated and the ship would return to many of these ports in the years to come. For large numbers of evangelicals in many countries, the *Logos* became an international evangelical symbol.

Many government and media figures were also aware of and intrigued by this unique 'International Educational Ship'. A report in the *Ethiopian Herald* in October 1973 described how 'His Imperial Majesty' Haile Selassie I, had attended a reception staged by 'the staff and crew of the International Educational Ship'.[49] Another regular feature became the International Night. This started in Istanbul, Turkey, in 1975, when Frank Fortunato, who was responsible for the music on the ship, put together a concert with a choir and cultural contributions – folk dances, songs – from the thirty nationalities on board.[50] Enthusiastic praise from his Highness, Sheikh Isa bin Sulaman Al-Khalifa, ruler of Bahrain and its dependencies, was reported in 1977.[51] In preparation for visiting Sierra Leone that year, Stan Thomson, who did the line-up, was able to arrange an interview with the president, the prime minister and other leading officials. The *Logos* was mentioned on radio every day and TV programmes also featured her. On the last Sunday, 5,400 people visited the ship.[52] The story was similar elsewhere in West Africa. In Liberia, the ship was given thirty minutes of prime TV viewing time. In Ivory Coast, Bernd Gülker, later director of OM Ships, and Peter Conlan, coordinating the West Africa line-up, negotiated a nationwide broadcast of the ship's morning worship service.[53]

New people joined the *Logos*. George Herbert Paget, a very well-known and respected retired British captain, followed Björn Kristiansen, who decided to move on. Fritz Schuler joined for a year in 1974 before returning to Germany to become OM leader there. In the same year, Allan and Rhonda Adams from Australia joined the ship in Puducherry, India, with Allan taking the post of *Logos* programme director. Allan Adams, a medical doctor, had a particular concern for hurting people.[54] This led to a significant counselling ministry within OM and beyond. Mike and Jorie Stachura joined in 1974, in Indonesia. They were soon involved in leadership; Mike as book exhibition manager and in line-up. Irma Svensson, from Sweden, joined the leadership team and developed the work with women. David Hicks, who with his wife Cathy had worked with OM in India since 1967, moved to the *Logos*, working alongside and then (from 1977) succeeding George Miley as director.[55]

The general expansion of OM in Asia was very significant, and in particular more East Asians were becoming part of OM. Rodney Hui, from Singapore, heard David Adeney, who was a missions spokesman within the Overseas Missionary Fellowship (OMF) and was Dean of the Discipleship Training Centre in Singapore, speaking at his church. Part of the message referred to OM, and Rodney felt called into OM's work. He joined the *Logos* in 1975 and later worked with OM elsewhere – in Malaysia and in Bangladesh, where he assisted Mike Lyth, the OM leader.[56] Rodney Hui and Geraldine Lee were among those who would go on to take major regional responsibility within OM. In the later 1970s, hundreds of East Asians (for example from Singapore) brought a new culture that OM had to absorb. At the same time, Rodney argues, it was the ministry of the *Logos* that stimulated mission vision in the East Asia Pacific region, starting with short-term mission. However, it was realised that the *Logos* could not take all of the increasing number of Asian recruits. The vision grew of the ship as a catalyst to enable the sending out of missionaries 'not only from Europe and North America, but also from Asia, Africa and Latin America'.[57]

There was also an increased emphasis in this period on holistic mission – later often called integral mission. This had always been present in OM, going back to the early ministry in Mexico to people living on a rubbish dump. In his arguments for a ship, George Verwer included the possibility that it could be used for relief work in times of crisis or emergency. He saw the labour force on the ship as always being 'ready to serve others'.[58] Elaine Rhoton comments that in 1972, during ministry in Bangladesh, the 'lofty, idealistic plans to use *Logos* for relief work were brought down to reality', as it was recognised how complicated this was logistically. Dr Arrawattigi, the ship's doctor, however, and two of the nurses, set up clinics there.[59]

The most dramatic relief effort undertaken by the *Logos* was the rescue of ninety-three Vietnamese refugees in October 1980. The *Logos* had visited Vietnam in 1974, not long before the communist takeover, and the response in the city of Saigon had been huge. OM leaders had been warned of the problems of picking up Vietnamese refugees – the 'boat people' as they were called – since most countries did not want them, but when faced with the reality of people in such desperate need, actually alongside the *Logos* in small boats, it was decided to take them on board. The challenges of accommodating ninety-three additional people for what turned out to be eight weeks were enormous. There was a great deal of political wrangling about where they could be resettled. Local line-up leader Lloyd Nicholas, an Australian, talked with the British consul in Bangkok, and Peter Conlan with the Foreign Office in London. The first response was that 'the British government did not consider it their responsibility to resettle the refugees'. However, following the proposal of a united prayer vigil on the steps of the Foreign Office, the British government relented and agreed to guarantee their settlement. Eight years later, Graham Wells, the last director of the *Logos*, met a Chinese Christian in Birmingham who told him: 'The *Logos* saved my life.'[60]

A final new development for the *Logos* at the end of the 1970s was the first 'Operation World' conference, held when the *Logos* was in Singapore. The first edition of the book *Operation World* was written by Patrick Johnstone in 1964 – to provide pointers for prayer in the context of the work of the Dorothea Mission. In 1974, he enlarged the production and two years later George Verwer became involved, as a result of which *Operation World* was published by STL.[61] In 1977 Dave Hicks, as the *Logos* director, used *Operation World* to produce prayer cards, which were translated into a number of languages. An invitation by WEC International in 1978 to Patrick Johnstone and his wife Jill to become the Mission's International Directors of Research led to an opportunity for the Johnstones to spend 1979 working on and with the *Logos*. The conference in Singapore was named after the book. It embraced the themes often emphasised by OM – world mission and New Testament discipleship. Later, the publicity OM gave *Operation World*, especially through George Verwer as he spoke at large meetings, helped to lead to its wide distribution around the world, in six languages. The conference in Singapore provided a pattern for subsequent 'Operation World' conferences in several other countries, including Australia, South Korea, Japan, India, Germany, France, UK, USA and Brazil.[62]

On the move

Although the *Logos* represented 'a lot of ship', and certainly a great deal was accomplished through the ship ministry, it had limitations. In 1972, a British marine engineer met George Verwer at an OM conference and, with great enthusiasm, told him that half a dozen people were praying for a second ship. George was unimpressed, telling the enthusiast that he had 'no idea of all the tears and heartbreak' involved in the *Logos* project. The idea of a second ship began to capture the imagination of others in OM, however, and gradually George, who was both a visionary and skilled at weighing up possibilities, moved from rejection to beginning to ask practical questions. A key one was – who would lead a second ship? Around the same time, Dale Rhoton, who had supported literature work in Eastern Europe, began to think of something new. Much to their own surprise, in 1973 Dale and Elaine Rhoton wondered whether the ship might be right for them. At an OM leaders' conference in September 1974, it was agreed that moves should be made to purchase a second ship. The plan was that George Miley would assume oversight of both ships and Dale Rhoton would eventually become director of the new vessel.[63]

In April 1975, therefore, George Verwer presented an extended rationale for the purchase of a second ship for OM. The *Logos* had operated at a lower cost than OM could have expected: people were in fact operating more economically than they could have done on land. More books were sold and the impact on local churches was greater than OM could have imagined. There had been many openings in the mass media. Nationwide impact had been felt in countries where OM had not been present before. George also spoke about the major challenge of the Mediterranean and Black Sea areas – twenty countries and a hundred sea ports. A second ship would give support to countries such as Turkey, where much money and effort had been expended with little result. There were great possibilities for getting young people involved in eastern Mediterranean countries, where – although they would be limited as to which books they could sell – person-to-person conversation was still possible and worked well. Finally, OM already had potential crew members for a second ship.[64]

Already Frank and Anneli Dietz had left the *Logos* in order to prepare the way for a possible second vessel. They based themselves in Anneli's home country of Finland, where she had helped to make contacts for OM in the 1960s. Their time there in 1974–75 led to the establishment of OM Finland.[65] Mike Poynor, with his extensive expertise in marine engineering, investigated ships that were on the market.[66] But OM leaders were not yet unanimous, and in his memorandum of April 1975 George Verwer suggested that there was something to be said for OM going deeper, rather than continuing to expand. However, he was happy that George Miley had taken over the running of the *Logos* project and that Dale Rhoton was devoting himself to the possible new ship. In that year, the *Logos* visited South Korea, from where many future OMers would come, and Japan, where Prince Mikasa opened the book exhibition. George Verwer emphasised again the number of Asians wanting to come on the ship. The 'Third World', he said, was 'on the move'.[67]

South Korea was a significant example of this new movement. In 1975, when the *Logos* visited Incheon, the port city of Seoul, for the first time, it made a great impact across the nation. Korean churches began to send significant numbers of their young people for training with OM. Strategic partnerships emerged between OM and Korean agencies, including the Joy Mission and the Korea Harbour Evangelism (KHE), which was the first indigenous non-Western maritime mission agency in the world. Then under the leadership of Paul Ki-Man Choi, KHE became a channel for recruiting hundreds of cross-cultural missionaries. Perhaps the name most closely associated with the extraordinary growth of OM Korea is one of Korea's most distinguished Christian leaders, Pastor Oak Han Heum, founder of Seoul's SaRang Community Church. John Oak, as he is known internationally, became the founding chairman of the Korean OM Board of Directors. His vision was to renew lay ministry in Korean churches and, under his leadership, hundreds of Korean young people joined OM. Among them was Jihan Paik, who served with his wife in Turkey and helped found OM's ministries in the Caucasus, before becoming Field Leader for OM Korea in 2005.[68]

Although George Verwer was arguing in 1975 that the period of Anglo-Saxon dominance was over, with Asians, Africans and others ready to reach out across the world, and while recognising this development constituted part of the rationale for a second OM ship, he was still 'personally frightened by the whole idea'. He admitted he had fought against it and tried to forget it for two years. Others in OM, he noted, including George Miley and Dale Rhoton, were keener. George Verwer insisted that if OM leaders in each field were not united about the idea – 'like-minded' – then it was wrong to move ahead. His core belief, as always, was that the issue had to do with spirituality. It would, he argued, take 'spiritual renewal in hundreds of lives' before a second ship could become a reality. In the light of that, his ultimate call was to do the will of God and not 'sit back in ease and comfort'. 'Faith', he concluded, in a phrase that expressed OM's thinking, 'is the Victory.'[69]

Plans were now made for a German trust to be the legal owner of the new ship, when it was purchased, and Mike and Carol Ann Poynor and their family moved ashore ready to join the new vessel. In July 1977 an Italian ship, the *Franca C* was inspected – believed to be the oldest passenger ship of her size in operation. As the *Medina*, she was built in 1914 by Newport News Shipbuilding and Dry Dock Company for the Mallory Steamship Company of the USA. A Panamanian company acquired her in 1948 and converted her into a passenger ship, with cabins for 287 people and dormitories for an additional 694 people. In 1952, she was resold to an Italian company, the Costa Line, converted from steam to diesel power, and named the *Franca C*. Later she became a cruise liner. In December 1977 the purchase of the *Franca C* by OM (by *Gute Bücher für Alle*, the German trust) was finalised. The *Franca C* became the *Doulos* (Greek for 'servant'). Yet another new chapter in OM's mission was opening up.[70]

Conclusion

The story of OM and its venture into ships in the 1970s is a remarkable one. Other Christian organisations became interested in the idea. YWAM, after giving a significant amount of money to OM to help with the purchase of the *Doulos*, bought their own first ship, the *Anastasis*, in 1979. The story of the *Logos* in the 1970s and into the 1980s is one of amazing new opportunities opening up. Between October 1970 and January 1988, 7.48

million people visited book exhibitions connected with the ship and 370,000 people attended meetings held on board. About 51 million pieces of Christian literature were distributed, of which about 450,000 were Bibles and New Testaments.[71] Almost everywhere the *Logos* went, a significant impact was seen. One summary said: 'Presidents, Sheikhs and other dignitaries welcomed the ship to their countries. National radio and television carried testimonies, songs and messages. Large international rallies held at public stadiums also enabled many to hear the word of God. Numerous teams travelled inland in order to visit and encourage missionaries and local churches.'[72] The *Logos* and, as we will see, the *Doulos*, were crucial catalysts in promoting short-term training and providing opportunities for innovative ministry for many more people. The attractions of the ships were huge. Through book exhibitions, OM's ministry, pioneered by the *Logos*, was able to penetrate into regions where normally it could not have operated. The witness of such a diverse community also had a powerful impact on visitors. The pioneering work of the *Logos* has rightly been termed an 'extraordinary ministry'.[73]

Chapter 5

Spirit-Controlled Expansion

In moving from the 1960s to the 1970s, George Verwer had kept alive the concept of OM's involvement in 'total revolution'. In April 1971, he wrote to twenty-four key OM leaders throughout the world about the challenge of world mission. He was writing on the *Logos*, 'as we sail through the beautiful calm waters of the Mozambique straits', and drew attention to the amazing provision of the ship, but his vision for 'mobilising the Church' was far wider. His particular concern was for disciple-making strategies to reach the great cities of the world. To have these priorities would, he argued, 'mean a total revolution throughout the whole of Operation Mobilisation', and he warned that without openness to such changes, OM 'if we are not careful, will degenerate like almost every other Christian movement in history'. He was now talking about a 'revolution of love and balance'.[1]

Four years later, he developed his thinking about the future direction of OM in a letter (March 1975) that was intended to be shared with all OMers. He began by reflecting on the fact that it was twenty years since he had committed his life to Christ in Madison Square Garden. His response to all that had happened since then was summed up in a phrase (the title of a hymn by Fanny Crosby often sung in OM) – 'To God be the Glory'. This was not, however, a time for looking back. George offered OMers a phrase which he considered important for OM in the years to come. He wanted 'Spirit-Controlled Expansion', an expansion that took account of the past but that was open to new developments and that was 'led of the Holy Spirit'. For him, this meant an increase of 'true spirituality' in OM, an increase in 'like-mindedness', facing failures and weaknesses with 'a new dimension of faith and reality'.[2] This chapter will explore the practical outworking of these themes in the wider ministry of OM in the 1970s.

Something big

Although the *Logos* was central to the expansion of OM in the 1970s, there were many other developments not directly related to the ship. India was crucial. As OM leaders looked to the new decade, they envisaged 'something big, something that would catch the imagination of the faithful prayer partners across India and around the world', and would mould and unite the scattered teams around India.[3] Thomas Samuel spoke about the exhilaration of this period, as OM India continued pioneering and consolidating.[4] It was decided to launch in 1970 a programme across India, 'Operation 10 Million'. OM teams would distribute ten million Christian leaflets in south, north-west and eastern India. This huge venture was followed in 1973 by 'Project Ten', in which ten teams, comprising 150 young people, worked in Bihar.[5] In this period, many future OM India leaders and others sent by their missions to OM, received training. Courses lasted up to one year. In 1997, Marcus Chacko calculated that out of thirty senior leaders in OM India at that time, twenty had joined OM in the 1970s. There was an emphasis on developing leaders through involvement in mission and through structured training programmes.[6] George Verwer was already envisaging changing times: with foreign missionaries having to leave India, it was essential to have trained Indian leaders to take on OM's expanded mission.[7]

Changes were evident in the early 1970s. Thomas Samuel felt that there was 'something more' he wanted to do and he spoke to George Verwer. The opportunity arose to buy a small hunting lodge called 'Wild Heritage' in the Nilgiri hills, Tamil Nadu, which was used by OM for conferences and prayer retreats. The owners, Johnny Mendekhar and his wife, offered the property to

OM at a low price and Thomas Samuel saw this as fulfilling his desire for 'new exploits for the Lord'. The OM policy in that period was not to own property and when Thomas approached George about a possible purchase, the answer was 'No'. Money came, however, from other sources, and the property was purchased, then registered in OM's name. Thomas was ecstatic. His vision was for the centre, now called Philemon's Home, to be 'a multifaceted ministry hub'. There was disagreement, however, over the way in which Thomas was making known the financial needs of the project, a procedure which violated OM's rules at that time. Eventually, Thomas Samuel considered it was time to move out of OM and to set up ministry based at Philemon's Home, which he called Quiet Corner.[8]

Another Indian ministry was pioneered in this period by M. Paulose, who had joined OM in 1965 and, after basic training in south India, worked in north India, especially Bihar, and had 'intensive training' on the *Logos* in 1971. His vision was for church planting and, since OM India was not involved in this work at the time (although it did become important later), he left the movement in 1972. He and Sarojam, his wife, felt a call to the island of Rameswaram, known as the second most holy place for Hindus in India. There was much opposition to the ministry but, following through his early vision, he became involved in the initiation and growth of what developed into a large Christian congregation, and oversaw the planting of more than 150 other churches.[9]

In 1973, Ray Eicher and Alfy Franks took over from Thomas Samuel as OM India joint leaders, with Ray contributing particularly through effective administration and Alfy giving priority to personnel and pastoral care. Both continued the emphasis on large-scale mission and training. During 1974, the first major All India Outreach was organised. The state of Uttar Pradesh (UP), with 120 million people, was chosen as the focus. During the months of October–December, a huge mission was arranged, entitled REACH UP '74, involving all the OM teams. More than three hundred people took part. The teams were made up of a mixture of longer-term OMers, short-termers (those working for one to three months) and people from the *Logos*. David Lundy, from Canada, was central coordinator. Most teams had trucks, so that personnel and large amounts of literature could be transported. About half a million gospel packets, as well as Bibles, evangelistic books and many leaflets, were distributed throughout Uttar Pradesh. All the OM tracts, in line with procedures established in Mexico in the 1950s, included an invitation to write in for a Bible correspondence course. Many thousands of people signed up – in fact the administrators could not cope. Radio programmes were important for immediate follow-up.[10]

Although India was by this time OM's pace-setting field, the Indian ministry was closely related to OM's wider work. Europeans and North Americans were involved, generally travelling to and from India overland in OM vehicles. After REACH UP '74, a Volkswagen van left for Belgium: this journey ended in tragedy. Between Belgrade and Zagreb, in Yugoslavia, the van had a head-on collision with a truck. Four of the OMers were killed: a married couple, Chris and Hillevi Begg, both aged thirty, Jay Sunanday, aged twenty-four, who had studied in the USA and planned to stay on in India, and Sharon Brown, aged twenty-three, who had studied at Biola College and was George Verwer's secretary. Chris Begg, originally from New Zealand, had studied at Newcastle University, and Hillevi, who had been born in India, had studied in Sweden where she became a qualified teacher. They had helped to start OM's ministry in Bangladesh and were also gifted singers. Two others in the vehicle were injured, but survived: Fritz Schuler, who had come to India for the REACH UP programme and was about to take responsibility for OM's German office, and Frank Fortunato, Sharon Brown's fiancé, who was music director on the *Logos*. The loss of these fine OM leaders was a massive shock, and from OM India there were many expressions of heartfelt appreciation of them and their work.[11]

As well as the large-scale and concentrated outreach, teams continued to work in many areas all round the year. K.P. Yohannan had a passion for the unreached villages of the Punjab in the north. His experiences there included dramatic encounters, such as one with a young man who lay on the ground, in the presence of the team, tongue lolling out of his mouth. The team prayed for his release from evil powers and, as K.P. Yohannan describes it, Sundar John 'was delivered, gave his life to Jesus and was baptized'. Later he went to Bible college and subsequently was involved in planting several churches. In the 1970s, K.P. Yohannan set up Gospel for Asia (GFA), a church planting movement, which three decades later was deeply involved in training and supported more than fourteen thousand national missionaries in ten Asian nations. With many of its key leaders from an OM background, GFA has placed great emphasis on Christian literature.[12]

Like-minded leaders

In his letter of March 1975, his 'Third Decade Memo', George Verwer suggested that OM needed a 'more permanent core of like-minded leaders', some 'long-term people in administration' and then many more people who would 'only stay with us for a few years at the most'. He was in favour of mobility, and opposed any idea that those who stayed long-term were 'some kind of special elite' with 'all kinds of special privileges'.[13] India is a good example of people moving into and out of OM and of long-term adherence to OM. Among those who moved on in this period, several took up roles in other organisations. Enoch Anthony led OM's Delhi base before moving to the Gospel Recording Association; A. Steven founded the Cornerstone (World Challenge) Ministries; Ebenezer Sunder Raj became General Secretary of the India Missions Association; Naomi (Jeyaraj) Emmanuel took up work among prostitutes in Bombay; P.C. Alexander made an important contribution to the Pocket Testament League; and Thomas Mathai launched New Life Ministries.[14] Others settled in the West, although OM did not want to be a stepping stone in this direction.[15] The place of Western connections was the subject of much discussion. In this context, George Verwer pressed for workers in OM India to be supported financially both from within India and through help from the West.[16]

There was movement out of and into OM India, but there were also many people who provided continuity. This was crucial if momentum was to be maintained. REACH UP '74 was followed up in Uttar Pradesh by FOLLOW UP '75. In a moving gesture, Hillevi Begg's father, a missionary in Uttar Pradesh, donated the insurance money received after her death to UP '75. After UP '75, the work in Uttar Pradesh was firmly established. The following year saw a new programme, 'Love Your Neighbour', with teams working for several months in their own states. There was a strong emphasis on fulfilling OM's goal to work 'in partnership with the church', and wherever teams planned to go, they contacted local evangelical churches in advance. 'Love Maharashtra', which started in 1979, was a good example. About one hundred churches, organisations and mission agencies joined with OM. The outreach lasted three months. Hundreds of young people came to faith in Christ or had their faith renewed, and many received a call into mission. It was decided to have a major 'All India' outreach every three years, with the OM teams in India working together.[17]

The emphasis on training became even more marked in this period. WEC offered their Indian headquarters building, 'Birla House', situated in an ideal location in Lucknow (the capital of Uttar Pradesh) for OM to use. This became an important training centre. Eventually WEC generously gave the premises to OM as a gift. This period saw a large number of women joining OM India. Joan Beesley thought carefully about how to recruit and train women who had leadership potential and this vision gave birth to the innovative Women's Training Programme. The later 1970s saw Berit Johannson working alongside Linda Cowley, and then taking on the responsibility of training national leaders. As part of this leadership development, Joyce Cherian was trained to head the All-India Women's Coordinating Team.

Joseph D'Souza, from a Roman Catholic family in Karnataka, who became an evangelical Christian when at university, had his first experience of OM as a volunteer on the *Logos* in Goa in 1973 and then joined the movement. He was to be a shaping force within OM, a global missions spokesperson and a voice for the oppressed Dalit-Bahujan people in India. Building on what was being done for women in OM India, he promoted the idea of team members having biblical education alongside their on-going ministry.[18] The Intensive Training programme overseen by Frank Dietz was also a catalyst. Joseph D'Souza, when in his mid-twenties, became OM India's training coordinator, based at Lucknow, and he initiated significant leadership and vocational training programmes.[19] These were to help equip and connect many future evangelical leaders in India.

One of those future leaders was K. Rajendran. He joined OM in 1970, impressed by the lifestyle of an OM team. His initial plan was to stay six months, but he became a long-term team member. While in Tamil Nadu, he met OM leaders, Chacko Thomas and Ebenezer Sunder Raj, who spoke to him about the needs of Bihar. This led him to work in Bihar and he later commented that he was 'a Tamilian by birth but a Bihari by choice', at home in both places. On one occasion, in 1976, he was preaching to a large crowd and realised that an equal number of Hindus and Muslims were listening. He began his message by speaking about 'one true God', at which point the Hindus present started objecting but the Muslims agreed, then went on to talk about Jesus as the Son of God, and here the Muslims present objected but the Hindus kept quiet. With some difficulty but without causing a riot, he concluded his message. K. Rajendran later worked for seven years on the *Logos*, with his wife Pramila, from north India, and then joined Joseph D'Souza, becoming OM training coordinator at Lucknow.[20] These 'like-minded' leaders were committed to integrating field work and biblical education. Barriers between practical and academic were, as far as possible, broken down.

OM also continued to work hard to ensure that there were no barriers between those from the West and those from India, or between OMers who had different callings. One example of how this model operated was the way in which both Westerners and Indians were involved in supporting OM's fleet of vehicles. The culture within OM was so vehicle-orientated that the work of a mechanic could never be seen as secondary. Mechanics could be from any background and many were multi-skilled. Thus Enoch Anthony moved from the OM garage to recording, and his successor, Mike Wheate, later became OM's International Personnel

Officer. The OM garage provided vital support to keep all of OM India on the move. During much of the 1980s, the garage was led by Edward Ammanna, Ray Cooper and Maitan Ekka.

Ray Cooper's introduction to OM India was in 1979. He arrived at the garage in Ranchi, equipped with fine tools, and asked about the trucks. There were none. Frustrated with having nothing to work on, he then saw a derelict Jeep and asked if he could set to work on that. There was no money for parts. Then a telegram arrived saying that an OM truck had broken down in Orissa State. Itching to 'really help the team', he and Edward Ammanna headed off on a gruelling, all-day journey in an over-crowded bus; by the time they arrived Ray was exhausted. The Indian team spent the next three days reviving him with bananas, coconuts and glucose biscuits. He quickly learned that he would receive from India much more than he could ever give. Ray and Sonja Cooper were to spend several years in India before moving to Afghanistan.[21]

To heed this challenge

Although India was a clear OM priority in the 1970s, Europe remained a centre of OM's activities. In George Verwer's April 1971 letter, which had 'mission in the city' as its main theme, of the twenty-four key leaders to whom he wrote, eight were in European cities and seven were in India. The eight in Europe were Derek Virgin (London), Mike Evans (Paris), Jonathan McRostie (Brussels), Stuart Park (Madrid), Daniel Gonzáles (Barcelona), Giovanni Definis (Pisa), Heinz Strupler (Zürich) and Dale Rhoton (Vienna). Within Europe, there was particular interest in 1971 in OM's mission in France's small cities, towns and villages. Literature distribution on a massive scale was undertaken, enti-tled 'France '70–'71', with the aim of visiting and placing evangel-ical literature in every home in the small cities, towns and villages across the country.[22] Over eight hundred people came to help in France in 1970, in thirty teams. Eight million Christian leaflets were distributed. Many local churches cooperated. In 1971 about

1,300 people, working in fifty teams each month, were involved. By the end of the summer, five thousand people had responded to the offer of a correspondence course or of spiritual help in other ways.[23]

George Verwer appreciated the huge effort by Mike Evans and the team in France and urged other OMers 'to heed this challenge'.[24] Similar summer outreaches were held across Belgium in 1972, with the theme 'God is not far', and in 1980 with a different theme: 'Jesus in your heart, revolution in your life!' Leo Proot was one person who came to faith in Christ as a young man through the street ministry of OM in Belgium and he later became Belgium OM Field Leader, initiating creative outreach in music and drama. For three summers, from 1972 to 1974, OM teams also worked in all the towns and villages of fewer than two hundred thousand people in Italy.[25]

Attention was also given to mission in Britain. In 1972 Mike Evans, who had a strategic wider role within OM in Europe, drew together evangelical leaders in the north-west of England to plan for OMers to work with local churches. The programmes undertaken were typical of the range of activities undertaken by OM and by a growing number of churches in Britain and elsewhere in Europe in this period: visiting homes; a walk of witness; evangelistic coffee bars; a holiday Bible club; the showing of films; a team going round pubs and clubs; and literature distribution. In this case the chairman of the local committee was A.B. Baldwin, who was from the Brethren, and evangelical Anglican and Nazarene ministers were also involved.[26]

Many of those joining OM in this period were contacted through student Christian Union groups (known as CUs and affiliated in Britain to the Inter-Varsity Fellowship, or IVF, which later became the Universities and Colleges Christian Fellowship, or UCCF) or through well-known student churches.[27] Several initial British OM contacts had been made in Cambridge and Oxford, but the range of contacts spread, with OMers active at major IVF conferences. In April 1972 in Exeter University, for example, the CU held a 'missionary weekend' and two CU members who had been with OM in France spoke, calling for more students to serve with OM. Nigel Lee, who had been in India in the 1960s, was now one of the key coordinators of OM's links with the university CUs and he helped to set up OM prayer groups in several universities.[28] He later had senior responsibility within UCCF. On the mainland of Europe, OM student teams helped launch the work of IFES (the International Fellowship of Evangelical Students) in both Spain and Austria. Kees and Toos Rosies, from the Netherlands, organised outreach opportunities, including student outreach, in Belgium and Luxembourg, seeking new, innovative possibilities. Kees also coordinated the crucially important OM training conferences.[29]

The three areas of evangelism, training and literature continued to be central to OM's vision for Europe in the 1970s. There was an increasing interest in reaching immigrants, which would later become a much greater challenge. OM realised early on the importance of witness in immigrant areas. A team under the leadership of Les and Dot Wade, who had international OM experience, worked in the 1970s with Asians in England and attempted to draw local churches into the ministry.[30] This ministry became 'Friends from Abroad', then OM LUKE (Love United Kingdom Evangelism) and then OM Lifehope. Another OM team was based in Germany, seeking to make contacts among the one million Turkish immigrants.[31] Randy and Margie Lawler, who had served in Sudan, founded the Turning Point ministry among Arabs in London, joined by Norm and Joni Brinkley, who later gave many years to ministry in the Middle East and North Africa. OMers worked with London youth fellowships, including a Cantonese fellowship, with the hope that Cantonese young people would reach Asians in Britain.[32]

Several long-term OMers were heavily involved in taking meetings across Europe, which led to more young people joining OM. George Verwer travelled incessantly, speaking at major events and challenging people to discipleship and mission. At OM training conferences, some outside speakers were utilised, such as Ralph Shallis, a Brethren missionary in France and North Africa, and Homer Payne from the USA.[33] In 1975–6 there was a further summer mission in France, known as 'One Way', to reach out to the cities of more than fifty thousand. Tens of thousands of copies of the booklet *One Way* were distributed. A publishing house called Farel was established.[34]

The literature arm of OM, Send the Light, directed by Gerry Davey, was growing rapidly. In the 1970s, several STL bookshops were opened and STL became the largest evangelical book wholesaler in Britain. Premises in Bromley, Kent, were redeveloped to make STL offices. Of the profits that were made through books – the wholesale operation and the shops – 90 per cent was sent to assist in work in other countries.[35] OM's multifaceted ministry became widely known.

A particular challenge was to take Christian literature into Eastern Europe. In 1964, Dale Rhoton and other OMers met Richard Wurmbrand and his son, Michael, at a meeting in Bucharest. Richard Wurmbrand, recently released from prison after fourteen years of imprisonment for his faith, asked the OM team to bring Bibles into the country. Later, Richard Wurmbrand spoke of OM as the first organisation to 'smuggle Bibles behind the Iron Curtain'.[36] The language of 'Bible smuggling' became common. In 1968, a garage was opened in Germany to build special vehicles for carrying literature. The 'Greater Europe' (GE) OM team moved into Vienna, setting up a base for travel into Eastern Europe. As an example of the scale of the operation, in one year a million leaflets were distributed in Czechoslovakia. In 1970, some of the team moved to St Pölten, outside Vienna, for greater security.[37]

Dale Rhoton made contacts with other missions such as Underground Evangelism, Open Doors and *Licht im Osten*, who provided literature in Russian, Hungarian, Romanian, Czech and other languages. Experienced engineers and mechanics – initially Mike Koch and Ray Hill, and later Dave Babcock, Louis Huveneers, Terry Jarvis and Bob Craton – constructed vehicles with false floors or cavities in which literature was hidden. The GE teams, under the direction of Dennis Wright and John Hymus, who spoke Russian, transported not only millions of Bibles, tracts and Christian books but also parts to make printing presses. One printing machine was delivered in parts over the course of thirteen trips; it functioned for seventeen years. Other items for printing purposes, such as paper cutters, staplers, and cleaning chemicals, were transported. There were tense moments, arrests and expulsions (one of these even making the front page of the *Daily Telegraph* in 1969), but most journeys were successful.[38]

A remarkably creative venture, operated jointly by the Finnish Lutheran Mission and OM, was to send ready packed wooden houses from Finland to Greece and Cyprus, via Russia and Romania. These had Bibles stacked in spaces in the packing; twenty to forty thousand Bibles were sent with each truck. About six hundred thousand Bibles or equivalent-sized pieces of literature were transported as a result of this scheme.[39] Yet another idea was to sail a boat, with Bibles hidden on board, down the Danube through several communist countries, but a trial run, in which the boat had to go through forty-five checkpoints, showed this was not feasible.[40]

One 'out-of-the-box' plan was to get literature into the closed country of Albania by releasing helium balloons with packages of gospels from the *Logos* as it sailed along the Albanian coast. A test run conducted on the Danube was promising, but when it came to the real thing, it was realised that the test had been conducted with a stationary vessel and that the movement of the *Logos* created a down current which pulled the balloons into the water. Later, over five thousand Albanian-language gospels were packed into plastic bags, taken into Yugoslavia, and deposited in rivers flowing to Albania. Eventually border guards installed wire netting to stop the material. There was no way of knowing whether the literature in these packets was read, but after the end of communism, some OMers in Albania met a former border guard who had searched the rivers for such literature to burn it. He had not read it at the time, but he later became a Christian. One packet of literature even found its way into the Museum of Atheism in Tirana.[41] The challenge was to adapt mission in Europe to the very different contexts across the continent.

A broadening ministry

A short history of OM in 1984 reported, under the heading 'a broadening ministry', on growth in OM in the 1970s. The number of people on OM teams (excluding summer campaigners) in this period reached 1,600, with teams working in several countries in Europe (Britain, Ireland, Belgium, Austria, France, the Netherlands, Sweden, Finland, Norway, Switzerland and Germany), in the Middle East/North Africa (Turkey, Cyprus, Jordan, Israel, Egypt, Tunisia and Sudan), and in the Far East (Pakistan, India, Nepal, Bangladesh, Singapore and Malaysia). OM was also in the USA, Mexico and Canada. This was not a complete list, since OM was careful not to publicise its work in some places (for example in Eastern Europe) where such publicity could cause difficulties for local Christians.[42]

Between the twin poles of OM in the 1970s – India and Europe – several OM and OM-related enterprises were taking place. Key personnel noted in a survey in 1971 included Steve Richards in Istanbul, John Ferwerda coordinating work in Beirut, Bob Cook in Jerusalem, Virgil Amos in Iran and Victor Gledhill in Kathmandu. Across the Atlantic from Europe, Paul Troper was in New Jersey, Ron George in Los Angeles, Dick Griffin in Mexico City and Chuck Wilson in Toronto.[43] For two years, from 1970 to 1972, Greg Livingstone, after leading the Zaventem team, was involved in OM's ministry in Beirut and his gifts as a powerful recruiter were used to good effect. OM work grew very rapidly. Among those involved in this period were Bertil and Gunnel Engqvist, Mickey and Kathleen Walker, Terry Ascott, Birgitta Gustafsson (later Conlan), and Peter and Grace Ferguson.[44] There were over fifty OMers in Lebanon and work extended elsewhere in the Middle East.

Greg Livingstone's vision was for church planting, but others focused on literature, among them John Ferwerda and Terry Ascott, who set up Middle East Media.[45] In 1972 Greg and Sally Livingstone moved to Toronto to establish OM Canada. Greg's concern for the Middle East continued and in 1977 he became North American Director of North Africa Mission (NAM), subsequently recruiting David and Linda Lundy, who had been with OM, into NAM. After leading NAM-Canada, David Lundy returned to OM, leading OM Canada until 1994.[46] OM had many strategic wider connections.

By the early 1970s, OM had been involved in a number of countries for over a decade, including several countries where establishing a presence was sensitive and difficult. OMers later spoke of interrogations at borders, being held up at gun point, near-miss car bombings, expulsions, abduction, imprisonment, and highly ingenious ways of smuggling tracts. Interwoven with such experiences were many opportunities to offer personal witness and give out literature; occasional opportunities to speak to groups of people; the discovery of individuals who had come to Christ and the work of discipleship among new Christians.[47]

In Turkey, OM attempted to take advantage of a change in the law in 1973 which increased freedom of speech. Books formerly banned were being sold in 1974. OM produced a book, *The Third Alternative*, for free distribution, which was sent to five thousand Turkish leaders and intellectuals – Members of Parliament, university professors, writers, lawyers and newspaper editors. The book engaged with a common perception among Turkish intellectuals that the alternatives facing people were traditional Islam or Western materialism, and argued that there was 'a genuine third alternative – the Christian way'. The whole project was entitled 'Operation Intellectual'.[48] By the end of the 1970s, a few evangelical fellowships had been formed as a result of the work of OM teams, which had been present since the 1960s, and of other agencies that gradually began to work in the country. As others arrived, OM's policy was to cooperate with them.[49]

During the 1970s and 1980s, Denis Alexander was influential in helping to develop wider work in the Middle East. Howard and Nora Norrish also served in significant ways, over a long period of time, in ministry based in the region. In the 1970s, an Arab world coordinating team was established in Cyprus, with Bertil Engqvist from Sweden as leader. OM work emerged in the mid-1970s in Egypt, and then in Sudan, with the involvement of Kamal Fahmi. In Iran, the situation was seen as promising. OM teams had started serving in Iran in 1963, as had WEC, and OM cooperated with other agencies, such as the Bible Society, in widespread distribution of gospels. Dick and Shan Dryer, Paul and Jean White and Virgil and Martha Amos were among key personnel in Iran in the early days. Virgil Amos, as Field Leader, was one of the few African Americans to be a senior figure in OM. His successor, Ron George, went on to pioneer other significant outreaches to the Muslim world. An OM document in the 1970s described Iran as 'a land of revolutionary social and economic change at the crossroads of Asia'.[50]

In 1977 Mickey Walker became Field Leader in Iran, and spoke of teams selling around twenty-five thousand copies of the Gospel of Luke all around the country. The end of this ministry came suddenly in 1979 with the return of Ayatollah Khomeini and the Islamic revolution. OMers hurriedly packed to leave. Law and order was breaking down and petrol was rationed to a few litres per person. One of the girls in the team queued all night at a petrol station, and when she got to the pump the following morning she filled up her van's tank, and then the barrel in the back of the van. The crowd was too bemused by this foreign woman's actions to intervene. The team drove to Pakistan, leaving their enormous literature stock to Iranian Christians who were able to distribute large quantities in the chaos of the following months.[51]

Other ministries opened up in the 1970s. The suffering that was experienced by refugees as a result of the 1971 Pakistan–Bangladesh war led to OM becoming involved in Bangladesh. Millions of refugees poured into West Bengal and camps were set up along the border. The relief agency World Vision provided food, blankets and tents, and OM provided trucks and teams. Some fellowship groups were formed among those who turned to Christ in the refugee camps and when they returned to Bangladesh, they asked the OMers they had met if they could help. Teams of OMers began serving in Bangladesh, therefore, helping people to rebuild their lives. Mike Lyth, who had done significant work in India, moved to Bangladesh with his wife Elsie, and became Field Leader. Phil and Jennie Bushell served there for many years. Developments in Bangladesh represented an important step in OM's increasing involvement in meeting practical needs and in pioneering the contextualisation of the Christian message in diverse local settings.[52]

In the same period, OM work in Pakistan was started, an initiative that had been advocated by Ron George. In 1979, in Lahore, Mike and Kerstin Wakely (Mike from the UK and Kerstin from Sweden), together with a small number of short-term foreigners, started OM Pakistan. They were soon joined by Pakistanis and slowly won the confidence of both missionaries and church leaders, though many regarded OM's work as something of a high-risk operation. OM Pakistan later became almost entirely Pakistani, with national leadership. There was a particular focus on two areas – evangelism and training. After the earthquake of October 2005 in Pakistan, 'holistic' ministry developed, as teams sought to address the pressing needs of the Pakistani people, within and beyond the Christian community.[53]

OM's 'broadening ministry', both geographically and in terms of the range of ministries being undertaken, inevitably demanded more administration. The 1975 version of OM's Leadership Manual emphasised that OM's aim was to keep administrative costs to a minimum. Much of what was needed for effective administration – for example, equipment – was given to OM free of charge. By that time, there were boards of directors in eight OM fields and the work of these fields, covering twenty-five countries in which OM had teams, was registered with the appropriate governments.[54] Each team appointed a treasurer to handle money and keep financial records, which were submitted to national OM offices. From there, records were sent to the Central Accounting Office (CAO) at Zaventem.[55] Steve Hart, in charge of the CAO, was legendary for his attention to detail and this approach was affirmed by George Verwer, who warned that 'inefficient office operations' were 'deadly'.[56]

Very little money was spent on property during OM's first two decades: many of the properties OM used were rent-free. In 1975, George Verwer wrote a six-page memorandum, 'Thoughts on why we should not get involved in buying property'. He wanted

OM to continue to trust God to provide property, and pointed to the way in which this provision had been seen in (for example) Manchester and Bromley in the UK. 'I personally believe', he stated bluntly, 'that as OM gets into property, it will tend toward corruption.' For him, it was important to remember that 'most of our teams are living in the backs of trucks out in India, or in other difficult situations'.[57] This rigid policy, however, was to change. OM was acquiring property, even if – as in the case of Zaventem – it was bought for them by someone else. Not only did OM fields begin to have their own premises, but OMers were also encouraged to do the same. The emphasis in OM moved from a simple lifestyle to a 'moderate lifestyle'.[58]

In this period of expansion, George Verwer appealed for investment of personnel in wider coordination.[59] Dale Rhoton and Jonathan McRostie had a significant wider international role in OM. Greg Livingstone, after serving with OM Canada and then North Africa Mission (later Arab World Ministries), launched a new mission. His experience from 1982 in experimental work with NAM led him, with encouragement from NAM's leadership and George Verwer, to begin a new agency, Frontiers.[60] Within OM, informal leadership teams gave way to a formal group, gathering in International Leaders Meetings (ILM).

The appointment of Peter Maiden as British Director of OM was important in this period; his gifts in international leadership were increasingly recognised. Peter Maiden, from the Hebron Hall assembly, Carlisle, had worked in industry in an administrative capacity, and had been with an OM team in Spain in 1967 and seen considerable growth in a very small church in Cullera. During the next few years he was an itinerant evangelist and Bible teacher, working mainly in British universities and with Brethren assemblies. He had met George Verwer at the funeral of Keith Beckwith, a fellow-member of Hebron Hall, and in 1974 he accepted an invitation to join OM, to lead OM UK. From 1985 he began to work alongside George as OM's Associate International Coordinator.[61]

Revival or survival?

By the 1970s, OM was an established part of the wider evangelical scene. In the 1960s, there had been some concern expressed by some established missionary societies about its activities,[62] but by the early 1970s, OM's work was widely appreciated in Britain and elsewhere. At London Bible College (LBC), Gilbert Kirby, the Principal, encouraged OM leaders, as he had done in his previous position as General Secretary of the Evangelical Alliance. Among the OMers who studied at LBC was Bill Musk, who had been in Turkey and would later work with the Church Mission Society and the Episcopal Church in Egypt. He wrote important books on Islam.[63] Another was Peter Hill, who spearheaded the Festival of Light.[64] As in OM, evangelicals generally were becoming more involved in social action. In Britain, Tearfund, under George Hoffman, was to grow at a remarkable rate.[65] George Verwer and George Hoffman found they had much in common. Internationally, the integration of evangelism and social action was given considerable impetus by the Lausanne Congress of 1974. OM leaders were among the 2,700 Lausanne participants, 1,200 of whom were from the Two-Thirds World.[66] George Verwer, who was there, felt the impact of Lausanne's call for a holistic approach to mission. Of particular significance for him was the increasing awareness that world mission was not the responsibility of Anglo-Saxons or northern Europeans alone, 'but of the WHOLE church'.[67]

Within OM, however, questions regarding its internal culture were beginning to surface. Following visits with George Verwer to many OM teams around the world, a memorandum to OM leaders written in 1968 from Kathmandu by Peter Conlan raised a number of issues. Despite OM's emphasis on 'esteeming others' it was submitted that over-zealous team leaders too often failed to appreciate their team members properly. There was also a suggestion of inappropriate pressure to 'confess all' on some teams. While 'walking in the light' was good New Testament teaching, people needed space for personal privacy. Under the heading 'Contemporize or Fossilize', those on mission with OM were encouraged to remain in touch both with current events and the 'real' world.

A perhaps lighter question was OM's economical and conservative dress code. While valuing the unique role of 'Charlie', OM's second-hand clothing stores (to be found at all OM bases), the memo suggested that 'dullness and dowdiness are not signs of dedication'. There was also a hint that OM's militant approach to team life might succeed in workers 'enduring to the end' in a given campaign, but was less likely to encourage people to return for a second year. A plea was made for OM to become an international 'family' rather than a global 'regiment'. Finally, the memo urged OM to be less hesitant about the language of 'revival', arguing that fear of extremism and division had made this 'a hushed up and even unpopular word in OM circles'. Rather than a 'survival' mentality, sometimes less reliant on the work of the Holy Spirit and more linked with OM's disciplined regime, there was a call to heed George's frequent heart-cry for 'daily revival'.[68]

George Verwer himself stressed the challenge of change, but also wished to remain faithful to OM's original vision. One area of debate related to OM's caution about making known financial needs. OM's strict policy on this was being questioned and in time would change. In 1972, George wrote to William MacDonald, author of *True Discipleship*, to ask for his comments. The response was circulated. William MacDonald stated that the 'first and foremost argument against this practice [publicising financial needs] is that it does not have any scriptural precedent or support'. The apostles, he argued, 'never made their needs known'. He considered that the subject was 'closely linked with the life of faith'. The writers he cited to support his position were almost all Brethren authors. One, G.H. Lang, was quoted as saying that early Brethren leaders abandoned accepted methods of raising money to give 'the disbelieving world and an unbelieving church a fresh proof of the reality and faithfulness of God and the power and sufficiency of faith and prayer'. William MacDonald's approach to financial needs was that there should be 'information, but not solicitation'.[69] OM's financial policy over the next decade continued to be that OMers could not make their financial situation known unless they were approached about their specific needs.

It is clear that a degree of Brethren influence on OM's spirituality continued. This had been present in the North American roots of OM and had been reinforced in Britain. Keith Beckwith, in 1966, had written in typical fashion in the Brethren magazine, the *Witness*, that OM must avoid becoming 'some kind of man-made organisation'.[70] A decade later, notes published for a Brethren conference in Britain spoke about the denominational make-up of OM and described the Brethren representation as 'by far the largest'.[71] But OM was far from being a revival movement within the orbit of the Brethren. There were other powerful spiritual influences. In the 1975 Leadership Manual, a major aim was 'to be a company of praying people, hungry for daily revolution, reality, righteousness and world evangelism, especially in terms of the book, *Calvary Road*'.[72]

In the experience of George and Drena Verwer, the spirituality of the Keswick Convention, with its emphasis on a life surrendered to Christ, was crucially important. They had encountered Keswick's holiness teaching in the late 1950s, principally through George Duncan, a British minister who gave a week of ministry at Moody. George Duncan was the leading international Keswick speaker of the time. OM circulated tapes of messages given at the Convention. George Verwer also spoke at the Convention several times. In 1980, for example, he issued an impassioned plea to evangelicals meeting at the Convention to preach holiness and the Lordship of Christ – two of the central themes at Keswick.[73]

Writing to OMers on 11 November 1978, George Verwer set out his personal commitment to Keswick spirituality. He commented on the 'high percentage of us in OM [who] have been greatly blessed through some of the sermons of Keswick which have been distributed in printed form', and informed his fellow-OMers that STL would publish the 1978 *Keswick Week* – a volume that was produced each year with sermons from the Convention. His concern was to link people with Keswick's 'very Christ-centred, balanced and outstanding biblical message'. In addition, his letter emphasised several books, such as *Operation*

World, produced by Patrick Johnstone,[74] *No Easy Answers*, by Eugenia Price, *The Logic of Faith*, by Dale Rhoton,[75] and *From Now On*, by Ralph Shallis.[76] These were regarded by OM as basic at that time.[77]

In commending a wide range of authors, George Verwer was intentionally aiming to break down divisions in the evangelical community. His commitment was to having Calvinists and Arminians, charismatics and non-charismatics, working together. OM continued to draw its speakers from across the evangelical constituency. With the help of Tony Sargent, who fulfilled an important role within OM India as a visiting teacher and mentor, Martyn Lloyd-Jones agreed to speak on board the *Logos*. Lloyd-Jones, minister of Westminster Chapel, London, was highly influential within Reformed circles. The tape of his sermon on 'Word and Spirit', which addressed the polarisation that could take place over this issue, was widely distributed. Lloyd-Jones' commentary on the Sermon on the Mount was used within OM to counter Dispensationalist arguments that the Sermon was not applicable to contemporary Christians.[78] George Verwer was concerned about divisions between more traditional evangelical churches and 'the new and more spontaneous house groups and movements'. His prayer was that 'somehow we in OM may help bridge this gap and be used of the Lord to maintain deeper fellowship, understanding and appreciation between different groups and different movements'.[79]

Conclusion

The 1970s was a decade in OM's life in which the character of the movement was significantly changed and the vision broadened. The vision became 'Spirit-controlled expansion'. This expansion was principally due to the *Logos*, but there were other factors that contributed to the ongoing reshaping of OM. The role of India was crucial. Here was a model of the principles of internationalisation and indigenous mission work that were highly prized by OM. At the same time, Europe was a crucial base, not least for recruitment, and it was from central Europe that mission reached into the East European communist countries. As well as Eastern Europe, the Arab countries remained a priority for OM, and in these countries there was some progress. However, setbacks were also experienced, notably in Iran.

As OM moved into more and more countries, the calls issued in George Verwer's 'third decade memo' of 1975 were of critical importance. He called for a commitment to 'spiritual revolution', the life of faith, simplicity of lifestyle, team relationships, service to the churches, brokenness and compassion. He did not imagine that large numbers of Christian people were going to maintain a 'revolutionary lifestyle' but he did not wish to see OM lowering its own standards. At the same time, he was wary of spiritual pride, and called OM to humility. His message in 1975 was about a 'Revolution of Balance' to be set alongside the theme 'Revolution of Love'.[80] The life of discipleship, he argued, demonstrated 'not firstly in word, but in life and practice', was the key to effective mission.[81] Although OM was a movement that had world mission as its goal, the *Calvary Road* of surrender to Christ and his will always came before the missionary road.[82]

Chapter 6

The Enormous Value of Teamwork

The purchase and fitting of the *Doulos* was a massive financial step for OM to take, and some tensions were to result. George Miley commented that 'as with *Logos*, there are the financial mountains which loom so often before us'.[1] The agreed purchase price was $770,000, and although this was considerably less than the asking price, OM did not have the necessary funds when the contract was signed. However, on the due date, the money was paid in full. The next step was dry dock, which cost $100,000 – one-third of what had initially been estimated.[2] Another pressing need was for personnel. It became obvious that more people were going to be needed than had originally been anticipated. A great advantage in the initial stages, however, was that there were skilled people who had worked together on the *Logos* and in fact a 'second ship team' was in place. 'Once again', said George Miley, 'we see the enormous value of teamwork.'[3]

Gradually the necessary people started coming on board the *Doulos*. First there were about thirty-five adults, including families with children, among them Mike and Carol Ann Poynor and their four daughters, two of whom were six-week-old twins. There were initial struggles: there was no water on board the ship, the weather was freezing cold and, to make matters worse, the ship was not generating any electricity. Morning devotions were held in the main auditorium, which was big enough to seat five hundred people, and the small, shivering group seemed rather insignificant. Soon, however, the numbers of people reached fifty, and then eighty. For the maiden voyage there were 150 on board, more than had ever been on the *Logos*.[4] The number would grow to about 320, from up to forty countries. Through the ships and through other OM teams, the 1980s, which is the focus of this chapter and chapter seven, would see OM's ministry reaching further than ever before.

Latin Americans involved in missions

On 28 February 1978 the *Doulos* sailed to Bremen, Germany, with all bills paid. There the ship received a comprehensive refit. The swimming pool area was replaced by what was the world's largest floating book exhibition and bookstore. The *Doulos* was to carry up to six thousand different titles, with many thousands of books stacked in the holds. The early crew and staff included George Miley, director, who coordinated the work of both ships; Mike Poynor, marine and engineering superintendent, who also immersed himself in the re-fitting; Rex Worth, chief engineer; George Booth, first mate; Ebbo Buurma, chief steward; Stan Thomson, chief electrician; Mike Stachura, book exhibition manager; Frank Dietz, assistant director; Allan Adams, programme director; Manfred Schaller, personnel director; Peter Conlan, Robert Clement and Bernd Gülker, all line-up; Johannes Thomsen, first engineer; Randy Jury, welder; Francois Vosloo, carpenter; Nocha Mares (Myers), women's leader; Bernhard Erne, purser; and Martin Keiller, administration. Others who soon augmented the team were Dale and Elaine Rhoton, with their strong sense of call to the ships; Chacko Thomas from India; and Carl Isaacson, who later became captain. In 1979, Dale Rhoton became *Doulos* director.[5]

The focus of most of the leaders within OM, as they thought about operating with two ships, was on ship ministry in Asia. However, a small OM team, led by Robert Clement, had been exploring possibilities in Latin America and was in favour of the *Doulos* going there. Many in OM were unaware of the contemporary massive growth taking place among evangelicals in many Latin American countries.[6] In fact, there was controversy in OM about opening up fresh work there. OM had ongoing ministry in Mexico under the leadership of Dick Griffin, along with Mexicans like Samuel Castro, who had served on the *Logos*, and two brothers, Duane and Darrel Grasman, from the USA. Later, Darrel became Field Leader of Mexico and then of Central America, based in Costa Rica. Duane became the first OM Area Coordinator for Latin America. Concerns in the later 1970s about extending Latin American work included whether OM was spreading itself too rapidly and too thinly; whether it was losing its focus; whether Latin Americans would come to the ship; and the cost of taking the ship there. The arguments made in favour of further Latin American involvement were accepted, however, and Frank Dietz flew to Mexico to help with prior recruiting. Among those who joined OM at this point were Juan Daniel Espitia and Pablo and Jane Carrillo, who had experience in the Muslim world.

On 24 October 1978 the ship left England, calling at 'her birthplace', Virginia, USA, and then Tampico, Mexico. One contact made in Tampico was Ramón Martínez, head of the dockworkers' union, who had a life-changing spiritual experience, and when the *Doulos* returned to Tampico three years later he was there to help. Four churches sprang up in Tampico in part as a result of the 1978 *Doulos* visit.[7] The larger vision for Central and South America was also taking shape. At Veracruz, the leading Latin American evangelist, Luis Palau, held meetings in conjunction with the ship. From Mexico, the *Doulos* headed to Colombia. David Greenlee, a twenty-one-year-old American who had recently joined OM, had the job of line-up preparations in the land where he had grown up. The use of young and often quite inexperienced people for responsible jobs remained typical of OM, but experienced line-up help was available: in this case from Peter Conlan and Frank and Berit Fortunato. Ronnie Lappin, then on the information desk, later moved into line-up and had a major role in this area.[8]

Although David Greenlee had grown up in Colombia and spoke Spanish fluently, he had to master the complexities of obtaining a berth, permits to sell books, making contacts with churches and many technical details. Like others, he learned the value of George Verwer's maxim: 'Faith doesn't have just Plan A and Plan B.' George commended having Plans X, Y and Z as well.[9] Through unexpected help from a lawyer for customs, permits for the *Doulos* were granted at the last minute. Although not all the stories ended positively – soon after this the *Doulos* was refused entry to Trinidad – the recurring picture was of seemingly insurmountable obstacles being overcome. As with many other ports in Latin America, the stay in Barranquilla, Colombia, was a success, with conferences held on board and many people visiting the book exhibition. Leaders within OM became aware that the Latin American evangelicals were young, enthusiastic and ready to move into new work, but that in general they had not been given a vision of world mission. This was precisely what OM offered.[10]

The book exhibition, with between three and four thousand titles available for viewing and purchase (and half a million books in total on board), was a major attraction when the ship berthed in a port. Mike Stachura, book exhibition manager, with his teams, often had to deal with enormous numbers of people. A publisher in Spain was pessimistic about achieving much in Guayaquil, Ecuador, but the sales there in 1980 were astounding. The queue at peak times stretched for two miles. In Peru, the country's President, Fernando Belaúnde Terry, turned up early one Sunday morning without warning. Many of the ship leaders were asleep. Later he invited some of the team to the presidential palace. Many of those who visited the *Doulos* – about a million people a year did so – wanted to purchase from the large stock of general educational books. There were books on family issues, children's books and specifically Christian books.[11] It was clear that, with the very high volume of sales, the systems of accounting and management were inadequate, and through a group connected with Taylor University, USA, with Gus Vandermeulen as the link, a computer was donated to the *Doulos*. In 1981, when the *Doulos* was in Argentina (an OM office was established there),[12] the computer system was introduced; for Mike Stachura, who would later use experience he gained in leading OM USA, this was 'a turning point in moving from a small business to a multi-million dollar operation'.[13]

But at its heart the ship ministry had to do with people. Mentoring, which was provided by leaders and peers, was emphasised.[14] Humberto Aragão, who became leader of OM's work in Brazil in the later 1980s, and George Booth, *Doulos'* first mate, were examples of those given opportunity to develop as preachers while serving on the ship. There was also structured training through the Intensive Training (IT) scheme, which combined tests in physical and spiritual endurance. On the *Logos* Allan Adams introduced Rotating Ministry Training (RMT) and Special Ministry Training (SMT). He was concerned that too much stress and pressure did not help people. He also observed a tendency to equate success in IT with greater spirituality. In addition, not everybody had the chance to have such training because of work requirements on the ship. RMT and SMT opened ministry training to more people.[15]

Another crucial aspect of people-ministry was personal contact with individuals when the ship was in port. Roger and Yvonne Malstead rejoined OM in 1978 and became involved in the *Doulos'* work, with Roger heading up on-shore evangelism. Later, the Malsteads worked for several years at OM's international headquarters in London. 'Billy the Boxer' (Billy Jones, a former boxer), who had joined OM in 1963 at the age of fifty-two, had a tremendous impact – on people within OM and those to whom he witnessed personally about Jesus Christ. In Recife, Brazil, for example, in 1979, Billy went ashore and was soon in conversation with a local lawyer, who as a result committed his life to Christ. Billy and he kept in touch, and two years later, when the ship visited Argentina, they were able to meet and Billy's witness led to other members of the family making Christian commitments.[16]

Finally, a very significant aspect of the ship's ministry in Latin America was 'getting Latin Americans involved in missions'.[17] This included mission in Europe. In Rosario, Argentina, Frank Dietz commented that so many Argentineans wanted to join the ship (there were over three hundred applications) that it could have been filled with Argentineans. Subsequent to this, George Miley discussed with Frank the possibility of recruiting some from Argentina, Uruguay and Brazil for mission in Spain and Portugal. As a result, in a venture coordinated by Jonathan McRostie, George Miley, Frank Dietz and others, the *Doulos* carried sixty Latin Americans on its next trip to Europe: the Latin Americans worked with churches in Spain and Portugal and were well received.[18] Future influential Latin American leaders included Pablo and Jane Carrillo, who would recruit many Latin Americans for world mission; Daniel Bianchi from Argentina, later to be heavily involved in wider mission work; and Decio de Carvalho and Humberto Aragão, who would both take significant roles not only in OM Brazil but beyond: all were part of the *Doulos* team.[19] Within Spain, Pedro and Antonia Arbalat joined the ship, later returning to Spain to give leadership for twenty-seven years. The rise of 'global Christianity', not least in Latin America, was changing the face of mission.[20]

One ministry

Although a great deal of attention was paid to the *Doulos*, it was also realised that the two ships were 'one ministry', and consequently a ships' HQ was established in Germany.[21] OM Germany played a significant role in developing OM's European ministry and has been a major sending and resourcing base for a number of OM fields, including the ships. The German 'office' began in Belgium as 'the German desk' at the OM European HQ in Zaventem, with Mike Ponsford from the UK as its pioneer and first coordinator. The office moved in 1973 to Heilbronn in West Germany where a rent-free office had become available. OM's early association with Adelshofen Bible School and with Christian leaders, such as the publisher Friedrich Hänssler, encouraged Germans, especially Lutherans but also those from other denominations, to support the work.

Two factors contributed to rapid growth, especially in the 1970s and 1980s. The first was the drive and vision of Fritz Schuler, who became Field Leader in 1974. He oversaw the impressive conversion of the old Mosbach flour mill into the beautiful German head office, with the OM Ships HQ in adjacent buildings. Later he played a key role in the foundational stages of initiatives such as 'Love Europe' and 'TeenStreet',[22] before a divergence in leadership styles led to his eventually moving on into further ministry out of OM.

The second factor was the presence of OM Ships and especially visits to Germany by the *Doulos* in the late 1970s. Bernd and Margaret Gülker, lining up for the *Doulos* visit to Bremen in 1979, reported: 'Church groups came for the first time to an OM event from all over Germany, resulting in a massive increase in our prayer partner base.'[23]

In 1980 and 1981, George Miley, Mike Poynor, Martin Keiller, Ebbo Buurma and Mike Stachura, with their families, became part of the team at Mosbach. Lloyd Nicholas played an important role in supporting ship line-up teams from Mosbach, and Peter and Birgitta Conlan, who had gained experience in many aspects of OM's work, also became shore-based. It was recognised that younger line-up and ship-based personnel needed to work under the supervision of experienced people for the work to continue effectively. Francois Vosloo, from Johannesburg, South Africa, who joined the *Doulos* as a carpenter in 1978 (his family had a furniture business), took leadership of the team at Mosbach in 1981. Sigge Johansson, who had been chief engineer on the *Doulos*, supervised internal reconstruction at Mosbach so that the building could be used not only for offices but also as a Christian conference centre.[24]

During 1979 and 1980, as the *Doulos* was covering the countries of Latin America, ambitious plans were being made for the *Logos* to go to China. This idea was first raised in 1978, when some from the *Logos* had been able to visit China, and in early 1980, when the *Logos* was in the general area of China, Peter Conlan and Go Teg Chin, who was Chinese – from the Philippines – booked a ten-day tour of the country. In preparation, Peter Conlan went to Singapore to meet a businessman, A.C. Toh, who had top level contacts in Peking (now Beijing) and to receive advice. This was that any approach to the Chinese government should emphasise that the *Logos* team could offer scientific books, international friendship, youth activities, English classes, cultural events, and books that the Chinese government wanted. As a result of the contacts made through A.C. Toh, Peter Conlan and Go Teg Chin were able to spend ten days in China, including three in Beijing and two in Shanghai, and met with a number of senior government officials, including a Vice-Premier. It was clear that if the venture was to go ahead, it would need to be spearheaded by a fluent Mandarin speaker like Go Teg Chin.[25]

Peter Conlan and Go Teg Chin were also able to make contact with Chinese Christians, including eighty-year-old pastor Wong Ming-Dao, who had just been released after more than twenty years in prison. Peter was the first Westerner he had seen and to celebrate this amazing event he sang, in perfect English, the hymn 'All the way my Saviour leads me'.[26] After more visits to China by Go Teg Chin and then by Peter Conlan, involving negotiations with the three government departments coordinating book imports, shipping and tourism, by February 1981 the position looked clearer and even reasonably promising. One of the government ministers had been interested in the educational books, in the simple lifestyle of OM and in the international nature of the work. The transcripts of some of the discussions that had taken place appeared in Beijing's leading publishing and book magazine. The *Logos* was described as the 'Wisdom Ship'.[27]

The terms of the possible agreement from the government for the *Logos* to visit China included allowing a small book exhibition – about one thousand books. These would have to be given free to the Chinese government, with no guarantee of future purchases. A booklet could be made available offering an English language course. Although what was likely to be allowed by the government was very limited, it was felt within OM that at least it was a beginning.[28] As well as the useful meetings held with government officials in 1980–1, it was also possible to build on initial contacts made with Chinese Christians. Go Teg Chin and Peter Conlan made two visits to Ni Kwai-ting, then aged eighty-five, and he and his wife vividly described the pre-communist days when Watchman Nee (whom they knew well) was a powerful Christian leader in China. They also described the terrible suffering and persecution which the Christians had experienced, from the 1950s onwards. The year 1966 had brought the horrors of the Cultural Revolution, with Bibles burned, churches devastated and Christians humiliated, tortured and often killed.[29] But was China now changing? There were some signs that this was the case.[30]

Finally, after a year of uncertainty, signed invitations were issued for the ship to visit China, a move described by one respected China watcher as the first official recognition that the Chinese government had given to any Christian activity.[31] At the conclusion of the negotiations, the OMers were even unlikely guests of honour at a banquet.[32] Allan Adams had become the *Logos* director in 1980, a year before the visit to China, and he reported on the great excitement and gratitude to God that was evident as the *Logos* sailed up the Huangpu River into Shanghai. A book exhibition was set up in the National Art Gallery in Beijing. By OM standards, this was very limited, with only seven hundred titles, and among those only thirty Christian books. Also, books could be read at the tables provided but could not be sold. An OM leaflet about the ship, in Mandarin and English, was distributed, entitled 'The Wisdom Ship'.

By contrast with the large numbers that usually visited the ships in port, only government officials were allowed to board in Shanghai. However, these visits in themselves provided a witness: in particular the Chinese visitors noted the simple lifestyle of those onboard.[33] Members of the ship team were also able to visit seven local churches. The churches in China were divided between those in the China Christian Council, which was recognised by the government, and the unrecognised house fellowships. The two groups tended to be critical of each other, but the *Logos* was accepted by both.[34] From OM's point of view, the ministry in China, as on the ships, was 'one ministry'.

The *Logos* continued in the years that followed to visit countries that presented many different challenges. There were moments of high drama, such as a visit to Lebanon in 1982 at a time when the Israelis had invaded the country. Egyptian authorities had withdrawn their permission for a *Logos* visit to

Mrs Dorothea Clapp who prayed
for George Verwer's high school.

JACK WYRTZEN
DIRECTOR

15th Anniversary Rally
WORD OF LIFE HOUR

WITH

BILLY
GRAHAM

CLIFF BARROWS
Song Leader

BEVERLY SHEA
Soloist

MADISON SQUARE GARDEN
THURS. MARCH 3, 7:30 p.m.

New York rally where George
Verwer committed his life to Christ.

Orientation for Mexico outreach,
led by George Verwer, 1958.

George Verwer and original Send The
Light (OM) literature vehicle.

Walter Borchard, George Verwer and Dale Rhoton – first team to Mexico.

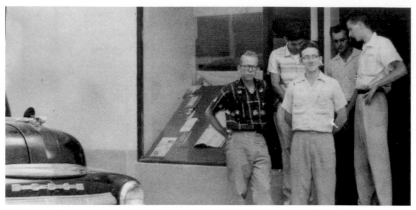

Dick Griffin, George Verwer and team at La Victoria, OM's first bookstore, Monterrey, Mexico, 1958.

Dick and Helen Griffin, Fuente de Vida bookstore, Veracruz, Mexico, 1961.

Wedding of Blanca and Baldemar Aguilar, OM Mexico director, 1960.

Leaflet advertising US meetings following arrest of George Verwer and Roger Malstead in the Soviet Union, 1961.

Hand-drawn map of 'Journies [sic] of the Spain Team', 1961–1962.
Upper left: First OM team in Spain. Lower right: OM's Spanish bookmobile, 1961.

OM summer training conference
Lamorlaye, France, 1963.

Jonathan McRostie, coordinator
for OM in Europe.

Gerry Davey (right) and outreach team
in France, 1963.

Bruce Littlejohn, OM mechanic
in Zaventem, 1960s.

Prayer and preparation, Lamorlaye, France 1963.

Overland to India, 1964.

Drena and George Verwer
in India.

Harry Charles, John Hymus, Chris Begg
and team in Kathmandu, Nepal, 1969.

OM India coordinator Thomas Samuel
and Mike Wiltshire (left).

All India Conference, Ranchi, 1970.

Bombay OM literature manager, PP Daniel (right) with 'banana cart' book table.

George and Hanna Miley, India and ships pioneers.

Long-time OM India trustee and leader Alfy Franks and family.

Peter Conlan and George Verwer, street meeting in India, 1968.

All India Conference, Ranchi, 1970.

Nigel Lee and Chacko Thomas.

George Verwer's historic ship memo, October, 1969.

Captain George Paget and Chief Engineer Mike Poynor (right) with *Logos* crew and staff, Glasgow, Scotland, 1976.

Literature coordinator Philip Morris addressing naval officers, on *Logos*, in India, 1971.

Emperor Haile Selassie and *Logos* Book Manager, Harley Rollins, Ethiopia, 1973.

Chilean newspaper reports of *Logos* accident, 4th January, 1988.

Visitors to *Logos II*, Nicaragua.

Logos Hope Project Director Lloyd Nicholas with Bernd Gülker and Mike Hey.

Logos Hope, Kiel, Germany, 2008.

Alexandria and the ship anchored off the Egyptian coast in international waters with nowhere to go. Somewhat discouraged, ship leaders were asking 'What next?' The entire region seemed to be in turmoil. It was then that Bertil Engqvist, from Sweden, the OM Coordinator for the Arab World, called the ship office to say: 'I really feel that God wants *Logos* to go to Lebanon.' He had been in touch with Lebanese Christian leaders who were desperate for *Logos* to come in their hour of need. Allan Adams agreed. Senior line-up man, Lloyd Nicholas, who quietly thrived in 'God or nothing' situations, was immediately dispatched to Beirut. He later said: 'As I arrived in Beirut, the Israelis were bombing the city.' As it transpired, it was a unique window of opportunity. Thousands of Lebanese came on board and the visit brought encouragement to many suffering people.[35]

There is no doubt, however, that it was the ground-breaking visit to China which had the most impact on the wider evangelical world. David Adeney, who had been a missionary in China before the communist revolution, was invited to be part of this visit, and he later wrote about the significance of the *Logos* being in Shanghai harbour. He commented on seeds sown through the visit, contacts made between Chinese Christians and the West after thirty years, and the public display of the Bible in the National Art Gallery. Peter Conlan reported on China at the Keswick Convention, and the implications of all of these new developments were discussed in October 1982 at a consultation on China organised by the Evangelical Missionary Alliance in Britain, with David Adeney and Peter Conlan present.[36] The 1990s would see seismic changes in China, especially related to economic growth, and the OM ship ministry would return to a very different China – one with an increasingly globally aware and mission-orientated Christian community.[37]

Financial crisis

While the *Logos* was riding high, the *Doulos* was ploughing into serious financial difficulties. There were challenges as early as

1979, with George Miley writing: 'When *Doulos* arrives back in Europe, we face another financial crisis. Fuel costs this year have tripled.'[38] A year later, as the *Doulos* went round the Latin American continent for a second time, it seemed that the situation was deteriorating. Elaine Rhoton writes: 'The economy of country after country was falling into shambles. In Ecuador the currency devalued 50 per cent while the ship was in the country. *Doulos* sales plummeted. Income from book sales had been expected to meet a large part of the expenses of the ship, but that money was instead tied up in stock sitting in the book holds of the ship.'[39]

Many high level officials (including the vice-presidents of Brazil and Bolivia) had attended events connected with the *Doulos* in Latin America and hundreds of thousands of people had come to meetings on board, but OM was only just beginning to develop the strong links with evangelical churches in Latin America that it had established over time in North America, Europe and India. This had financial implications. The hope was that the ship would serve the churches, but meaningful relationships had to be established. This was how OM had operated in India. There was a fresh realisation that it took time to develop such relationships and build trust with local church leaders.[40]

In theory, every person on the ship, like every person in OM generally, had a certain level of regular financial support, usually from friends, churches or family members. The intention was that this paid for all the ship's expenses, but in practice many on the ship received only part of the amount needed. Thus the ship depended on selling books. Also general donations were important. In all of this, prayer was always central – on the ships and in all of OM's life – and on the *Doulos* there were, in this period, examples of dramatic provision at times of need. There was also a willingness on the part of those on board to live with only basic necessities. Yet the needs of families on board were a concern. It is important to note, too, that prayer was never seen as a magic formula. Serious thought was being given to what should be done.

The team at Mosbach agonised over the situation. In Chile, in 1982, prices were escalating and book sales were significantly reduced, compared with the last visit the *Doulos* had paid to the country. On the other hand, port fees and other expenses had gone up considerably. George Miley sent a telex from Mosbach to all OM's offices: 'I feel *Doulos* is in a situation needing emergency prayer. The financial situation continues to worsen ... I sense entire *Doulos* ministry in jeopardy.' While the ship was in Chile, it was decided to make an audacious move: to seek an audience with President Pinochet and to ask him to waive the port fees – $180,000. Captain Isaacson, John Jenkins and Robert Clement, who oversaw the programme department including line-up, were given the interview and were ushered in and then out, with the fees completely waived.[41]

The OM policy, derived from stories of heroes of faith and in part as a reaction against extreme methods of fund raising, was that financial needs should not be publicised. Clearly this rule was being ignored, since those outside the churches (in this case a country's president) were being approached to help the *Doulos*, and in fact the policy of individuals 'looking to God' had always been applied flexibly. Richer fields in OM helped poorer fields. In the early 1980s, however, serious rethinking about finance took place.[42]

A key figure in this process was Ingemar Emker, who had served with OM in the mid-1960s in the Middle East and India. He later worked at the United Nations in New York as First Secretary in Sweden's Permanent Mission to the UN. He then 'reconnected' with OM and married Irma Svensson, who had served for many years in leadership with the ships. His grasp of financial systems and international management structures impacted the ships and then, by extension, the rest of OM in the early 1980s. Given its philosophy of 'looking to God', OM had always found the concept of budgeting difficult, but Ingemar suggested that without this OM might not survive. He proved that, though unpredictable, OM's income followed a pattern upon which a budget could be based. This not only led to changes in the ships' funding philosophy, but also influenced George Verwer and led to fundamental shifts in OM's thinking. Ingemar Emker was tragically killed in a car accident in Sweden in 1984.[43]

In early 1983, information about the financial needs of the ship ministry was circulated; there was concerted prayer and realistic assessment. OM was losing about $2,000 a day in the total ship ministry. Some bills were several months overdue and more were piling up in Mosbach. It was decided that the *Doulos* should return to Europe. Of the roughly one hundred Latin Americans on board, those who had not been able to find their full financial support – about $150 per month – were interviewed by David Greenlee, as personnel director. Sending churches were contacted and every attempt made to find workable arrangements for each individual's future. As a result, about one-third of the Latin Americans were able to stay on board. Rafael Lopes, who had been leading OM's work in Brazil, moved on to another Brazilian mission, turning over leadership of OM in Brazil to Decio de Carvalho. He was joined by Humberto Aragão. Later, when Decio and his family moved to the Middle East, Humberto Aragão took the leadership of OM Brazil, combining this with Baptist pastoral ministry in São José dos Campos.[44]

However, the fact that in many cases churches that had sent people out with great hopes were not able to fulfil the promises made when they sent them – something OM had earlier been able to overlook – meant that the very painful decision was made that those people could not stay on board. This was particularly hard because of the commitment to 'getting Latin Americans involved in mission'. Two-thirds of the Latin Americans had to return home. Later, David Greenlee commented: 'It took *Doulos* years to recover from this serious blow because, in cutting down the numbers so drastically, we completely eliminated much of the training.' Intensive Training had been providing a flow of leaders, but this was now significantly reduced. On 22 June 1983, the *Doulos* left Brazil, heading back to Europe.[45]

During 1984, 1985 and 1986, the *Doulos* was kept around Europe, relatively near to the German headquarters, where expenses could be controlled. Ministry was mostly to Christians, with ship members speaking about world mission, although during four months in Italy, for example, contacts were made with people from many different backgrounds and nations.[46] Visitors were less interested in the books on sale, as Europe was well supplied. Donations for the ship ministry came in slowly. In the meantime, however, Latin America was not forgotten, and Frank and Anneli Dietz moved from the ship ministry to become OM leaders for the Latin American work, helping from 1985 to develop further the ministries in which they had been involved while on the *Doulos*.

The emphasis was not only on OM's work in Latin America but more widely on keeping a clear mission vision before the growing Latin American evangelical churches. This was done by OM as it worked in conjunction with other missions, for example at Latin American missions conferences. Rafael Lopes and Humberto Aragão helped to organise the 1982 *Operação Mundo* (Operation World) conference in Sao Paulo. The international nature of OM was of great importance in this area. OM also placed a strong emphasis on training to develop character.[47] Humberto Aragão spoke about his own experience: he left a good profession as a chemist to join the *Doulos* and found himself peeling onions or cleaning up grease in the ship's galley, working for a leader on the ship whose vocabulary did not include the word 'please'. The development of character included resisting the desire to punch the leader on the nose.[48] Frank Dietz also had an interest in helping missionaries from Latin America to go as tentmaker missionaries to some of the difficult parts of the world.[49] A financial crisis had, at least in part, stimulated new expressions of teamwork.

It was a tape in 1985 by George Verwer, entitled 'Financial crisis', which was the crucial turning-point in this area. In this tape, which was widely distributed in OM, George offered powerful arguments for a change in OM's approach. It had often been said that everyone in OM should 'believe God' for finance, and that the finance would come, but George stated bluntly that this had simply not worked for many people. This was not necessarily because of a lack of faith: OM could have failed to inform supporters properly. George noted that Oswald Smith, a strong influence on him, had encouraged pledged giving to mission. It was also significant that the 'name it and claim it' movement was now saying: 'If you have faith you will receive.' OM did not want to be associated with this. Partly in the light of the growth of OM and the complexity of its worldwide activities, what was needed, George argued, was a financial policy which combined faith with common sense.[50]

This tape generated enormous feedback, which confirmed that a change was needed. The emphasis that subsequently came to the fore was on encouraging supportive individuals, and especially the many local churches that were linked with OM, to be financial partners of those in mission. George Verwer suggested that this theme was more prominent in the New Testament than the much-repeated theme in OM of 'looking to God alone'. Indeed, as he reviewed the past, he suggested that this theme and the policy that flowed from it had sometimes produced feelings of superiority and 'super-spirituality' within OM. The revised OM view was that appropriate and responsible actions should be taken to share information about finances. Fundraising was now seen as part of teamwork.[51] As George put it later, OM came to believe 'that we should show our esteem for our partners in the local church by sharing our needs with them so that they can join with us in prayer and in giving'.[52] The change in OM's approach to financial support was of enormous significance.

Look at the fields

New impetus was evident in OM. In September 1984, at the OM conference in Belgium, Allan Adams was asked by George Verwer, George Miley and Dale Rhoton to take on the role of director of the *Doulos* and 'turn the bow of the ship towards Asia'.[53] Early in 1985, after leaving his role as *Logos* director, Allan Adams took responsibility for the *Doulos*, with Mike Stachura as associate director. Within a year, the ship team leaders and the Board of Directors believed the ship should move out again. There were many discussions about the ship ministry's wider future, including the possibility that it would become a separate ministry from OM. In the end, this option was rejected.[54]

After visits in early 1986 to Gibraltar, the Canary Islands and the Cape Verde Islands, there was a longer stay in Senegal, the first predominantly Muslim country that the *Doulos* had visited. Local missionaries were somewhat discouraging, suggesting that the lack of French speakers on the ship meant that the team would not be of much help. In response Kenny Gan, from Singapore, leading the line-up team, explained that the *Doulos* had a vision to reach the capital city of Dakar. This was regarded locally as unrealistic, and maybe it was, but the teams that went out into the streets of Dakar with tracts and correspondence course applications were swamped in the scramble to receive literature. This part of Africa was literature-starved. By the time the *Doulos* sailed, two and a half weeks later, 990 people had signed up for a correspondence course, churches reported that members were more committed to mission, and the ship's doctor trained several Senegalese women (who would train others) in essential health care and infant nutrition.[55]

As the ship moved from country to country in West Africa, the sale and distribution of literature was central. By the time the ship reached the Gambia, the bookshop staff had moved book displays from English to Spanish to Portuguese to French and back to English. Mike and Jorie Stachura had not seen anything like the conditions in the Gambia in their fourteen years of living in and visiting cities in many countries: there were only a few pipes for running water, not all working, and houses were made of patched-together corrugated steel. The best-selling item of literature in the Gambia proved to be a small packet containing a New Testament, an evangelistic booklet, children's tracts and a postcard of the *Doulos*. Four thousand sold for the equivalent of an hour's wage. In addition, literature was produced for the six thousand school children who came to programmes on the ship. Later, in Liberia, more literature was distributed than in any other part of Africa. Often, too, there were Russian ships in the ports and the sailors gladly received Russian Bibles and other Christian books in Russian.[56]

Although well-established methods of communication, such as literature, proved very effective, new methods were also utilised.

Ray Lentzsch, who was a highly motivated evangelist, noted that cassette tapes were immensely popular in Africa and thought of selling cassettes with messages from Gospel Recordings. They were sold for slightly more than a blank cassette. The cassettes could also be used in evangelism in the villages. Some teams, for example in Togo and Ghana, went inland from the ports. As a result of the range of activities undertaken in the ship's journey round Africa, the teams found that many people were willing to decide to follow Jesus Christ.

There were questions, however, about how long-lasting the decisions were. In Sierra Leone, for instance, three thousand decisions were reported during the three weeks in which the *Doulos* was in the country. Four years later, however, when another West African tour was contemplated, those doing survey trips were asked to investigate what lasting impact there had been from the *Doulos* visit in 1986. The results were disappointing: they found very few people, if any, who were faithfully participating in a church directly as a result of the *Doulos'* ministry.[57] However, in 1991 a team member was pleased to meet someone who had come to Christ in Liberia through the *Doulos*, had then spent two years at Bible school, and who was working in Sierra Leone among refugees who had escaped from the horrors of the civil war in Liberia.[58]

As a result of the survey of the West African experience, emphasis was placed, when the OM ships were in a port for a longer period, on following-up alongside local churches. Cooperation already happened, and for many OMers it was a broadening experience. Teams spoke in small churches in Sierra Leone and Liberia that worshipped in distinctively African ways, expressing joyful praise in loud songs and dance. Mike Stachura had never experienced this kind of spontaneity, nor the joy and generosity that was evident – among very poor people. By contrast, when preaching in the Ivory Coast, in a large Methodist church, Mike encountered a grand pipe organ and rather formal worship. In Ghana, however, when he preached in the largest Assemblies of God (Pentecostal) church in the country, the service lasted four hours, with the offering alone (during which worshippers danced to the front to give their offerings) taking twenty minutes. He wrote: 'I think there were more lessons that I learned from the churches and church meetings in Africa than any place other than India when I first joined *Logos*.'[59]

OM had always emphasised working closely with local congregations. OM's Leadership Manual stated: 'Almost all our work is closely linked with that of local Bible-believing churches and assemblies, so that the fruit of our evangelism can be adequately cared for.'[60] It was in part a 'high view of the local church', as George Miley put it, that led him and Hanna, after having given so much to the ship ministry, to leave OM and form the Antioch Network in 1987. There had also been some tensions between George Miley and some other OM leaders over OM's direction and in particular the role of the ships' leadership.[61] In their new ministry, the Mileys were committed to encouraging local churches in their sending of people into mission.[62] Also, in Hanna's home area in Germany – from where she had escaped in 1939 as a young Jewish refugee – they established a ministry of prayer and reconciliation.[63]

Within OM, the traditional links with the Brethren assemblies were becoming less significant, although some links remained. Teams doing line-up for the *Doulos*' first visit to Latin America in 1979 took 'letters of commendation' that opened doors to Brethren assemblies. The Pentecostal churches were, however, much more numerous, and in Latin America OM increasingly worked with Pentecostal and Baptist congregations. The same was true in Africa. More and more people from Pentecostal and charismatic backgrounds joined OM from the 1980s.[64] The changing configuration of evangelical churches around the world began to affect OM's global witness.

A rainbow in the clouds

In late 1986 and early 1987, the *Doulos* spent time in South Africa, and then moved on to Kenya and Tanzania. This period was to be significant for OM work in southern Africa. An incident in South Africa illustrates the *Doulos* team's desire to stimulate local churches across the world to more adventurous mission. Preaching in one half-empty church, the OM team leader asked: 'How many of you would like to be missionaries?' In true African fashion, his question elicited an enthusiastic 'Amen!' Immediately he asked the people to go out and find other people to come to watch a film. Within half an hour, the church was packed.[65]

OM's work in South Africa, under the leadership of Francois Vosloo – who moved from Mosbach to become the South Africa Field Leader in 1984 – expanded significantly. Peter Tarantal joined OM in 1987, thinking that he would work on the *Logos*, but he responded to the challenge of mobilising South African churches, which at that stage had sent out very few missionaries.[66] In the coming years, South Africa would supply hundreds of people for wider mission through OM alone, and the influence of OM would be felt around the southern African countries. From South Africa, the *Doulos* went to Kenya, where the Doulos Gospel Film Festival drew large crowds to Mombasa, and then on to Tanzania, where one of the ship's visitors was Iran's Ambassador, who presented the *Doulos* with a Qur'an, on behalf of Ayatollah Khomeni of Iran.[67] From Africa, as planned, the *Doulos* moved to Asia, where she would spend the next few years and where much was to be done to consolidate and extend the OM work which had begun in that region over two decades before.

Although OM's presence and work in India had been crucial for OM's identity, most of those on the *Doulos* had never been to the country before and were shocked when they saw the slums and overcrowding in Bombay. Many OMers did not go ashore. One who did was a young Korean woman, Prisca Ahn, from a Buddhist background, who felt a call to India. Tragically, her calling was never fulfilled: a bus she was boarding in Bombay lurched forward and she fell backwards onto the street, struck her head and, after being on life support for three days, died. This was a huge shock for the *Doulos* community. Allan Adams, as *Doulos* director, established communication with Prisca Ahn's family in Korea. She was cremated in Bombay (in accordance with her family's instructions) and Allan Adams took her ashes back to the distraught family members in Korea.[68] *Doulos* and *Logos* reports in this period emphasised 'storms and tears' rather than 'plain sailing'.[69]

After the anguish in Bombay, the *Doulos* faced enormous problems and anxieties in obtaining permission to visit Malaysia. The ship was within three days of arrival when Stan Thomson, who was responsible for line-up, reported that permits had finally been granted. The ship's visit was debated in the Malaysian parliament, with supportive voices ultimately prevailing. One of the older members of the country's founding political party announced his interest in going on board, and a retired former Prime Minister said: 'We are a Muslim nation, but we are also a multi-cultural, multi-ethnic nation.' Finally the government agreed that the ship's book exhibition could be open to all, and the queue of people wanting to board the next Sunday was three miles long. Interest continued unabated for three months.[70]

Over the next two years, the *Doulos* visited fourteen countries in the Asia Pacific region – Thailand, India, Sri Lanka, Singapore, Indonesia, the Philippines, Taiwan, Hong Kong, Papua New Guinea, New Zealand, Australia, Vanuatu, Fiji and Tonga. In this period Rodney Hui, leading OM's work in Singapore, saw many from this region choosing to work with OM in Europe, the Middle East, Central Asia, North Africa and on the ships.[71] Inevitably, there were many high and low points.

One high point was in Thailand. A Thai woman, Boonsian Chaiyasakorn, who had been with the *Doulos* in the ship's early days, came on board for a few months and became excited about the possibility of the ship making contact with the Thai royal family. She had a friend who knew Princess Maha Chakri Sirindhorn and, as a result, the Princess visited the ship. A crash course in protocol followed for all the crew and staff involved in the visit. The Princess chose books for the royal library and took a particular interest in the school that operated for the children on the *Doulos*.[72] After her well-publicised visit, thousands of people wanted to visit the ship.[73]

But there were also low points. As the ship made its way from Papua New Guinea to New Zealand in autumn 1989, it was clear that many on board were exhausted. The ship's director and the assistant director had changed over, there had been rough voyages and delays, and there were relationship tensions. Captain Dallas Parker, in line with OM thinking, instigated extra prayer. At one Friday night prayer meeting, led by Marcus Chacko, a time of openness and confession began, and this lasted until two o'clock in the morning and continued the next evening. The atmosphere on board the *Doulos* was transformed. Authentic community was crucial to authentic ministry.[74]

As the *Doulos* concentrated on Asia, the *Logos* was in South America. There was excitement about spiritual revival taking place in Argentina. In Ushuaia, southern Argentina, nine thousand visitors came aboard the *Logos* and many Christian books and Bibles were sold. Ushuaia was the *Logos*' 401st port of call and as she left on 4 January 1988, at 7.30 pm, there was no way of knowing that it would be her last. At 11.55 pm, however, as a result of a very strong current and heavy winds, the *Logos* struck the rock shelf in the inter-island waterways of Tierra del Fuego, Chile. Those on board not called to emergency duties went to the dining room as part of the normal emergency plan and joined in singing and prayer, not knowing what was going to happen.

Everything possible was done to save the *Logos*, but water began pouring in and, at 5.00 am, the captain gave the order to prepare the lifeboats. Although there had been weekly lifeboat drills, the evacuation had to take place with the ship listing badly. It was an extremely hazardous operation, which could at the very least have ended with injuries, but by 5.30 pm all six of the lifeboats, with everyone on board, had safely reached Chilean naval boats and the launch that had carried the Argentinean pilot, about a quarter of a mile away. As they looked back at the ship, people wept. All the 139 people on board, ranging in age from six weeks to fifty-nine years, had been saved, and none was harmed. There had been a brilliant rainbow in the sky that morning and when David Greenlee had seen it, he had thought of Ezekiel 1:28: a 'rainbow in the clouds': a reminder of God's glory.[75]

The loss of the *Logos* was a huge blow to George Verwer, to the whole of OM, and most especially to the people on board, who lost all their possessions and – even more difficult – their home. Chief Engineer Dave Thomas had been on the maiden voyage of the *Logos* seventeen years earlier and it was on the *Logos* that he met his wife, Joy, and they had begun bringing up their family. Jonathan Stewart, the captain, felt the loss very deeply. The Chilean naval authorities conducted a thorough investigation, which Captain Stewart found absolutely exhausting. The decision, after the production of the report into the accident, was that no charges should be brought against the captain, the ship owners or the pilot.

Meanwhile, in Britain, America and elsewhere, the accident caught the attention of news reporters and was featured for days. Franklin Graham and his organisation, Samaritan's Purse, generously covered the cost of the repatriation of all *Logos* personnel. There were messages of sympathy and support from around the world, and Christians in many countries began to offer money to OM to replace the *Logos*. The more open policy on fundraising within OM also helped. The replacement of the *Logos* was the largest financial project OM had faced up to that point. On 23 September 1988, OM was able to announce the signing of a purchase agreement by Educational Book Exhibits Ltd for a twenty-year-old 4,900-ton Spanish ferry. It had been known as the *Antonio Lázaro* and had been sold by Trasmediterranea to a Greek company and renamed *Argo*. OM named it *Logos II*. It was renovated in Amsterdam and set sail in April 1990.[76] There was a rainbow in the clouds.

Conclusion

The combined effect of OM having two ships in operation for most of the 1980s was to create a complex web of relationships within OM that reached across every continent. The original vision of the enormous value of teamwork in global mission remained but, by the end of the 1980s, there was a very different set of teams to the one that had taken shape thirty years before. Many of the developments were positive. The vision that George

Verwer had for missional leadership emerging across the world was becoming a reality in remarkable ways, with the ships playing a central role in mobilising and training people from many countries. At the same time, it was difficult to see OM's ministry as 'one ministry' when it was so dispersed. Much depended on the leaders working well together, in centres such as the London offices, Mosbach or on the ships.

However, the personnel involved in OM's work – whether connected with the ships or with the wider work on all continents – was always changing, and as well as this logistical challenge, there were also inevitable leadership tensions. It was not easy to replace leaders like George Miley, who exercised a great deal of influence on the ship ministry, on OM as a whole and on many individuals. The extension of the work of OM also meant that when financial issues had to be addressed, these were on a much larger scale than before. The potential for a globalised OM to affect the life of the churches was greater in the 1980s, but at the same time OM itself was changing, not least as the worldwide evangelical community grew and new recruits and supporting churches brought new expressions of Christian spirituality into OM. Having seen the way the ships reshaped OM's ministry in the 1980s, the next chapter will also focus on this period and will look at other significant new directions that OM took in its life and mission.

Chapter 7

Trusted and Appreciated

The world of the 1980s was a generation away from the world in which OM had been born. In a wide-ranging memorandum dated 27 August 1986, Nigel Lee, one of those in OM working most closely with students in universities, examined its state. The immediate concern was a drop in the numbers of those involved in OM's European summer missions. Among the strengths of OM, on the other hand, was the way the movement appeared to be 'trusted and appreciated by a wide cross-section of missions and church leaders, certainly more than 15–20 years ago'. By this time, many of OM's leaders had been around for over two decades and instead of being radical young people, as they had been in the 1950s and 1960s, they were now the same age as many key evangelical leaders – and often involved in leadership in the wider evangelical community. However, this age factor could also, Nigel Lee argued, cut OM off from young people. It could be seen as the establishment, not a 'radical protest movement, as we were in the 60s'.[1] Clearly, after almost thirty years, OM was in transition. The ships represented a ministry which attracted many evangelicals, but in other areas questions were being asked about possible changes that OM needed to make. This chapter concentrates on three of the areas in OM's work which dated back to the 1960s – Europe, the Middle East and India – and then looks at global organisational developments and certain changes in emphasis in the area of spiritual experience that were taking place in OM in the 1980s.

Original vision

George Verwer spoke in a report in March 1981 about a trip of eight thousand miles that he had recently undertaken in which some of his 'original vision' had been rekindled. This included concern for countries such as Yugoslavia, 'one of the first lands God put on my heart when I was a student'. As early as 1962, David Borman went to Yugoslavia with OM, but later moved out of OM and was now in Italy. Although such early visions had not been lost, George acknowledged that he had 'thrown so much of my time and effort and emotional energy into the ships and then into basic survival' that other work had been neglected in his thinking. A few from Yugoslavia had been with OM in the summer of 1980 and George had been able to take meetings in Hungary, where the tensions in the churches, especially between charismatics and non-charismatics, had dismayed him. Yugoslavia and Hungary were more open than other communist countries: his report noted that there were 'many OMers and associated people and friends' in Eastern Europe, but that it was not appropriate to speak about their work.[2]

It was, however, becoming more difficult to fulfil the original vision of mobilising young people for challenges such as Eastern Europe. The decline in the numbers coming to OM's European summer missions had serious knock-on effects, since, for twenty-five years, the majority of those joining and remaining with OM had come initially through being on OM's summer teams. OM's ability to attract young people from countries such as Britain (the largest single recruiting country), Sweden and the Netherlands appeared to be declining in the mid-1980s.

Nigel Lee, in his 1986 memorandum, identified two major new trends within the churches that were contributing to this. The first was the strong emphasis being put on friendship evangelism. There was a perceived need to spend time with new contacts: selling a book or giving a tract, as OM had always done, was beginning to be questioned, since such activities did not seem to express how Christians should value people. Nigel and Tricia Lee had both worked with OM in India, and were aware that some approaches were only appropriate in some cultures. However, the immediate concern was Europe, where the 'modern young Christian is far less responsive to the old challenge to spend many hours in footslogging literature evangelism'. The concept of a literature 'blitz', Nigel argued, appeared to many younger evangelicals to belong more to the cults than to 'a caring church'. New recruits to OM expected that mission would involve a meaningful 'relationship dimension'.[3]

A second major issue for OM was the international growth of the charismatic movement.[4] Nigel Lee noted that, by the mid-1980s, charismatic renewal had become 'a widespread influence in all our recruiting countries'.[5] Through younger evangelical leaders such as Clive Calver, General Secretary of the British Evangelical Alliance, charismatics in Britain became more involved in the wider evangelical world.[6] There was also the growing influence of Black-majority churches.[7] Most of these were Pentecostal in their spirituality. Significant numbers of Baptist churches were also involved in charismatic renewal by the mid-1980s.[8] George Verwer was appreciated as a speaker within Pentecostal and charismatic circles – speaking at Assemblies of God, Elim Church and Baptist events – but OM did not always appear well-adapted to charismatic spirituality: some OM leaders suggested that alongside YWAM, OM seemed 'out-of-date ... belonging to that wing of the church which is already on the defensive and shrinking'.[9]

At the same time, there was affirmation of the strengths of OM: its cross-cultural dynamic, its non-denominationalism, which attracted young people, and its proven willingness to give young people responsibility. Frank Fortunato, the primary influence on worship in OM in this period, commended 'wholehearted clapping, singing, dancing, shouting' in worship, as well as the 'often overlooked' dimension of silence. He welcomed new experiments, citing – from OM India – S.D. Ponraj's use of local Indian songs and local musical instruments, and he also appreciated a Brethren Assembly's *a capella* style.[10] Nigel Lee suggested new possibilities for OM: one proposal, related to charismatic issues, was to aim for conferences with a 'taste of really meeting God'.[11] These were major challenges.

OM rose to these challenges by launching something new. Within a month of Nigel's paper, Peter Conlan set out ideas for a new summer outreach event, named 'Love Europe', which he hoped would draw five thousand people into the 'OM experience'. His vision was to 'challenge and excite a whole new sector of young people'.[12] He followed this up with an extended paper on how Love Europe would differ from the existing OM summer missions. He envisaged attracting much greater numbers of young people in the churches. He also saw the possibility of Love Europe expressing God's love in new ways to people in Muslim communities, communist countries and great cities. Another important suggestion was that there should be a greater emphasis on the theme of friendship.[13] A crucial new feature of Love Europe was partnership between OM and other missions. Greg Livingstone, one of OM's shaping figures, who had for several years been leading the mission agency Frontiers, wanted to be involved.[14] In promotion and advertising, OM wished to show evangelical churches that something exciting and genuinely new was happening. There were to be attempts to involve groups rather than simply individuals, to attract people from developing countries and those from charismatic fellowships. The conference to launch the initiative would have 'top communicators', music would 'play a much greater part than in normal OM conferences' (with Frank Fortunato bringing in leading musicians), and young people would be offered a vision of 'THE cutting edge of mission for the 90s'.[15] OM's desire to regain the cutting edge was driving it forward in imaginative ways.

There were some hesitations. A number of leaders expressed their doubts to Peter Maiden, as Associate International Coordinator, about whether the hoped-for huge increase in recruits was realistic.[16] However, the enthusiasts were persuasive and Stuart McAllister, based in Vienna, who was Love Europe coordinator, sent out details at the end of 1987. The launch would be in July 1989, in Offenburg, Germany, and would involve six days of training, ministry and worship. It was anticipated that five thousand young people would come together, from fifty nations: in fact, about seven thousand came, from seventy-six nations. Steve

Chilcraft administered the event, with Peter Conlan, 'on loan' from the ships, leading the programme.[17]

A network of regional 'Love Europe Committees' was established in connection with the new venture, to plan the evangelism and recruit the participants. George Verwer saw Love Europe as 'the greatest step of faith that we in Operation Mobilisation have taken since the launch of MV Doulos'. He was delighted that major speakers from outside OM took part. Luis Palau from Latin America gave a keynote address. Among the well-known North American speakers were Melody Green, Tony Campolo and Floyd McClung, the International Director for YWAM. European speakers included Brother Andrew, known for his work behind the Iron Curtain; Ian Coffey of the Evangelical Alliance and the song-writer Graham Kendrick. After the congress, five thousand young people fanned out across Europe, in three hundred vehicles, 'to make friends and share Christ'.[18] The original vision of OM, birthed in Europe, had been renewed.

Many different directions

After his 1981 visit to Yugoslavia, George Verwer went on to Turkey, where OMers had been present since 1961. There had been many difficult times, and in 1979, one OM member, David Goodman, was shot on his doorstep and died, during a period of strong anti-American feeling. George Verwer reported that about eighty evangelical Christians from abroad were working together in Turkey. Twenty-five were with OM and several more had been OMers. Many were 'tentmakers'. Activities in this period included Bible translation, a correspondence course, discipling work and camps. Small Turkish fellowships were growing slowly in major cities. George asked how more could be done in places like Turkey, which had been a primary focus for OM, when OM was 'moving in so many different directions'.[19]

OM had established a Bible correspondence course in Turkey in the 1960s, and, during the 1980s, Dave Wilson used it to pioneer imaginative ways of reaching the wider population. Against the advice of many, he opened a postbox in Istanbul to receive course enquiries, and persuaded newspapers to run advertisements for the course. He was arrested several times, usually when he went to visit people who had written about the course and whose relatives turned him over to the police. He was always released after a few days in the cells. The correspondence course students who showed interest were followed up by other OMers on church planting teams. Julyan and Lenna Lidstone, who had been challenged about Turkey by the death of David Goodman, worked in Ankara from 1980 onwards. After the police obtained an address book with Christian contacts, Julyan Lidstone's name featured in a popular national newspaper in February 1988. He was accused of organising camps at which he offered young Turkish men money and foreign women if they converted to Christianity. In March, twelve evangelical believers in Ankara were taken for interrogation – seven foreigners (including Julyan) and five Turks – and after three days in custody, their case came to court. The ludicrous charge of making financial gain was dismissed.[20]

In this period Koreans and Latin Americans began to arrive in Turkey, bringing with them their experience of church growth. Turks and Koreans both trace their ancestry to Central Asia and South Koreans recognise the role of Turkish soldiers who stood with them in the Korean War.[21] Latin Americans brought a warmth and understanding of family ties that equipped them to form deep friendships with Turks and other Middle Easterners, more easily than Europeans and North Americans. These new arrivals also introduced new ways of witness – one Korean missionary offered Tae Kwon Do (combat sport) classes to young men in his street. One came to faith and became an elder in a church in Ankara.[22]

In other countries in the Middle East and North Africa, where OM teams had been serving in various ways since the 1960s, the picture was mixed. When George Verwer visited Syria in 1981, there was an interest in Syrian young people coming on OM for training. In the same year, across the border in Lebanon, Jamil Saffouri, a former OMer, was murdered.[23] By the 1980s, there were those who had worked in various countries in the Middle

East for a long time. Among the pioneers who went on to gain extensive experience in the region were Peter and Grace Ferguson. In a reflection on events since 1970 when they graduated from college and had come to the Middle East, entitled 'Keeping on for the long haul', Grace Ferguson wrote movingly about some of the hard experiences: 'arrested, questioned and blacklisted' during their first year of language study; Peter put in prison with three others during their second year of marriage, at the time of the birth of their first child; and the death of one of their sons. 'Suffering', she wrote, 'has given us a heart link with Middle Eastern believers who suffer for their faith.'[24]

In the midst of the suffering, OM's work in the Middle East gradually expanded in the 1980s. OM's intentional internationalism created new opportunities in the region, for example through the ships and the work of summer teams. OM's leaders gained experience and skills as they moved around, taking on different ministries. Kamal Fahmi, who joined OM through the *Logos* and had been in India, moved to Egypt in 1975 and soon felt that he should seek workers for Sudan. Others questioned this move, but Bertil Engqvist encouraged him and Kamal began to lead the work in Sudan from 1976. Between 1976 and 1995 around three hundred people served with OM in Sudan. The first team included Christina, from Sweden, who a few years later married Kamal.[25] When Howard and Nora Norrish went to Cyprus in 1984, becoming involved in and leading the Arab World Team, there were forty-nine OMers in the Arab world. In 1991, when Howard and Nora moved to other roles in OM, there were 175, serving in sixteen countries. OM leaders played a significant behind-the-scenes role in drawing evangelical leaders together across the region.[26] OM's work in this region was increasingly trusted.

The practice of 'tentmaking' was crucial to establish a Christian presence in predominantly Islamic countries and had been encouraged in OM from the beginning. Howard Norrish believed that the recognition of the important role of the laity in mission, often using their gifts in 'secular' occupations, was something 'gifted to OM by God through our Brethren roots'. Theologically, he argued for an 'incarnational' understanding of mission that exhibited 'deep identification with people in their culture and in their pain, frustration and troubles', seeing this as increasing the credibility of the gospel. In the light of this theological perspective, he considered that OM should put tentmaking 'at the heart of its ministry'.[27]

Howard and Nora Norrish used their professional expertise as part of their witness over many years. By the 1980s, the tentmaking approach that Howard Norrish had been advocating and had practised was becoming more common. In 1979 Christy Wilson, a teacher working in Afghanistan, wrote an influential book, *Today's Tentmakers*.[28] In the same year, OM launched a training programme, Operation Tentmaker. A year later, as a response to the plight of thousands of Afghans fleeing the fighting in their country between resistance groups and the government forces assisted by Soviet troops, Gordon and Grace Magney set up a relief and development agency. One project was creating a solar oven so that refugees could prepare meals without destroying trees. This approach became a model when OM began wider integral mission work in the later 1980s and 90s, and other development agencies were founded.[29]

New initiatives were also evident in Eastern Europe. In the later 1980s, with signs of political change across the region, summer outreach through OM teams became possible, for example in Hungary and Yugoslavia. In Kiev, the capital of Ukraine, an OM team associated with Love Europe attracted large crowds in 1989 when they sang and spoke in the city's Revolution Square. OM had contacts with several Baptist and Pentecostal churches in Kiev and local Ukrainians joined the team in the square. On one occasion, some uniformed militia guard and plain-clothes KGB agents started shouting and grabbed one of the OM team. However, a *babushka* (grandmother) took hold of a militia man's arm and shouted: 'How dare you stop these people from speaking the truth?' Another joined in: 'We have a right to hear this, you go away.' In this period of dramatic change in the Soviet Union, officers who had previously wielded such power were unsure how to react, and when several more *babushkas* grabbed them and (with the help of members of the crowd) pushed them away, they left. Later, a contingent of officers arrived looking for 'these Western Christian propagandists' but the OM members were shepherded to safety by Ukrainian Christians.[30]

A number of countries in Asia, too, were increasingly important within the wider work of OM. During Love Europe, 143 Koreans participated, taking advantage of tourist visas being more freely available. Asians were adaptable and quick learners, and their spiritual maturity had a significant impact on OM. Koreans were committed learners of field languages and their role in OM was to be a major one. The rather Eurocentric outlook that had characterised aspects of OM up to the end of the 1970s, with major events taking the European viewpoint into consideration first, began to change.[31] Asians were increasingly recognised and appreciated in the 1980s as having a crucial missional contribution to make around the world, including in Europe.

Among the Asians who came on Love Europe, one young Indian, Moses Parmar, was allocated to a team working in Poland. He found that the European members of his team were unused to public witness and so he 'showed how we did open airs in India'. OM India's investment in training was paying dividends in Europe. He discovered that being Indian was a source of curiosity in Poland: most Poles had never seen an Indian before. Crowds of up to two hundred gathered and scrambled for the Gospels offered by the OM team. It was noted that the democratic movement in Poland, 'Solidarity', had reported on Love Europe in one of their leading newspapers.[32] The concepts developed in Love Europe spread to other regions, including the Middle East. New possibilities in cross-cultural mission were evident by the late 1980s.

Recruiting and training

Although OM India occasionally had an impact on Europe, most of its work was focused on India itself. Ten years before Love Europe, as we have seen, OM India had (in 1979–80) 'Love

Maharashtra', an outreach to Maharashtra state. In 1983 there was GO 83 – Ganges Outreach – to Eastern Pradesh, Bihar, and Bhojpuri-speaking areas. Whereas Europe was aware of Outward Bound training, Asia had an 'Eastward Bound' programme, later called Asia Challenge Teams, led by Gary and Sue Dean. These offered two years of work in India, in Nepal, where Dave and Connie McBride took up the national leadership, and in Bangladesh.[33] This was a time of significant response in the region. The vision of OM had always been for local leadership and this had worked well in India, with foreign workers continuing as valued partners. As well as providing personnel, OM's wider resources helped OM teams in India by bringing in foreign trucks, which could carry large quantities of literature and bigger teams.

Up till 1984, citizens of countries belonging to the Commonwealth of Nations could work in India without a visa, but during 1984 the government changed the visa policy and most Commonwealth citizens were told that they had to leave India in the next six to eight months. Those OMers who left included Mike and Heather Wheate, who had worked with the vehicles' team; John and Leena Brown in Bihar; Philip and Rosemary Morris and Des and Lynne Harper, all serving in Bombay; Martin and Mary Powell in Ranchi and Linda Cowley, who was leading women's ministries.[34] There was a profound sense of loss after what had been a fruitful two-decade partnership within OM India's ministry between Indians and foreigners.

The need for new leadership meant, inevitably, a fresh emphasis on recruiting and training. This had always been important in OM and especially in OM India, but it was realised there that the seminaries in India were not focused on preparing people for mission and OM India decided to invest more resources in developing its own specialised training. Attention was given to training in church planting; courses on friendship evangelism; training for reaching high caste people; other 'special people group' training and the development of worship groups. Although only some potential leaders went through courses of this kind, there was ongoing training for all OMers. Every three months, teams would come together for a ten-day study seminar.[35]

Pro-active recruitment and then training provided a flow-through of new leaders in the 1980s. An example was S.N. Shankar, who studied English Literature at university and was told by his Hindu professor to read the Bible. Later he became a Christian, joined an OM team and was trained. He became leader of OM's work in south India.[36] The later 1980s was a very significant time for the leadership of OM India. Ray Eicher and Alfy Franks had ably served as All India Coordinators since 1973 but they saw the necessity of affirming younger leadership. Joseph D'Souza became executive director, with Ray and Alfy continuing within the executive council of OM India. One of Joseph's concerns was to find the best 'recruiting and training strategies' for national mission.[37]

It was during 1988 that the OM India leadership felt there must be a response to the needs of suffering people, and as a result the 'Good Shepherd' ministry was launched in Hyderabad. It spread to a number of places – Bombay, Bhopal, Lucknow, Dharmapuri, Bangalore, Chennai and Secunderabad. The vision was to proclaim the love of Christ in word and in deed, and to see caring Christian commitment being worked out, especially among the poor in India's urban slums. In partnership with local churches and mission groups, OM India set up (for example) medical clinics, primary schools for children, literacy classes for adults, various kinds of vocational training for men and women, training in small business skills for groups such as single mothers, other development-related projects and fellowship groups. It is significant that alongside the help offered in the name of Christ, there was the emergence of new Christian communities among the poorest of the poor.[38]

By the end of the 1980s, about 350 long-term OMers were involved in a very wide range of ministries in India, with all of the personnel being Indians. As well as stressing holistic ministry, Joseph D'Souza brought his experience as OM's Uttar Pradesh state coordinator and OM India training coordinator to bear on the structures and emphases of OM India's wider ministry.[39] Changes to administrative arrangements were initiated. An Administrative Council was formed under the OM India Board to carry on the daily administration and decision-making. With the ongoing growth in OM India, it was decided to create five different fields: North India, South India, India Centre for Every People (Hyderabad Centre), OM Books and the ARPANA women's ministry.

Juliet Thomas, who started ARPANA, had a vision for mobilising interdenominational prayer networks across the nation. She was also involved internationally: from 1984 she was a member of the international Lausanne Committee and later became chair of its Intercession Working Group.[40] OM India had led the way within OM as a whole in training young women. ARPANA developed into a network of over five thousand women's groups across many states in India, and specific training for women was established in Bangalore. Joseph D'Souza's post-graduate studies had been at the Asian Center for Theological Studies in Manila, and he was committed to indigenous training and development, in line with Asian needs, rather than imported from the West. India was now the leading country in OM in terms of producing long-term team members.[41]

Many of these team members continued to be engaged in activities that had been the focus for OM's work from the beginning. Literature remained crucial. In 1987 it was decided that English book sales in India, which had been a great success, should be a separate department bearing its own costs. It was able to generate enough profit both to pay its expenses and give substantial amounts towards other ministries of OM India. Indeed OM Books became the largest Christian books publisher in Asia. Alongside this, bookshops were established in eighteen Indian cities.[42] Local teams continued to work across the nation, identifying closely with the people.

In many cases individuals who came into contact with these teams later joined OM. Apurva Tiwari, for instance, who was brought up in north India in a Hindu family, became a Christian in 1988 through someone from the Indian Evangelical Mission and then joined an OM team. He suffered physically because of his faith in Christ, but this did not deter him and he continued serving with OM. Having completed the basic OM training programme, he began to work among high-caste Hindus in Orissa, dressing in the traditional garb of Brahmins and abstaining from eating meat.[43] As well as local ministry, larger-scale OM outreach also continued. In 1987–8 there was RUN '88, 'Reaching Unreached Neighbours', in Uttar Pradesh and Bihar, and this was followed in 1989–90 by Project Light, concentrating on north India. Eastward Bound became Love India, with foreigners coming to India for six months, the maximum duration of a visa. The support of OMers from outside India was important, but OM India's leadership was seen to be thoroughly indigenous.

The body of Christ

Although each OM field had its own distinctives, there was an awareness that OM as a whole had been called to emphasise certain ministries. Literature distribution was prominent. STL in the UK not only distributed books and other products through virtually all the Christian retail outlets in Britain, but its sales representatives, Dave Armstrong, Howard Hall and Jaap Fontijn, made annual extended trips to bookshops and missions in English-speaking Africa. An important ministry aspect of STL in Britain continued to be giving help to work beyond the UK. From 1967 to 1985, during the period when Gerry Davey was the director of STL's ministry, about $4,000,000 of STL's profits were used to support ventures in other OM fields (principally India, the *Logos* and Greater Europe), and various Christian ministries outside OM.[44]

In 1981 Dave Brown, as Publishing Manager, reported on the continuing vision of STL to publish books that emphasised faith, obedience and mission. STL was also reprinting titles that had gone out of print. There was still strong encouragement within OM to read A.W. Tozer; in 1980 five of his books were made available under the STL imprint. There were also new authors being recommended, such as David Watson, a leading Anglican charismatic leader. Internationally, OM was producing very large numbers of 'bookazines' in English, Korean, Bengali, Spanish and

French. It was not unusual for one hundred thousand copies of titles such as Billy Graham's *Peace with God* to be printed in 'bookazine' format. Message cassettes by John Stott, Joni Eareckson, Elisabeth Elliot and others were also produced. Over fifteen thousand tapes were being sold in a year.[45] OM sought to continue its well-established wider ministries.

In the same year, George Verwer emphasised in a 'special communication' to all OM leaders that, as OM went through a period of rapid expansion, there was a need to focus on 'individual spiritual lives'. The danger, which had been underlined recently by OM's early mentor, William MacDonald, was of OM becoming 'too big'. George was concerned about the identity and authenticity of OM. 'We are not some secular company called OM', he wrote, 'but we are the Body of Christ, pressing forward in full fellowship with other members of the Body.' He reported that he had recently spoken to 6,500 people at the growing British Christian festival, Spring Harvest. This event was to grow to eighty thousand people and became highly significant for the shaping of British evangelicalism.[46]

OM had many connections within the orbit of British evangelical life in this period. New developments took place. Tony Kirk took over leadership of OM UK, and subsequently served in wider leadership as OM's Western Europe Area Coordinator. The OM UK head office moved to improved facilities at the Quinta Christian Centre in Shropshire. An important part of OM UK's work in the 1980s was a series of National Leadership Conferences. These featured leading OM speakers such as Peter Maiden, Nigel Lee, Viv Thomas and Jack Rendel, whose main ministry was in the Spanish-speaking world, as well as those from other evangelical agencies, such as Floyd McClung of YWAM, J. John, the Anglican evangelist, and David Harley, later Principal of All Nations Christian College and then General Director of OMF International. OM established particular links with certain mission agencies, such as WEC and OMF. Len Moules of WEC, for example, had been a valued OM conference speaker. Chris Wigram, who had been on the ships, became OMF's UK director.[47]

The international coordination (and, as has been seen, financing) of OM was becoming much more complex. George Verwer set this out in a memorandum in May 1984, explaining that in terms of international coordination, the 'base' was now a combination of Bromley (STL and an International Coordinating Team – ICT), Belgium (Zaventem) and Carlisle, where Peter and Win Maiden lived. Mosbach was also central. Zaventem was still the hub of OM's transport, but several other countries now had transport bases. George stressed the expertise OM had developed in literature (three hundred million pieces of literature in fifty languages had been distributed), in research into world mission and in 'special projects'. Often research generated new special projects, and in the 1980s OM could list over sixty of these. In the area of finance, Peter Maiden was for some time the acting financial manager, working closely with Steve Hart and the CAO in Zaventem.[48]

Even in the midst of international growth and increasing complexity, people have always been central to OM's work. Jonathan McRostie, a key figure from OM's earliest days and someone with a remarkable grasp of OM's finances, personnel and transport, was involved in a motor accident in Spain in 1982 which left him paralysed from the chest down. In his subsequent struggles, Jonathan found George's personal encouragement invaluable.[49] He always stressed that OM was a relationship-centred movement. The development of policies had always to be seen within this framework.

George Verwer referred in his memorandum of May 1984 to a 'Policy Manual' which was in draft stage. It was to go to OM's emerging General Council, a body composed of OMers who had been in the movement for five years or more. It was generally understood that there would be differences in how OM policies were implemented from country to country. George instanced the 'social policy' (regarding permission for dating) as something he felt had to be adapted for different situations. In the event a single, fifty-page document was agreed, covering the roles and responsibilities of OM staff at all levels, as well as the roles of Boards and Committees. The document set out policies on matters such as personnel development, holidays, training, dealing with serious disability or death in service, social policies, relationships between people from different cultural backgrounds, pensions, insurance, ownership of property, kidnapping and ransom demands, budgeting, internal audit and personal financial support.[50]

A great deal of the work on this Policy Manual, including the rather daunting task of seeking to have it ratified by the General Council, was steered through by Peter Maiden. He helped to place OM on a secure organisational and financial footing. His tasks included chairing the Council and, subsequently, the OM International Executive Committee (IEC).[51] David Cummings, President of Wycliffe International, was an invaluable consultant, not only in helping to clarify OM's structural issues but in wider matters of leadership development and communications training.[52] People with the necessary expertise implemented new policies; the policy area was not static. Viv Thomas reshaped the personnel function, later becoming OM's international coordinator of leadership development.[53] Through David Cummings, OM was invited to send participants to Wycliffe's 'Townsend Institute'. With significant involvement from Marc Kretzschmar and others, this course came to be known as 'Leadership Matters'. The two-week programme emphasised leadership, management, communications and relationship-building. Later, there was a wider consortium involved in the programme. Over one thousand people have completed the course.[54]

As OM's ministry expanded, there was a need to foster new leadership at international as well as national level and to resource new work. In addition to the posts of International Coordinator and the Associate Coordinator, six (soon seven) posts of Area Coordinator were established. This group operated from the mid-1980s as OM's executive body. In the 1980s, OM work was formally organised in Australia and Argentina (both 1980); Quebec (1983); South Africa, under Francois Vosloo (1984) and New Zealand (1989). In the same period, OM USA moved to fine new premises near Atlanta, Georgia, and began to play an increasingly significant role within OM's international operation.

David Hicks, one of the Area Coordinators (for North America) noted that only one of this group, Joseph D'Souza (India), was from a country outside the Western world, despite one-third of OMers being non-Western by this stage. Most of the forty OM Field Leaders, however, were citizens of the country in which they led OM's ministry. Under 20 per cent of OMers were North American, but the roots of OM in the USA were evident in the fact that four of the nine members of the early executive were from the US – George Verwer, Dale Rhoton (OM Ships), Dennis Wright, who had worked in Turkey and Eastern Europe (Europe), and David Hicks. One, Allan Adams, was Australian (East Asia Pacific), and three were Europeans – Peter Maiden, Mike Wakely (South Asia, including Asia Challenge Teams and the Afghan Refugee Ministry) and Bertil Engqvist from Sweden (Middle East).[55] Although the Policy Manual saw a role for women in wider leadership, there were no women on the executive body. Greater diversity would become evident later.

The rest of faith

In 1983 George Verwer published *No Turning Back*, which built on thinking in previous books (notably in his *Come! Live! Die!*, which became *Hunger for Reality*, and in his *Revolution of Love*), and in the first chapter he advocated a spirituality that took seriously 'the rest of faith' (Heb. 4:9, 10). This might seem strange, coming from someone who was the epitome of evangelical activism, but he argued that it was this kind of rest that enabled him to survive. 'In dealing with Operation Mobilisation business', he remarked, 'I frequently work very long hours. I could never do so if I didn't know the rest of faith.'[56] The phrase was one that was often used in the early Keswick movement, although it has not been so commonly employed by those who have shaped other strands of evangelical spirituality.[57]

In George Verwer's book there were familiar themes: the 'revolution of love', good and open relationships and Scripture memorisation. But there were also new emphases. George had been reading Richard Foster's *Celebration of Discipline*, before it became well known in the evangelical world, and strongly recommended its approach to the classic spiritual disciplines.[58] Drawing on Foster's work, he spoke of disciplines such as disappointment, danger, delay, dependability, doubt and disillusionment as all having a part to play in Christian growth. Instead of extremes in spirituality, he advocated balance between crisis experiences and the process of growth; between discipline and freedom; between submission and individual guidance; between activism and the rest of faith; between reckless faith and common sense and between 'anointing' and training.[59]

How did this work itself out in OM operations? There was an increasing awareness that the call to people to '*Come! Live! Die!*' had to be accompanied by a care for them as unique individuals. This became more prominent in the 1980s. In 1981, George Verwer urged that people within OM should not be seen in terms of their roles 'but firstly as people'.[60] His own policy of spending significant amounts of time with those he was seeking to mentor was deeply appreciated.[61] The 'gofers' who assisted him were one part of this mentoring commitment. In 1984, he commented that far more time, effort, money, tears and prayers had gone into relationships in OM than most people would ever know.[62]

In this period, a number of people in the field of international mission, including Allan Adams, argued for greater attention to be given to the pastoral care of those in mission – 'member care', as it came to be known. This was a somewhat contentious issue in OM in the 1980s. Some considered that it could lead to self-centredness and could distract from the real work of mission: others saw its important benefits. A course entitled 'The Leader as a Person', developed by John Hymus and conducted in Rhyl, north Wales, was initially treated with a degree of suspicion by some within OM but was later warmly commended. Allan Adams taught on it for about seven years.[63] Subsequently the missionary environment became very different, and proper care for those in mission was to be seen as essential.

Another rather contentious issue, at least for some within OM, had been the charismatic movement. In 1988, a report from an OM Charismatic Working Group was circulated, which explored this dimension of spirituality. The report recognised that 'charismatic' was difficult to define: what for one person was a 'strong impression' was 'a word from the Lord' to others. There were also cultural complications. Some considered 'charismatic' to be associated with a particular approach to worship, usually informal and contemporary, but in Pentecostal churches in Korea, the style was often operatic. The report reiterated that no OM worker should propagate charismatic theology. However, the report encouraged openness to God speaking not only through Scripture but also through members of the body. Everything should be checked against Scripture. It was felt unwise to permit public use of tongues in OM meetings, although there was freedom for private use of this gift.[64]

Issues connected with 'the Lordship of Christ' were also debated in the 1980s. Speaking at the InterVarsity Christian Fellowship's huge Urbana '87 convention in Illinois, USA, George Verwer stated that OM, in common with other movements such as the International Fellowship of Evangelical Students (IFES), with which OM had a long-standing connection, firmly believed in the Lordship of Christ. He then referred to groups propagating extreme views on this subject. Some had been outside a meeting he had held on the east coast of the USA, handing out literature that implied 'hardly anyone is saved except them'. To know the Lordship of Jesus Christ, he insisted, was to be involved in 'a lifetime of constantly growing and repenting'. He recalled that twenty years earlier he had spoken at Urbana and four thousand people had responded. Over these twenty years, he had received about fifteen thousand letters from people challenged by his teaching on the spiritual life and affected by his open sharing of his personal struggles. His 1987 theme was 'Christ as Lord of all' – of a person's time, 'the tongue', the sexual drive, and resources.[65]

Although there were important debates within evangelicalism in the 1980s about a number of issues in the area of spirituality, OM leaders did not wish debates about points of difference to overshadow the central call to mission. OM's spirituality was a missional spirituality. George Verwer was deeply moved by the continuing resolute commitment to mission of Jonathan and Margit McRostie after Jonathan's serious injury in 1982, and talked about the way Jonathan had spoken from his wheelchair to seven thousand young people at Mission '83 in Switzerland. For his part, Jonathan spoke about the loving and supportive fellowship he had known, including a memorable communion service with Mike Evans from France, Margit and himself, while he was still in intensive care in Spain. As a result of his Mission '83 message, over seven hundred made 'deeper commitments to Christ and to the great task of telling the whole world about him'.[66]

The trust afforded OM by this time meant that the thinking within OM about mission, especially the desire for indigenous leadership, gained a hearing in other missions. This was a gradual process and at times OM leaders were a little reluctant to become involved in what could be time-consuming work with international mission bodies. Yet Luis Bush, a pastor in El Salvador and later International Director of the AD 2000 and Beyond Movement, saw OM as being at the cutting edge of 'a major fresh initiative of the Spirit of God – globalization'. For him, OM's 1982 *Operação Mundo* conference in Sao Paulo, Brazil, was a key event. Later, Luis Bush was to join a committee of leaders in the USA that helped OM by advising on the replacement of the *Logos*, and Dave Hicks was to become a member of the AD 2000 USA committee. From the Latin American perspective, Luis Bush considered that OM gave vision to many who launched COMIBAM '87 (*Congreso Misionero Iberoamericano*) in Brazil, which drew together over three thousand people.[67] This Two-Thirds World congress, with its theme 'From a Mission Field to a Mission Force', represented the new direction in world mission. The influence of OM and the COMIBAM movement, together with other movements such as YWAM and IFES, contributed greatly to the increasing globalising of world mission by stimulating missional enterprise from Latin America.[68]

Conclusion

As OM's activities proliferated in the 1980s, the leadership faced huge challenges: to consolidate the ministry in areas that had always been a particular focus, to reach out in new ways and new places, and to coordinate many different activities. The situation in Europe in this period required a fresh initiative to be taken. This was done through Love Europe. Work in the Middle East continued, inevitably in a low-key fashion. OM India became more and more significant within the whole movement. Important structural steps were taken to ensure levels of excellence in OM management. There were also moves towards increased sharing of leadership, although bringing leadership from the Two-Thirds World into the new executive group did not happen as quickly as might have been expected, given OM's strong commitment to indigenous Field Leadership. OM had its tensions, for example over member care, but OM's emphasis on relationships enabled it to work through such issues. Above all, OM was committed to a missional view of the spiritual life. The 'rest of faith' was emphasised by George Verwer, to empower active service.

As OM was increasingly 'trusted and appreciated', its influence spread. This happened significantly through the ships but also in many other ways. In the rapidly changing Eastern European scene, OM's work found fresh expression. Brother Andrew, for example, took up OM's message, the 'Revolution of Love'.[69] The impact of OM was also felt in South America. At a 1988 Interdenominational Foreign Mission Association (IFMA) and Evangelical Fellowship of Mission Agencies (EFMA) Latin American Consultation, one of the leaders, Al Hatch, spoke rather dramatically about a 'veritable missions mafia of ex-OMers' in the Latin American mission scene.[70] George Verwer was concerned to challenge the evangelical community worldwide and brought that challenge in many places in his own unique style. At Urbana '87, he concluded his address with a statement which sums up OM's vision: 'Let us mobilize and let us go forth making Jesus Christ absolute Lord every day of our life until we are with him.'[71]

Chapter 8

A Thoroughly Global Organisation

The language of 'global organisations' and of 'multinationals' was commonplace in the business world by the 1990s, and in 1994 David Hicks, OM's North American Coordinator, spoke of how, as a member of OM's international leadership team, he had 'appreciated the enrichment and wrestled with the complexities of being part of a thoroughly global organisation'. He had captured something of the vision of this kind of organisation in 1971 when, as part of an OM team in India, he was working with a south Indian leader from a Hindu background, an Italian driver whose roots were Roman Catholic, a north Indian Pentecostal as team treasurer, a British Baptist leading the study programme and an Indian from an Islamic community in charge of literature. His report of this, written in 1971, highlighted how the concept of Christianity as a Western religion 'melts away'. 'People devoted to Christ from all nations', he wrote at that time, 'are going to all nations for Christ.'[1]

Over the two decades since the early 1970s, Dave Hicks, like many OM leaders, had realised the complexities of this process of globalisation, but the commitment to that vision within OM was stronger than ever. An OM Globalisation Committee was established in 1993, charged with proposing concrete ways in which OM could further globalise. Maureen Ma from Hong Kong, the chair of the committee, called for topics such as cultural anthropology, intercultural living and cross-cultural ministry to be covered in OM training conferences. OM's way of operating came under close scrutiny.[2] Huge geopolitical changes also affected

OM's global activity in the early 1990s. This chapter will look at the crucial period 1990–6, examining how OM responded to new challenges.

In the process of globalisation

In the early 1990s, a number of commentators on mission spoke about new realities which meant that a globalised approach to Christian witness was essential. These included the emergence of the 'global village', the fact that most Christians (perhaps three-quarters) were now outside the Western world, the significant growth in the number of cross-cultural mission personnel from the Two-Thirds World, and the recognition of the crucial role of national Christian communities and indigenous leadership.[3] Speaking in 1992 about 'churches of the [global] south, churches of the poor, churches of the Third World', one of the leading Latin American evangelical theologians, Samuel Escobar, argued that it was especially from these thriving and growing churches that new mission was emerging.[4]

Building on this kind of work, Dave Hicks suggested that for mission movements such as OM, globalisation involved more than 'operating internationally', and he proposed a vision in which the churches in diverse regions across the world needed to be involved fully in partnership for global witness. OM was, as Dave Hicks noted, a movement 'coordinating the vitality of sixty national entities'. There had been massive changes over the (almost four) decades of OM's life. Although it was now a global network with an emphasis on bringing people together and on transcultural relationship-building and leadership styles, he described it as still 'in the process of globalisation'.[5]

There were still obstacles to being truly globalised. A number of these were discussed at OM Field Leaders' Meetings held in Hyderabad, India, in January 1993. Dave Hicks presented a paper, based on the research he had been undertaking, and others contributed.[6] Mike Wakely, the OM Area Coordinator for South Asia, a strategic thinker, identified the predominance of Western culture, the power of Western economies and the Western approach to leadership as pervasive problems – from which OM was not exempt.[7] Speaking of OM's international business meetings, Maureen Ma from Hong Kong said in the report that was commissioned in 1993: 'In the West, often issues are presented with a rather pushy sales pitch ... Sometimes there is a confrontational attitude exhibited, making light of opposing viewpoints in order to substantiate one's own position. A culture that values relationships, not points of view, will find this approach abrasive.'[8]

George Verwer was not able to be in Hyderabad, as his visa did not come through, but Dave Hicks noted in his paper that, from the earliest years of OM, a certain philosophy that had been explicitly enunciated by George Verwer – for example in the Leadership Manual – involved three basic principles: world mission is the responsibility of the whole Church, not only the West; all workers, from whatever culture, must be esteemed as equals; and for a mission movement to be truly global requires intentional effort. Dave expanded on these points, emphasising the importance of working with the global church, being 'evangelically inclusive', affirming a multiracial approach, implementing teamwork, sharing resources and developing indigenous leadership.[9]

Although OM had fostered local rather than foreign leadership from the 1960s onwards, ahead of many other missions in the way it had enunciated these principles, the OM leadership, as it gave the issue fresh attention, was far from complacent. In May 1994, writing to OM leaders, George Verwer drew attention to the need for finance to help those in poorer countries take on cross-cultural mission. A great deal was being written about how personnel from the Two-Thirds World did not cost as much as Westerners, but George warned about trying to do mission work 'on the cheap'. Referring to Latin America, where former OMers were initiating new mission projects (for example Project Maghreb, set up by Pablo Carrillo), George asked: 'Are we going to get thousands of people from Latin America, where the church is so huge and motivated, without spending large amounts of money?'[10]

OM had, as George Verwer knew better than anyone, been doing precisely that for some time: allocating significant amounts of funds to enable work to be initiated in the Two-Thirds World. A few months after this May 1994 letter, in November, Peter Maiden, as Associate International Coordinator of OM, wrote:

> When I speak of globalising [OM], I look forward to the day when Indians, Latins, Africans, etc. can feel as comfortable and at home in our Area and International gatherings as Westerners do. I also look forward to the day when our meetings are conducted in a way which enables people from non-Western cultures to play a full part in our discussions. I recognise the danger of creating in OM a new-Western culture and we want to avoid that at all cost.[11]

By this time, there were 2,450 adults working in OM, of whom 36 per cent were Europeans, 34 per cent from Asia and 18 per cent from North America. Married couples comprised 1,018 of the total, with 726 children being part of the OM community. The largest single provider of personnel was India, with 437, with the second largest (and fast-growing) non-Western country being South Korea.[12] Of the very many Koreans who were serving with great effectiveness in over forty countries, including the Middle East and Central Asia, two eventually became significant Field Leaders. Within South Korea itself, Chun-Ho Choi led the OM work from 1990, followed by Jihan Paik. Daniel Chae, who was involved in the early connections in South Korea between OM and the Joy Mission, later gained a PhD at the London School of Theology and had wide experience in pastoral work, before rejoining OM with his wife, Helen, and becoming director of the *Doulos* in 2004.[13]

In 1994 over 60 per cent of OM's personnel were serving in South Asia, the Middle East and Europe. Another 22 per cent of OMers were working for the ships. The trend within OM over the decades had been to have more nationals in leadership in the countries in which OM worked, although this happened only slowly with the top-level leadership. In 1994, of fifty-two official or newly opened fields in OM, thirty-five were led by local people.[14] Up until 1992, all the directors of the ships had been British or American, with the exception of two Germans, Manfred Schaller and Bernd Gülker. With more than forty nationalities on the ships, this Western orientation did not convey the desired message about globalisation. This situation changed in 1992 when Chacko Thomas, from India, who had twice been the *Doulos* associate director, was appointed director.[15]

The statistics in this period showed that the finances for OM's international work came primarily from Europe and the Americas – about 40 per cent from each. Although OM could appear to observers to be rather chaotic, because of its rapid growth and turnover of people, a strong central accounting function and high accounting standards enabled money to be moved as needed. This helped to keep OM together as a global network.[16] Mike Lyth, who had been serving in Bangladesh, was appointed OM's International Finance Officer in 1989, and gradually took on more responsibility, becoming OM's Head of Corporate Services. His remarkable range of gifts and experience, which included working at the World Bank, ensured that OM transformed its accounting and communication systems for its global operations.[17]

From 1994, OM was also working to a strategic plan, 'Towards 2001', which was accepted by the International Leaders Meeting in Mosbach in January 1994. A consultant, David Schmidt, who had worked with well-known Christian organisations, denominations, churches and missions, gave expert help. Maureen Ma's globalisation committee was part of this process and among the commitments in the strategic plan were further globalising of OM's work, 'enabling each of the national entities to make a significant contribution to the movement in planning, decision-making, strategizing, and implementation'. The aim was that OM would 'not be dominated by any one country or culture' and would achieve 'substantial indigenisation in the leadership'. OM's overall purpose was defined: its 'role in the body of Christ' was 'to motivate, develop and equip people for world evangelisation, and to strengthen and help plant churches, especially among the unreached in the Middle East, South and Central Asia, and Europe'.

Specific elements within this vision included partnering with churches for mission, caring for OM's personnel, equipping world Christians and mobilising the next generation. The core values were identified as: knowing and glorifying God; living in submission to God's Word; being people of grace and integrity; serving sacrificially; loving and valuing people; reflecting the diversity of the body of Christ; evangelising the world; global intercession and esteeming the Church.[18] There were also key results that were to be sought, with responsibility for these given to certain individuals or teams. Overall responsibility for the plan's implementation lay with Peter Maiden and, in 1995, George Verwer stressed that his own work of leading OM was being done in partnership with Peter Maiden.[19] A globalised movement was one that operated with shared leadership.

Clash of civilisations?

The vulnerability of OM in its global ministry was emphasised by a tragic event on 10 August 1991 in Zamboanga, in the Philippines. During the *Doulos* International Night performance on that evening, two hand grenades were thrown among the *Doulos* personnel seated backstage. One grenade exploded and two young women serving on the ship were killed – eighteen-year-old Sofia Sigfridsson from Sweden, and nineteen-year-old Karen Goldsworthy from New Zealand. The International Night was taking place in a port terminal building and Chacko Thomas, the *Doulos* associate director, was giving a final message when the grenades were thrown. Twenty-two injured OM personnel, from fifteen countries, were airlifted to hospitals in Manila. Dale Rhoton and Peter Maiden flew out to Manila to be with the injured, and George Verwer spoke to each of them by phone. In an interview with the BBC World Service in London, Peter Conlan was asked: 'Where was God?' He replied that there were no easy answers, but that even in this situation God was there, as he promised in Matthew 28:20 ('I am with you always').

After this devastating experience, the *Doulos* moved on to Tawau, East Malaysia, where a memorial service was held for Sofia and Karen. Dale and Peter Maiden joined the ship there, as did Dr Marjory Foyle, for many years a doctor in India and a highly qualified psychiatrist, with much experience in counselling trauma victims in war-torn areas. There was great concern among OM leaders to give as full support as possible to all those who had been involved. Bernd Gülker, who had been director of the *Doulos* since 1988, while struggling with his own sense of despair, nonetheless gave crucial leadership and support in this period to all the crew and staff, as together they lived through the pain of the most traumatic and tragic event in the history of the *Doulos*.[20]

The newspaper *Malaya*, on the Wednesday after the bombing, carried this statement: 'The remarkable thing is that one of them [the *Doulos* victims] said he had forgiven "the people who did this" in true Christian fashion, while Muslims of Zamboanga issued a statement of apology and a disclaimer.' Although it was suspected that the bombing was the work of a Muslim group, at the time no one claimed responsibility. Two years later, members of a terrorist group which, inspired by ideas of an Islamic holy war, had carried out kidnappings and armed assaults on Christians that had left several dead, began to speak about their part in the bombing. More details were included in an *International Herald Tribune* report on 26 May 1995.[21]

By this time, much more attention was being given to the idea of a 'clash of civilizations'. The term was first used by Bernard Lewis in an article in September 1990, *The Roots of Muslim Rage*,[22] and was taken up by Samuel P. Huntington in 1993.[23] Huntington expanded his ideas in 1996 in what became a much-quoted book, *The Clash of Civilizations and the Remaking of World Order*.[24] His thesis was subjected to serious critique, but there was no doubt about the increasing tension between the Western world and elements within the Islamic world. OM, however, which had been present in a number of Islamic countries for decades and was serving (alongside others) in an increasing number of countries in the Middle East, North Africa and many parts of Asia, did not see itself as defending Western values but as offering credible testimony to a global Christian faith. In 1994, George Verwer stressed the importance of OM having 'a good testimony and credibility' in all countries.[25]

Against a tense background, OM continued to seek to witness sensitively. When the *Doulos* was in Kota Kinabalu, Malaysia, in May 1996, the invited guest of honour opened the book exhibition and encouraged people to 'purchase and avail themselves of these valuable and educational books'. Later, the first book he purchased was a Bible. The *Doulos* book exhibition donated about 150 books to a local orphanage.[26] The perspective among many Christians in Asia who were involved with OM was that, through the ministry of the ships and in other ways, OM was in touch with the 'grassroots' of church life and was 'challenging the grassroots' to seek ways to engage in authentic witness. It is also significant that one Asian leader suggested that 'the ships make OM truly global in its operation'.[27]

There were questions, however, about the extent to which OM could support the range of work being done by various agencies in the Middle and Far East. While the *Doulos* was in Malaysia, George Verwer was writing an 'urgent communication to OM leaders worldwide' in which he spoke about a financial crisis in 1995 that had plunged OM into debt. He pointed out that OM had encouraged many other missions and had been 'big hearted in regard to finance'. By this time, over one hundred agencies had roots (at least in part) in OM. George's specific concern was the extent to which OM could help one of these, Middle East Media (MEM), in supporting the launch of a new Middle East broadcasting venture, SAT-7. Many former OMers were involved in MEM, and the Middle East as a whole continued to be central to OM's concerns, but George argued that OM was 'very overcommitted and not able to meet our own obligations' and he was overwhelmed by the tens of millions of dollars needed to get SAT-7 up and running and developing. For him, the ships and India were among OM's current priorities.[28]

It was clear in the mid-1990s that the ships had a crucially important part to play in establishing and consolidating links in countries across the world, especially in the Middle East and Asia.

In April 1995, the *Doulos* was in Kuwait, and leaders from the ship were interviewed live for a television breakfast programme. Book sales were at record levels. In the following year, there were visits to various and varied ports in Southeast Asia – in Malaysia, the Philippines, Japan, Hong Kong and Taiwan, where fourteen teams travelled around the country. Rodney Hui, who had been involved in the work of the ships and in Singapore, had been travelling in East Asia, building up OM work. From 1990, he lived in Hong Kong, establishing the work of OM there as a springboard into Central Asia, Mongolia and China, where Lawrence Tong from Singapore was later to assume the leadership.[29]

A visit to China in July 1996, the first by the *Doulos*, was particularly significant, especially given the enormous changes in China over the previous decade. China was developing economically at a remarkable rate and assuming a more proactive role in global politics, and its Christian population was growing rapidly. One key purpose of the ship's visit to Shanghai was to build relationships and mutual trust with the Chinese authorities, as a basis for opportunities to do more in future visits. Andrew Sinclair and Peter Conlan, leading the line-up, reported that before the *Doulos* arrived, the Lord Mayor of London, who inaugurated a *Logos II* London visit, wrote to the Mayor of Shanghai (who had recently visited London) to say he hoped the ship would 'do much to promote international goodwill and understanding in your municipality'. Contact was also made with the Christian community. On the Sunday about sixty people from the *Doulos* visited several churches in Shanghai.[30] Daniel Bays, a historian of Chinese Christianity, considered that Christianity was probably growing faster in China than anywhere else in the world.[31]

The time in China was a good example of the way in which OM reached across cultures. Among the highlights was the International Cultural Concert which the ship team presented to one thousand guests in the Shanghai Majestic Theatre. One official stated that the team was able to 'get close' to ordinary people. Another highlight was a book exchange: the ship donated five thousand educational books to twenty-four Chinese institutes and was given several Chinese books. At a professionals' reception, Bernd Gülker, who from 1993 was managing director of OM Ships, spoke with great effectiveness to seventy guests on 'Succeeding in Life', using the parable of the prodigal son to illustrate that forgiveness leads to freedom. The last event was a special luncheon for invited guests. Huang Yue Jin, Deputy Secretary General of the Shanghai Municipal People's Government, expressed his appreciation of the visit and hoped the ship would return.[32] Important bridges were being built.

The courageous revolt of ordinary people

The Middle East and Asia were not the only parts of the world experiencing significant change in this period. The global mission of OM was profoundly affected by the fall of communism across Eastern Europe in 1989–90. The OM Greater Europe (GE) team followed events closely, not least 'the courageous revolt of ordinary people' (as Arlene Adams described it in a GE report) in Romania, and two members of the GE team made an exploratory trip into Romania in December 1989 to assess the situation. They encountered continued fighting around the city of Timisoara but they were able to reach Arad and took part in Christmas services, the first open Christmas services for decades. Soon OM committed itself to new projects across Eastern Europe. One of these, initiated by the International Bible Society, was for one million Russian New Testaments. It was a strange experience for the OM team to be in Leningrad (which later reappropriated its original name, St Petersburg) in 1991 to arrange to hand over New Testaments. Through OM's Greater Europe ministry, a team was established in the city. OM began to work with local churches in several countries, with a focus initially on Russia and Ukraine. Lloyd and Katherine Porter (Lloyd from Australia and Katherine from the UK) became the OM Russia leaders. The first half of the 1990s was seen as a time of spiritual hunger in Russia.[33]

Albania had been a completely closed country, and after the end of communism there was excitement in OM about new possibilities there. Mike Stachura, OM USA director, took a keen interest in developments in Eastern Europe, and used Albania as an example of the effectiveness of OM's short-term mission work. He described how an OM short-term team of three entered Durres, Albania, in 1991, with a commitment to learn the language and culture, to start three Bible-study groups and to see a fellowship of believers commenced. Within a year, they were making good progress with the language, had started twelve groups (with several national Albanians helping to lead) and were working with other agencies in evangelistic outreach in Durres. The team became involved in two new fellowships resulting from a large-scale mission. The evangelical community in Durres grew to 120 by 1994 and began to involve itself in short-term evangelistic outreaches to remote mountain villages.[34]

The ships were crucial to OM's work in the former Soviet Union. *Logos II*, which had set sail in April 1990, was in St Petersburg from 25 July to 8 August 1990. This was a historic visit. OM agreed to 'pay' the sum total of forty Russian Bibles for the use of a berth for *Logos II* in St Petersburg during this visit. René Rodríguez, line-up leader, and Ronnie Lappin travelled up the canals of St Petersburg with the two boxes of Bibles to pay for the Lieutenant Schmidt Embankment berth. At that stage, selling Christian books was not yet allowed, but eventually permission was obtained to give away literature in the city. About eight thousand Bibles, four thousand New Testaments and two million tracts were given to local evangelical churches. Team members took part in a public baptismal service. Ronnie Lappin, who had done many line-ups, considered this visit one of the greatest highlights of his years in ship ministry.[35]

A similar level of excitement was associated with the *Doulos'* visit, from 30 July to 10 August 1992, to Vladivostok, in the far east of Russia. This port, which operated in a highly secretive way because of its naval defences, opened to outside shipping in January 1992 and the *Doulos* was one of the first foreign ships to berth. Again, there was a sense of history. Ronnie Lappin, after being repeatedly told that it would be impossible to get a visa, was 'smuggled' into Vladivostok without a visa to have a talk with a shipping agent. He was then placed on a train out of the city about two hours later. Amazingly, the response was positive.

During the visit over three hundred thousand pieces of literature were given away. Also, seven thousand individually wrapped packages from Korean Christians (the ship had been two months in South Korea), with clothing and foodstuffs, were distributed. Interest across the OM world in the Vladivostok visit was so great that two OMers came from Kazakhstan to be part of the outreach. About seven hundred local people responded during the visit. There were some worries about follow-up, as the local evangelical churches had little experience in this area, but George Barathan and Ronnie Lappin worked hard to foster relationships with the pastors and by the end there was evidence that they had been given fresh vision.[36]

As the Soviet Union imploded, the countries of Central Asia that had been part of the USSR, of which Kazakhstan was the largest, claimed independence, and OM looked at the new possibilities in this region. In 1990, just before Christmas, Lenna and Julyan Lidstone and their family visited Baku, Azerbaijan, travelling via Tblisi in Georgia. OM had just one Azeri contact from a Muslim background in Baku, Lachin, who had become a Christian in the communist period. The Baptist congregation in Baku was almost entirely composed of Russians from atheist or Orthodox Christian backgrounds. Julyan reported on the work in Turkey during the Sunday service, challenging the leaders to reach out to the majority Muslim Azeri population. Within a few years, the Azeri Baptists had grown so rapidly that they were able to form their own congregation. And when *Logos II* visited St Petersburg, crew members were delighted to meet a man from distant Tajikistan who had received a copy of the Gospel of Luke years earlier and who expressed his hope that an OM team would come to his city in Tajikistan to speak about the Christian faith.[37]

Bertil Engqvist was energetically recruiting for this new mission frontier in the early 1990s, and in 1993 this bore fruit with an influx of OMers settling in Central Asia. Dan and Sue St John had already learned the Uighur language in China, but crossed the border to Kazakhstan because of the greater openness and freedom. They became leaders of the new Central Asia field. They saw many Uighurs turn to Christ and churches being planted in the Uighur villages of eastern Kazakhstan. At the same time, Dave and Pam Lovett moved to Tajikistan and others went to Uzbekistan.[38]

In 1994, the *Doulos* visited the city of Odessa, Ukraine, and met Gagauz believers from Moldova (which had also been part of the USSR), who felt the challenge to reach other Turkic peoples. Before and after being in Odessa, the ship was in Turkey. As part of the ministry to the region, some Turkish Christian volunteers sailed with the *Doulos* from Istanbul to Yalta (in the Crimea) in order to work among the Turkic Tartars in the Crimea. By this time, there was a greater awareness of the potential of links among people across the Turkic world. Lenna and Julyan Lidstone travelled from the ship to Almaty, Kazakhstan, to visit thirty members of OM teams meeting for retreat there. In the mid-1990s, OM was serving among Kazakh, Uzbek, Tajik and Uighur people.[39] By the end of the decade, there were OM teams located in every Central Asian country, working with other mission agencies and local Christians and finding many thousands of Muslims coming to faith in Christ across the region.[40]

OM's ship ministry celebrated its 25th anniversary in 1995, and in that year *Logos II* returned to St Petersburg. Onboard conferences were significant during this visit. Return visits were made during the same trip to other Baltic ports. Three years after the first ship visit to Tallinn, Estonia, an OM base was established under the leadership of Jyrki and Anna-Maija Raitila from Finland, and there was an international summer programme in place, 'Love Estonia'.[41] In 1995, as well as the anticipated outreach in the Baltic countries, crew members met a group of Chinese people who had come to faith while working in Tallinn. Soon, to their excitement, the crew members gave them tracts in Chinese.

Along the Baltic coast, in Riga, Latvia, a variety of churches and language groups actively participated in conferences. Peter Magnusson of OM Sweden described the responses as more 'than we can handle'. An unexpected number of people interested in joining OM had churches behind them that were willing to raise the necessary money in support. Literature was, again, crucial. Over 32,000 books were sold, and the churches, along with groups such as YWAM, took responsibility for distributing 250,000 tracts in Latvian and another one hundred thousand in Russian. The International Night was presented in the Academy of Science, known as 'Stalin's Church'. The invitation to Latvia came from the Latvian Baptist Union and the bishop of the Union also asked OM for help in organising evangelism training.[42]

Gerry Davey, who had led STL since the 1960s, was keen to be much more involved in the production of evangelical literature in Eastern Europe. Gerry and Jean Davey's efforts were redirected into work with EELAC (East European Literature Advisory Committee), an outgrowth of OM and IFES that was established to provide literature of enduring worth in Eastern Europe. More specifically, the EELAC vision was to work with evangelical Christians in Eastern Europe who wanted to produce and distribute Christian literature of their own. From 1989, through training, mentoring and the provision of needed capital, EELAC was able to assist in the establishment of national evangelical publishing houses in ten East European countries, with titles produced in fifteen different languages. Over time, publishing houses in Hungary, Romania and the Czech Republic became self-sufficient and assisted other East European publishers. Gerry Davey's experience in OM was crucial in guiding EELAC as it sought to operate in sensitive ways. Although EELAC's focus was and is literature, it played a significant role in equipping leaders in the post-Soviet era.[43]

In 1987, Keith Danby became chief executive of STL. Peter Maiden had met Keith, who was running a small family business in Northern Ireland, and had, he believed, 'a word from the Lord' that Keith should be the next STL chief executive. When he was approached, however, Keith offered several substantial reasons why he was not the person for the job. During the course of 1986, there were further meetings involving George Verwer and others and, in early 1987, Keith and his wife became convinced that the call to OM was a call from God. After his appointment, there was a strategic review of STL's operation, and the OM UK Board endorsed Keith Danby's proposals for a radical new direction. This involved a dedicated Board to lead STL, staff being recruited and compensated from outside the OM family and relocation of the operation. A strong team of senior executives and staff was recruited. The ministry relocated in 1989 from Bromley, Kent, to a purpose-built distribution centre in Carlisle. STL established its position as the principal supplier in the UK Christian book trade. Close links were maintained between STL and OM, with STL continuing to support OM world projects, particularly in India.[44]

Practical application

Ministry in the Middle East grew. Most was unreported but some became public knowledge. In the aftermath of the Gulf War of 1991, about five hundred thousand Kurdish refugees, including old people and small children, took refuge in the mountains of Kurdistan without proper provision of water or sanitation, fleeing from Saddam Hussein's army. Working through the OM network in Turkey, which helped to channel aid from two Christian charities, Global Care and Samaritan's Purse, about thirty people went to the refugee camps with supplies. In order to have an organisation under which to work, Operation Mercy was set up as a separate entity. The prime movers were Bertil and Gunnel Engqvist and Julyan and Lenna Lidstone. The Engqvists were artists, and within a day a logo had been designed and business cards printed.

Other aid groups were working with the Kurds, but many Kurds felt great spiritual hunger and distress and the Operation Mercy team, as well as meeting physical needs – often undertaking the most menial tasks – were able to pray and cry with the refugees. When the Kurds returned to northern Iraq, teams of Christian workers went with them and helped in various ways, such as staffing village clinics.[45] Later, Operation Mercy's work spread, taking in North Africa, the Middle East, the Caucasus and Central Asia, the emphasis being on community transformation through locally initiated work. Its vision is 'to positively impact societies with compassion and integrity through relief and development ministries'. The head office is in Sweden where the organisation benefits from Sweden's neutrality on the world stage.

OM India was another example of the way in which OM was giving more attention to humanitarian needs. Its leadership decided that as well as being committed to on-going holistic ministry, they should become more involved in responding to calamities and natural catastrophes, such as the terrible earthquake which claimed twenty thousand lives in 1993 in Latur, in Maharashtra state. This larger-scale work required funding, and in the early 1990s only 10 per cent of OM monies used in India originated there. In 1993 David Lundy, soon to return to India,[46] did a survey of thirty top OM leaders which showed that despite the reliance of OM India on money from outside for its ministry, 82 per cent of the OM leaders thought Indian churches viewed OM India as 'quite indigenised' or 'moderately indigenised' – and the OM leaders themselves concurred.[47] What was of particular importance was that OM India was setting its own agenda.

OM India teams were developing increasingly extensive holistic work among the poor in some of India's largest urban slums.[48] An example of this was Annamma, who joined OM in 1989. She wanted to start 'mercy ministry', and after prayer and discussion within OM India a team of five young women began a social programme in 1992, among people in an area of Hyderabad who were living without running water or proper sewage. The team started a Balwadi (nursery school), sewing classes and literacy classes. Slowly people also started coming to a small worship gathering on Sundays and in 1996 twenty-one of them publicly declared that Jesus was their Lord and were baptised.[49]

The OM ships were also involved in holistic ministry. A study by David Greenlee of the impact of the ships noted the effect on an orphanage in the Philippines when ship teams built fences and helped in other practical ways. A European who was leading a street children's ministry elsewhere in the Philippines greatly appreciated the ship teams that worked with him, including running a free medical clinic in his poor neighbourhood. An OM leader in the Middle East noted the impact when a team helped in cleaning up the hospital in Djibouti.[50] In August 1995, when *Logos II* visited Swansea, Wales, Jimmy Carter, former President of the United States, was guest of honour at the official opening and stated that the ship ministry was 'a demonstration of the practical application of one's religious faith'. At the time there was bitter conflict in the Balkans, and Jimmy Carter said to the *Logos II* team: 'If you could only go to Bosnia and let the people see the spirit that is exemplified in you, we would soon have peace there.'[51]

Later in that year, the *Doulos* was in Madagascar and, as was increasingly the case, a medical tour ashore was arranged. The ship's dentist, Issam Smeir from Jordan, heard the team doctor could not come and wondered what impact the team could have. But when he and the two nurses, Jamie Cheng from Hong Kong and Martina Berg from Sweden, met with the local translator, Fernand Ramahalison, they discovered he was a medical doctor. During the four days ashore, the team visited four villages, travelling by helicopter, and treated over four hundred people.[52]

Holistic ministry was not restricted to those whom the OM teams served. It was increasingly recognised that the teams themselves needed proper care. As we have seen, in the 1990s the place of missionary care was the subject of much discussion within missionary organisations.[53] In 1995 an issue of the *International Journal of Frontier Missions*, for example, was devoted to 'member care'.[54] Allan Adams, who handed over his East Asia Pacific Area Coordinator role in 1995 to Rodney Hui from Singapore, was International Pastoral Care Advisor for OM. He was responsible for the Oasis Counselling Services in OM Conferences and in Love Europe, and was also involved in the OM Leadership School. He noted that almost every evaluation conducted within OM Ships had pointed to a deficiency in pastoral care. In 1995 a survey showed 'two significant negatives in OM'. These were: 'People feel used. Communication is deficient.'[55]

David Greenlee, commenting slightly later, agreed that on the ships 'The most common complaint was the need for more pastoral care.' He suggested that it was 'probably impossible to ever provide enough pastoral care', but argued that the emphasis on such care was important, as was the need for care in 'balancing the many pressures of ship life, a perceived over-emphasis on work, and spirituality'.[56] George Verwer had always been concerned for people and, in many of his letters to international leaders in this period, he asked them to let him know of anyone who was struggling, so that he could get in touch with them. He regularly quoted from Charles Swindoll's book, *The Grace Awakening*, and insisted that the best pastoral care in the world would not deal with 'legalism, judgmentalism, disobedience and sin'. What was needed was 'grace-awakened forgiveness'.[57]

OM placed an emphasis on bringing people together for mutual care, not leaving them isolated. In 1994 George Verwer reported on 'Network 94' which had brought together many OM board members from around the world. He stressed relational support.[58] A significant change had been going on in OM, however, and this was dealt with in the strategic plan produced in 1994. This argued that 'as the influence of the founder of a movement is spread more thinly then the structure must increase'. It hastened to add: 'George Verwer is not diminishing!' However, OM now had 3,300 people, including children, working in sixty-four countries and therefore his influence was bound to be diluted.[59] In 1995, he argued that OMers needed to make 'greater efforts to relate to a wider range of people' in the movement.[60]

Leadership development

Another long-standing emphasis, considered and implemented in new ways, was leadership development. Here India was crucial. The Indian experience had shaped OM from the 1960s onwards. A large number of the Western leaders in OM had developed their ideas about leadership in their early days in India. Senior Indian OM leaders sustained a high level of trust in their Western counterparts at the same time as being given – and being willing to take – leadership responsibility themselves.[61] More formal training gradually developed in India, leading to the establishment of

OM's Asian College of Cultural Studies (ACCS), offering Bachelor of Ministry, Master of Divinity, and Master of Arts degrees, including a MA in Leadership. In 1995, an innovative joint venture came into being: David Lundy was asked to set up a MA majoring in Leadership and Management or in Missiology, offered through the Briercrest Biblical Seminary in Saskatchewan, Canada, and OM India. It was offered in India, focusing on the Indian context.[62]

The expansion of training in OM India was partly facilitated by the move of OM India's headquarters from Bombay to Hyderabad. It was possible in 1990 to buy a campus, Logos Bhavan, in the village of Jeedimetla, near the twin cities of Hyderabad–Secunderabad, and construction of the new premises was completed in 1994. Hyderabad was becoming known as a centre of cyber-technology. The fine OM facilities were made available to many missions and churches around India for conferences, meetings and training.[63] Gradually, more and more of OM India's 1,200 national workers became involved in training at ACCS, with the figure reaching 50 per cent. Under OM India's training philosophy, with its aim of promoting integrative learning, what was learned in the classroom was directly applied in practical ways.[64]

There was a keen awareness in the 1990s of the need to contextualise training and development, to learn from each other and to re-emphasise a core OM value – relationality. Viv Thomas, who was with OM's International Coordinating Team (ICT) and oversaw the coordination of personnel and training, argued strongly for new and flexible approaches: 'Different times demand different types of leaders; what looks like great leadership in one set of conditions can be inappropriate in another . . . You cannot drop Canadian leaders into North India and tell them to lead, or vice-versa. What works at one stage of an organisation will not work at another. Leadership Development must keep moving.'[65] Recognising the increasing complexity of OM and the need always to be learning from each other, George Verwer encouraged leaders to keep in touch through e-mail; he wanted to see all the main OM leaders on the network.[66]

An important contribution to the development of new leadership was made by a twice-yearly Senior Leaders Training Course, held at West Watch, a retreat centre in the south of England. Run for many years by Wayne and Hilary Thomas, this delightful English country house has been the setting for large numbers of international OM meetings. In the specific field of training, K. Rajendran chaired a training committee and, arising from its work, Christiane Böning (later Mackert) was appointed OM's International Training Officer. The OM Personnel Department relocated from London to Carlisle. Viv Thomas moved to consultancy work, and Peter Nicoll from South Africa, who had directed *Logos II* and then OM UK, became OM's director of International Personnel Services. In this period, Peter Maiden affirmed the way in which OM had embraced leadership development and training. Although keen to have local initiatives, he saw the need for central encouragement.[67]

In some areas of leadership and spiritual development, OM did not appear in this period to do as well as might have been expected. In India, many women were trained for leadership – the focus was on leading other women – but in OM as a whole, despite the remarkable contribution of so many women, few were given wider leadership, for example as Field Leaders.[68] In the area of spirituality, in earlier periods OM had contributed in distinctive and influential ways to evangelical spirituality but in the 1990s it seems to be reacting to initiatives by others. When the 'Toronto Blessing', with its controversial phenomena, became a source of intense debate in 1994, George Verwer suggested: 'We have people in OM from many different sides and we must ALL go the extra mile.'[69] This was helpful in terms of accepting others, but did not suggest a clear spiritual direction.

A further surprising aspect in this period is the lack of significant OM leaders emerging from Eastern Europe, given the huge investment of OM in that region. This contrasts with the experience of other evangelicals in Europe: the pan-European Baptist community, for example, produced a number of influential Eastern European Baptist leaders.[70] OM's policy of people raising their own financial support was one obstacle to overcome in this area.

Also many of OM's links had been with 'underground' unregistered congregations in communist-dominated countries, and these groups found it hard to adapt to new European realities.

OM was, however, giving clear direction in the wider world of mission leadership. In 1994, Dave Hicks offered an impressive list of mission founders or leaders of evangelical organisations who had been influenced by OM.[71] As well as those mentioned in earlier chapters in this book, he listed: Federico Bertuzzi, Misiones Mundiales; Ron George, People International and then World in Need; Daniel Gonzáles, Alturas-Cursos Biblicos in Barcelona; Marshall Moyle, Central European Mission Fellowship; Doug Nichols, Action International Ministries (the Philippines) and Heinz Strupler, New Life (Switzerland). As well as mission founders there were other leaders who had served in OM: Lindsay Brown, General Secretary of IFES; Rafael Lopes, Projecto America do Sul (Brazil); and Vishal Mangalwadi, author and Indian social activist. Many others who were still in OM were now involved in wider bodies such as national Evangelical Alliances and Evangelical Missions Alliances. Many former OMers were part of 'OM World Partners'. Dave Hicks noted that over eighty thousand short-term workers had gained experience in OM, and that summer missions – in Europe, Quebec, Mexico, Hong Kong, India, Pakistan, South Africa, Argentina, Brazil and Sudan – continued to offer such experience.[72]

George Verwer was committed to evangelical cooperation, and agreed to help lead the mission executives' track at the 'Global Consulation on World Evangelization by AD 2000 and Beyond' (GCOWE) Consultation of Mission Executives in South Africa in 1997. Frank Fortunato led worship there.[73] OM was also open to receiving insights from those outside the movement: as he looked at OM in the 1990s, Peter Maiden reiterated that the movement was evangelical, drawing from and representing a 'broad theological background and a range of gifting', and he referred to the important themes covered by John Stott in his revised and expanded *Issues Facing Christians Today*, which set out the challenges facing contemporary evangelicals.[74] John Stott was seen by George Verwer and others in OM as an important mentor. In

1995 John Stott and George spoke to a gathering of pastors and leaders on *Logos II*.

In this context, long-time favourite books in OM such as *Calvary Road* continued to be mentioned by George Verwer, but new books were also strongly recommended. In 1994, he praised Ronald Dunn's *Don't Just Stand There, Pray Something* (1991), 'a powerful book on prayer that I should have finished a long time ago', and Tony Campolo's *How to be Pentecostal without Speaking in Tongues* (1994), 'a great heart cry for reality, victory, balance and the Spirit-led life'. He was typically honest about John Stott's *The Contemporary Christian* (1992): 'A great book that I started over a year ago, but being a large book I got bogged down and did not finish it. Drena and I had lunch with John the other day so that got me all motivated again for his books.'[75] As always, George was keen to encourage OMers and the wider evangelical constituency to think seriously about their faith. For OM, the effective leader was a thoughtful leader.

Conclusion

This was an important period of globalisation for OM. Challenges remained. Even in the 1990s, there were some experienced OMers who felt that OM was 'still very Anglo-Saxon in orientation'.[76] However, OM was becoming more and more globalised. As examples: in the 1990s a Central Europe Field began; new OM work was formally established in Papua New Guinea, Central Asia, Japan, Uruguay, Puerto Rico and Chile; and five new OM Areas were formed. Far-reaching changes in the Arab world and Eastern Europe, both areas of concern for OM since its beginnings, led to OM recommitting itself to long-term, in-depth ministry in these regions. By the 1990s OM India, the largest of all OM's operations, was also one of the largest interdenominational networks across the nation. OM increasingly invested in holistic or integral ministry. The OM ships offered a unique platform for global ministry. It was generally recognised in Latin America that OM, and in particular the *Doulos*, had been a catalyst for world mission. Bill Taylor, Executive Director of the World Evangelical Fellowship Missions Commission, who had himself been affected by George Verwer when they were students together at Moody Bible Institute in 1958, reiterated Al Hatch's view of the significance of ex-OMers in the Latin American mission scene.[77] More widely, at least one hundred new ministries had been initiated by those trained in OM. The impact of OM on wider mission continued to grow and develop, and the launch of OM's Global Action programme in 1997 was further evidence of this development.

Chapter 9

Transforming Lives and Communities

In September 1997, as the news in many countries was filled with the deaths of Princess Diana and then Mother Teresa, it was clear that the world, East and West, was amazingly connected. The talk was of a 'global village'. As a reflection of this language, September 1997 also saw the launch of OM's new 'Global Action', with varied openings for service – two thousand specific opportunities, in seventy countries – lasting for six months, or one or two years. Global Action, which was designed to reinvigorate OM's short-term mission programme, had three tracks: action evangelism teams; special ministry teams, for example engaged in relief work or educational work; and opportunities in administration, finance or technical services. Everyone accepted was required to raise their own support. There was no upper age limit, and there was an intention to engage with those with expertise and 'life skills', but it was anticipated that most of those joining a Global Action team would be young and it was hoped that for many this would be the introduction to a longer term commitment.[1]

George Verwer viewed 1997 as one of the most significant years in OM's ministry, not only because of Global Action but also other events. He had spoken at the Urbana conference, which had attracted 19,500 people. At least fifteen thousand had made some kind of decision about their commitment to Christ.[2] In 1997, new OM ventures were developing across the globe. Significant new initiatives were taking place in India, for example, Christmas Project Light.[3] The years 1997 to 2002–3, the subject of this chapter, were ones in which the OM India leadership was also involved in initiatives that had global implications, with the setting up of the All India Christian Council (AICC) in 1999 and the Dalit Freedom Network (DFN) in 2002, with Joseph D'Souza as its International President.[4] There was increasing focus on the theme of 'transformation'. Speaking of actions that were being taken in this period in the area of social justice, Joseph D'Souza said: 'If we are not intentional about bringing change and transformation in lives and societies it will not happen. To love people is to act on behalf of them.'[5] This emphasis was taken up in the OM theme – 'transforming lives and communities'.[6]

In solidarity

India's Dalits (the 'broken'), who comprise 25 per cent of India's population, have been known in the past as 'untouchables'. Under the traditional caste system the Dalits have suffered greatly. They have been subject to violent attacks, which have included murder. Many Dalit women and children have suffered particularly badly. Compared to others, Dalit children have had little access to education.[7] The All India Christian Council (AICC), with which OM leaders have been involved, was set up in order to pursue 'proactive and not just reactive actions to help the Christian community and other minorities, as well as Dalits, tribals and backward communities'.[8] These were referred to as the Dalit-Bahujan people. One important focus for the AICC has been persecution of Christians in India. In January 1999, India was shocked when Graham Staines, an Australian who had served in Orissa for over thirty years, especially caring for those with leprosy, and his two sons, were burned to death. Christian groups, including OM teams, were attacked in different parts of India. The Indian Cabinet ordered an enquiry.[9]

It is significant that OM India's leadership contributed to the vision to pioneer the AICC as an Indian Alliance which cut across denominational barriers and was committed to putting faith into action. Many themes that had characterised OM from the very beginning – the 'revolution of love', working with those in need and effective team work – contributed to shaping this new initiative. There were also new emphases. The AICC aimed to 'mobilize' – the use of the word was significant – 'committed and talented people to put their energies into safeguarding these peoples through all constitutional means'. Through the many contacts that OM leaders had, the AICC was able to put together a large network of activists across India (including lawyers) who monitored discrimination and atrocities. The vision was to strengthen India's communities and promote equal treatment of people.[10]

Two terrible events took place in 2002 which had a massive impact. In February–March 2002, thousands of Muslims in Gujarat were massacred by Hindu fundamentalists. AICC staff, in the tradition of rapid response that characterised OM, set up camps in Gujarat, providing shelter and food for displaced and suffering Muslims. As a result, the Muslim community throughout India opened its arms to the Christians 'as never before'. Christian leaders received invitations to speak to large audiences of Muslims. The questions asked were: 'Why did you help us? What does the Bible have to say about human rights and justice?'[11] In the same year, on 15 October 2002, five Dalits were brutally murdered for allegedly killing a cow. Udit Raj, a Dalit leader (President of the Justice Party), turned to the AICC for help, and Christian leaders, including Joseph D'Souza, travelled to New Delhi within hours. They joined a protest and met families of the victims, providing them with humanitarian aid and with human comfort. This atrocity galvanised action for justice.[12]

OM leaders, as they have become more involved in standing with the Dalit-Bahujan people, have made it clear that there is no room for complacency about the role that evangelical leaders have played in the past in addressing issues of need and of injustice. Just as George Verwer had sought to challenge young evangelical Christians in the 1950s to respond to the challenge of world mission, so Joseph D'Souza argued a few decades later for a vision of, and a commitment to, Christian mission that involved appropriate political action. He spoke passionately of the way evangelicals had failed to challenge 'structures and systems designed to oppress, degrade, abuse, and kill others'. For him, 'Christians, especially evangelicals, have for too long over-simplified the problems of the world by claiming that if we just deal with personal sin, then the world will be changed automatically as a matter of course.'[13]

No one in OM denied that when the hearts of individuals changed there was an impact on society, but there was a fresh awareness in the later 1990s that, at times, the gospel had been presented in a rather narrow form, which actually diminished its power. Joseph D'Souza, speaking at a public meeting in Bangalore in 2001, argued that 'the caste system was antithetic to Jesus' teaching about the Kingdom of God', and admitted that in this area 'the Church in India was in the wrong and needed to repent'.[14] The themes of a radical following of Jesus and repentance expressed the heartbeat of OM. 'The father of the Indian constitution and of the Dalit liberation movement, Dr. Ambedkar, turned to the church for help', Joseph said, 'and found the doors closed to him.'[15] The church community had not been as radical as it might – and should – have been.

The desire that Christians showed to stand with the Dalits angered some Hindu extremist groups and Joseph D'Souza was the target of attacks. Some Christians were also critical of the AICC, suggesting that it was wrong to endorse large-scale conversions to (for example) Buddhism, but Richard Howell, General Secretary of the Evangelical Fellowship of India, said: 'Christians do not have any hidden agenda in supporting [the Dalits].' In the aftermath of a Dalit conversion ceremony he affirmed: 'They made a request to us for support ...We are in solidarity with them.'[16] Joseph defended his actions, making the following case: 'It is surely a better witness to stand with them, to let them know that they are loved by Jesus Christ and His followers, and that Christians will support their right to be free even when they choose Buddhism over Christianity, rather than the alternative: to walk away, disassociate from them, and refuse to love them unless they convert to Christianity.'[17]

While these wider events were taking place, the OM India leadership seriously reassessed the situation of OM teams in India after the murder of Graham Staines and his sons. It was evident that even missionaries with long service were vulnerable. There was no desire to abandon witness because it was costly. Graham's widow, Gladys, who had served with OM, showed great bravery in continuing their ministry, working with her daughter Esther (aged thirteen) and based at their simple house beside the Baptist church in Baripada.[18] After discussion and prayer about the changing context, OM India leaders decided that OM teams should no longer give priority to the kind of itinerant ministry across India that they had been engaged in for three decades, but should aim to stay in one place, working in cooperation with the local people.[19]

In place of the traditional travelling ministries, long-term OM teams were formed to work among specific peoples in both north and south India. The goal of these teams was to share good news in an in-depth way with the people of each community. They have been involved in house visitation and setting up fellowship groups and prayer meetings. As local home groups emerged, OM India's Good Shepherd ministry, which was already in operation, began to broaden. The local emphasis, coupled with the support for Dalit-Bahujan people, produced significant growth from the late 1990s. People began to follow Christ in large numbers across the nation and needed fellowship and discipleship. OM India realised that OM's work in the country over forty years had produced significant results. The leadership training and experience that had been developed (in which twenty thousand workers had been trained) and the wide cross-section of Indian leadership which OM now had across the nation, had enabled OM to play an important role in the Dalit movement for salvation and empowerment.[20]

In the light of this, in 2003 OM India made the decision to begin a home-grown, fully indigenous church movement. The leaders of this new movement chose the name 'Good Shepherd Community Church Movement' (GSCC). The term 'Shepherd', referring to Jesus, made a specific connection with the Dalit-Bahujan peoples, as the caste system considers shepherding a low caste occupation. The word 'Community' was important, because OM India realised that the movement had to engage in holistic transformation, touching the spiritual, communal-social, economic and physical aspects of life of the people. The word 'Movement' was significant because, from the beginning, the aim was that every local GSCC fellowship would be a missional church, setting aside a significant portion of its income, however small, to support a new church planter or worker in a neighbouring area where Dalit-Bahujan people lived. Over a short period of time, this new, vibrant national church movement has seen rapid growth.[21]

As part of the wider commitment to transformation, OM India partnered with other agencies to assist victims of the Orissa super-cyclone (1999) and the Gujarat earthquake (2001). In Orissa, OM workers built more than seventy-nine houses, and after the Gujarat earthquake they constructed 910 houses. OM's project was the first to be completed.[22] Another aspect of transformation has been the provision of schools to educate Dalit children. Initially fourteen were set up, with between fifty and two hundred students in each.[23] OM India leaders, such as Kumar Swamy, South India regional director of OM, have been involved in supporting the DFN in these and other projects. It is recognised that the DFN and the AICC have been able to implement large-scale work among the Dalit-Bahujan people because they draw from the experience and expertise of OM India and their Good Shepherd ministry at local level.[24] These wider developments were – at least in part – the fruit of seeds planted in OM's earliest ministry in India.

A field led movement

In various fields new directions emerged for OM between 1997–2002. There was continuing concern for Eastern Europe. In Albania, OM helped plant four evangelical churches and trained national pastors to lead the churches. Albanian-led churches then established additional fellowships. In 1997, during a time of serious anarchy, and in 1999, during the Kosovo war, OM Albania's holistic ministry was of great importance. Led by Dane Hanson, Field Leader for OM Balkans, the work in Albania had a focus on training local Christians through Action Team training programmes. OM Albania also became involved in teaching sewing courses to women; working with the Emmanuel Clinic, a medical facility in Durres; running summer camps for children; reaching out to street children; slum and gypsy housing projects; building children's playgrounds and renovation in local schools. There has also been a project to develop and build water collection points in remote villages.[25]

In 1998, OM began working in Bosnia-Hercegovina, which had been part of Yugoslavia and was the scene of horrific ethnic cleansing during the Balkans War a few years before. OM teams focused on church planting, along with local evangelical (particularly Pentecostal) churches, through friendship evangelism; teaching language courses, computing, guitar and skills in crafts; humanitarian aid distribution; one-to-one discipleship; sports activities and ministry to children and youth. OM took responsibility for a youth centre in Sarajevo.[26] The province of Kosovo, in another part of former Yugoslavia, came to international attention during a war that ended in 1999 and resulted in half the population being displaced. Many organisations assisted the Kosovar people in post-war rebuilding. An OM team was established to keep in contact with individuals that OM had come to know through aid distribution in refugee camps. The team helped to establish evangelical churches in two towns. OM Kosovo has offered opportunities for short-term service to people from many countries.[27]

Another former communist country which struggled not with war but with poverty was Moldova. With a population of 4.5 million, Moldova is the smallest of the former Soviet countries and considered the poorest nation in Europe. The 1990s saw considerable evangelical church growth in Moldova and the work of the OM Moldova team involved assisting local churches in evangelism, discipleship and church planting. A twice-yearly discipleship and mission training programme was initiated, called 'Challenge into Missions'. Food distribution ministry was important, in the light of the widespread poverty. Several local Christians joined the OM team in Moldova, and young people from Moldova began to serve with OM in parts of Central Asia and the Middle East. Sports ministry was developed as a major aspect of OM Moldova's ministry, with several KidsGames programmes launched – a kind of 'Olympics for kids', drawing communities together.[28]

In some parts of Eastern Europe, including parts of the former Soviet Union, OM established work in the early1990s which was well developed by the end of the decade. This was particularly the case in Russia and Ukraine. In Russia, OM developed under the leadership of Lloyd and Katherine Porter, and held various outreaches and mission events. The St Petersburg and Novosibirsk teams grew to thirty members. Several Russians served with OM within Russia and in other places, especially on the OM ships. A rehabilitation centre for alcoholics was started in conjunction with local churches in Novosibirsk.[29] In Ukraine, where separate OM work was established, orphanage and sports ministries became important. An OM team reached out to over thirty orphanages in the Vinnitsa region. One major challenge for OM in Ukraine was how to mobilise Ukrainians for wider mission, given that the country has so many evangelical believers. The question that was being asked in OM was why more Ukrainians were not involved in seeking to fulfil the vision for global mission.[30]

Along with Eastern Europe, OM continued its commitment to the countries of the Middle East. In 1995, there was a change of Area designation in OM, with the Middle East Area, which had been comprised of the Middle East, Central Asia and North Africa, being split into two Areas: Middle East and North Africa (MENA) and West and Central Asia (WACA). From 1995, Kamal and Christina Fahmi coordinated OM's work in the Middle East and North Africa. Kamal's vision was for OM, as a 'field led movement', to see its work 'born in the different cultures and nations', so that it was genuinely 'incarnating the gospel'. Rather than having a predetermined set of answers which would be inappropriate in the Middle East, the key was 'adapting to the way of life of the people we work among'.[31] Alongside long-term work in these regions of the world, visits by the ships were important. In 1998, for example, the *Doulos* spent time in Bahrain and the Yemen. In Bahrain, over thirty thousand visitors came on board and many meetings were held.[32]

Western and Central Asia, stretching from Turkey to north-west China, essentially comprised the Turkic and Persian people groups. Bertil Engqvist, who had pioneered the early work in this region, was the obvious choice to be OM's Area Coordinator, and Julyan Lidstone followed later. Bertil's emphasis on holistic mission was even more relevant in the light of the economic challenges for the region that followed the collapse of the Soviet Union. OMers became involved in development programmes, teaching English, setting up small businesses or training people in job skills. A particular concern was disabled children, who had been ignored and hidden under the communist regimes. Bertil was committed to indigenous mission and finding creative ways in which those from outside the region would contribute. An example of the latter was the Love Silk Road summer outreach.[33]

At this time, there was considerable debate over how much Western missionaries should be involved in mission in cultures with which they were completely unfamiliar and where they might be insensitive: the Middle East and West and Central Asia being good examples. There were also financial issues for Western missions, given the cost of supporting foreign missionaries. George Verwer's argument was that there were 'people groups among whom the church barely exists: the Uighers of western China, the Afghans, the Kurds, the Baluchs', and he considered that, in such cases, the argument that the Western church should give support to local nationals, rather than sending missionaries, was at its weakest. 'In many of these places', he argued, 'there are no nationals to support.'[34] OM's flexible missional policy was a key to its effectiveness.

East Asia Pacific was an instance of an OM Area in which local energy for mission was marked. Writing in 2000, Rodney Hui, the Area leader, noted the growth of Asian Field Leaders within OM. By then they comprised about twenty of the leaders, out of the

110 OM fields. His own vision was to 'maintain a genuine and mutual assistance philosophy between the first and third worlds, north and south'. He saw OM as one of the few missions with a worldwide ministry that was offering Asian Christians substantial experience for service outside their region. Rodney was committed to 'the myriad short to long-term opportunities for all sorts of people with all kinds of training and background' that were available through OM. Also, OM had a role in bridging across some of the denominational divides. In the East Asia Pacific region, OM sought to work with all the major denominations and had built relationships with many denominational leaders.[35] Some denominational bodies are very large, for example the Presbyterian churches in Korea, and many East Asian OM recruits have come from these denominations.

Southern Africa, under the leadership of Francois Vosloo, as Area Coordinator, had also become a vibrant area of OM's work by the later 1990s. The hub of the activity was South Africa, where Peter Tarantal was Field Leader, with outreach taking place to other countries. Peter was one of the coordinators of the World Evangelization Network of South Africa, bringing black and white evangelical groupings together.[36] This was an important indicator of OM's wider commitments. A significant six-month missionary training course was developed in South Africa, with seventy to eighty people participating in each course. These conferences included teaching and practical field work, such as working with the poor, ministry to those of other faiths, relief work, evangelism and collaboration with local churches. This programme drew numerous participants from other parts of the OM world.[37]

South Africa sent many people into the ship ministry, and in 2002 the *Doulos* had a significant few months in southern Africa, working with local teams. In Mozambique, teams worked with communities in desperate poverty. Donations by South African churches enabled rolling water carriers to be given to those most in need. An AIDS Prevention Day for church and youth leaders was held in Maputo, with representatives present from many AIDS-awareness groups, including the UN. When the *Doulos* underwent dry-dock and lay-up in East London, South Africa, many volunteers became involved. In Durban, in the same period, OM teams joined in 'Operation Sunrise Africa', seeking to bring the Christian message to fifty million people in fifty African cities over fifty days. A 'Pure Relationships' programme in Port Elizabeth emphasised living morally pure lives, and this aspect of ministry was to be taken further through OM's AidsLink.[38] Experiences in South Africa are indicative of how each Area/field was developing in its own way.

Unusual open doors

The huge diversity of work within OM by 1997 might have appeared to question the movement's ability to stay together. But George Verwer was upbeat about developments. As he reflected on what he called 'one of the most significant years in our ministry' – 1997 – he highlighted many 'open doors across the globe'. He was delighted that Area and Field Leaders had more responsibility. His own ministry, as had always been the case, stretched well beyond OM. During the year, as well as speaking at Urbana, he and Drena had been at three large Campus Crusade regional events in the USA – a reminder of the early contact with Bill Bright, the Campus Crusade founder – and then at a student conference in Canada. He had also been speaking in New Zealand.[39] In thinking about global issues, not least in relation to OM, George drew from David Lundy's book, *We are the World*, published a year earlier, in which Lundy noted that about one-third of OM's short-term and career missionaries were from the Two-Thirds World.[40] George spoke about OM's great diversity, with 2,800 workers from eighty different nations, and the need to have people serving in strategic ways.[41]

In his 1999 end of year letter to OM leaders, George Verwer recommended Patrick Johnstone's new book, aptly titled *The Church is bigger than you think*. The note of praise was strong in his letter, as it had been in the previous year: 'This has been a fantastic year and we have so much to thank and praise God for.' In the light of all that had happened, George said that he wanted to shout: 'To God be the Glory.' The number of those who had been on OM was by now over one hundred thousand. George was keen on new technological developments that aided communication within OM. The year 1999 was declared 'The year of the Internet', and he hoped to increase OM's involvement in the internet tenfold. His phrase was 'Operation Hyperlink'. In thinking about strategic doors for OM, he stressed Europe, the Middle East, Central Asia, North Africa and the ships.[42] There were certainly 'unusual open doors'.

Although there was much to be thankful about in the later 1990s, there were also problems or, as George Verwer put it, 'complexities'. In 1997 he reported that many OM projects in dozens of languages had been held up due to lack of funds. Part of the funding issue was that there had been investment by OM in a fund called 'New Era'. This was highly recommended by evangelical bodies in the USA, and had proved to be a sound channel for return for many groups, but New Era collapsed. However, George was able to report in 1997 that 75 per cent of the lost money had come back, and later most of the rest was recovered.[43]

There was a particular focus in this period on effective fundraising and Ted Hilton, a Canadian Christian business leader and supporter of OM, spoke to OMers about aspects of this subject. His ideas were set out in a book, *Building a Support Team*. In 1998, George Verwer spoke about 'some breakthroughs in finance', but acknowledged that OM was 'over-committed and stretched'.[44] An increasingly professional approach to fundraising was characteristic of this period. Bernd Gülker spoke about OM embracing 'an active fund-raising attitude'. This was expressed through new initiatives such as the Fuel Project, fundraising dinners on the ships and at other venues, a ship entrance fee being charged and an executive team focusing on building a new OM major-donor base.[45]

The themes of finance and fellowship continued to be prominent features in George Verwer's thinking in 1998–9. OM's International Coordinating Team (ICT) began operating from offices in Forest Hill, London, that had been given to OM; and

John Bendor-Samuel, President of Wycliffe, came to speak at Forest Hill on questions relating to fund raising.[46] During the summer, OM conferences were held in five venues in Europe, involving 1,400 people, and George Verwer, while greatly appreciating these, commented that he and Drena found it difficult because there were many friends they would have liked to spend time with, but the numbers were overwhelming. The leader could not have the same depth of relationship with all the team, as had been the case earlier. George recognised that OM was changing, but insisted that everyone in it was needed and had a part to play. He wrote: 'The message and ministry of our feeble, ragamuffin fellowship is needed across the globe as much as any time in our history and each one of you who reads this is a vital and integral part of that.'[47]

OM would continue to expand but, in 1998, George Verwer announced at the International Leaders Meeting in South Africa, in a message entitled 'The Way Forward', that he wanted to relinquish the international leadership of OM when he reached sixty-five (in 2003) and allow others to find new ways forward. There was, of course, considerable discussion about the idea, but Area Leaders and others affirmed the decision. George had no plans to leave OM, but he wanted someone younger in his job.[48] Peter Maiden, as the Associate International Coordinator, was already sharing many of the tasks of international leadership with George, and he was subsequently nominated to be the next International Coordinator when George relinquished the post. This nomination was approved by the International Leaders Meeting and then subsequently by the General Council in 2001, with a view to Peter Maiden taking up the position in 2003.

Flexibility and openness to change were key to OM's continued expansion. After the first Love Europe in 1989, this new concept had spread to many different countries and had a huge impact. This expansion coincided with fresh developments in worship within OM. Bill Drake joined OM in 1991, becoming the movement's music minister, and his distinctive contemporary worship style had considerable impact.[49] A further innovative development, initially within Europe in the later 1990s but also subsequently spreading elsewhere, was TeenStreet. This was under the dynamic leadership of Dan and Suzie Potter. George Verwer saw the importance of this new and growing OM ministry to teenagers and in 2002 he enthused about the fact that TeenStreet, held in Offenburg, Germany, was attracting about 2,800 young people. He also drew attention to the 'Missionary Teens Only' (known as MTO) event for OM kids, which was held each year. Dan and Suzie Potter were also the leaders of MTO, which influenced many children of OM families.[50]

Another development that was mainly (though not exclusively) connected with young people was a new sports ministry. OM was involved in offering chaplaincy services at the 1996 Olympic Games, and after this George Verwer announced at an OM conference at De Bron, in the Netherlands, that OM had been given funds to start a sports ministry, had a vision to see this happen, but knew of no one to head it up. Martin Bateman, from Britain, who was present, responded to the possibilities of this 'open door'. He had given up sporting involvement after university when he joined OM, but he now began to find out as much as he could about sports ministries around the world and to motivate OM fields to think about working through sport. It became evident that there were already people in the Middle East, Pakistan and Eastern Europe involved in children's ministry, professional sport and hosting tournaments. The name SportsLink was given to this initiative. Two international events were held for all co-workers involved with sport in OM. By 2002, SportsLink was having a significant influence in several countries.[51]

In the light of serious global political tensions in 2002, with many expressions of antagonism evident across the world, George Verwer made plain his view that hatred towards anyone, Jew, Arab or anyone else, was 'equally wrong'. OM's concern was to cross over divides. George referred to David and Ann Zeidan, who had led OM's work in Israel, and spoke about OM's ministry among Muslims in London.[52] In many places work was being done by local leaders or by those who had lived in a region for a long time. In Bangladesh, for example, Roger and Jackie Adkins served for nineteen years, and most of the workers were

Bangladeshi. OM served in this region in a number of ways, for example offering vocational training for office skills, management and accounting, dressmaking and farming. Asia Challenge Teams (ACT) worked with young women to help them learn basic computer skills. ACT teams would spread elsewhere. In terms of OM's wider South Asia ministry, Mike and Kerstin Wakely gave overall leadership, and one of the initiatives was Starfish Asia Fund, to provide material, spiritual and educational help to poor and hurting people in Pakistan and other South Asian countries.[53] In this time of tension, OM involved itself at the grassroots in areas of the world that were regarded by many in the West as 'off limits'.

A tremendous staff

The ships, with their five hundred staff, continued to be an integral part of OM's ministry in this period. In 1997, the *Doulos* was in Papua New Guinea at a time of heightened activity because of elections; if anything this made the visit of the ship even more of a talking point. During a two-month period, 185,000 people visited the book exhibition and twenty-five thousand people attended conferences on board. People from Papua New Guinea were recruited into OM's wider work. The *Doulos* went on to Manila, in the Philippines, where training for local churches was a major focus. Emiliano and Marilyn Namuco, having returned from many years serving on the ships, were key figures in OM's growth in the Philippines. When *Logos II* was in Acapulco, Mexico, in 1997, teams were able to participate in sessions of COMIBAM '97, which drew 2,200 Christian leaders from across the Ibero-American world. OM's International Night, which was open to all (not an official part of COMIBAM), virtually filled a seven thousand-seat venue – provided free of charge by the Acapulco Mayor's office.[54] *Logos II* teams also became involved in relief efforts in the aftermath of massive damage in Acapulco from Hurricane Pauline. Local people spoke of the physical and spiritual help they received.[55]

For twenty-five years, OM ships had attempted to visit Myanmar (formerly Burma) without success. But in December 1998 the *Doulos* was able to be in Yangon, primarily because a significant number of Christian leaders inside Myanmar believed this was the right time. Representatives from the medical, educational and business communities attended on-board receptions. Myanmar has the largest Protestant church community between India and China, and a reception brought together pastors from all denominations for the first time in thirty years. Teams from the ship distributed packages of toys and school supplies to children in fifteen orphanages. A team of carpenters, plumbers, electricians and general labourers worked at Agape Orphanage, constructing much-needed buildings. Over twenty thousand books were donated to seventy-four libraries, universities, Bible schools and theological seminaries. Teams participated in services in thirty-two churches throughout the city. Steve Brown's report suggested: 'In the history of the *Doulos* there have been few Sundays like it.'[56] The stronger links made with the churches in Myanmar were to continue.

Regions covered by the ships in 1999 included South America and the South Pacific. In Uruguay, there was a meeting on *Logos II* for politicians and civic leaders. In Brazil, OM Ships celebrated the thousandth port visit of an OM ship. Bernd Gülker, who took over from Dale Rhoton in 1999 as director of the Ship ministry, noted the increasing emphasis in South America on mobilising churches for mission. An amazing three thousand individuals wrote to the OM Brazil office for information about joining OM and getting involved in missions.[57] Four months of ministry in Australia and two in New Zealand by the *Doulos* generated great interest: two hundred thousand visitors in Australia and one hundred thousand in New Zealand. An OM delegation had been in China in 1998, and while the *Doulos* was in Australia, a delegation of the China Christian Council spent two weeks on board. This was another step in developing a relationship with the Council. In New Zealand, George Booth, OM Field Leader, commented on the impact of the ship on secular people. Over fifty New Zealanders were serving with OM by then. During meetings on Bougainville, Papua New Guinea, the example and message of the *Doulos* moved warring islanders to seek peace. The UN representative spoke about the crucial role of the ship in the process.[58]

The year 2000 saw the *Doulos* in Japan, Taiwan and China. The visit to China, which had been prepared over a considerable period of time, was the second by the *Doulos*, and included historic visits to Shanghai and Nanjing. A Ship to Shore Exhibition was held in the Shanghai Municipal Library – the largest library in Asia. Mr Mi Yong-jin, Director of the Foreign Affairs Office of Jiangsu Department of Education, spoke warmly at the official welcome about the ship's work in the area of cross-cultural understanding. More than 120 ship members went out on Sunday morning to visit four different churches, where they found large crowds at the services. At the presentation ceremony on the last day in port, Lloyd Nicholas, as the *Doulos* director, expressed the hope that one day the bookshop would be open to the Chinese people.[59] Important visits for *Logos II* in this period included Monrovia in Liberia, where seven hundred pastors attended conferences on board and sixteen teams went out on construction and agricultural assignments,[60] and Italy, Croatia, Albania and Lebanon. In Beirut, more than 82,000 visitors came on board. One Lebanese woman spoke about how she had come to Christ through a book on the life of Joni Eareckson-Tada, given to her in 1982 in Nigeria by a Sudanese friend who had purchased it on the *Logos* a decade before.

During the next two years, the ships were able to connect with well-known people such as Her Serene Highness Siriwanwaree Mahidon, daughter of the Crown Prince of Thailand, who officially opened the *Doulos* Book Fair in Bangkok. There was considerable media coverage, and the *Doulos* welcomed over ninety thousand visitors. In South Korea, Mrs Lee Hui Ho, the First Lady of South Korea, officially opened the book fair and described her fond memories of the ship's visit of 1992, concluding: 'May all your activities continue to bring God's peace to the world.' There were important return visits to Vietnam and Myanmar. In Vietnam, academic textbooks and dictionaries were among the twenty thousand educational books donated to Ho

Chi Minh City libraries and universities. The Director of the General Science Library said: 'These books are so precious. They are like treasure for the people.' The International Night was held in the grand Ho Chi Minh City Opera House and Lloyd Nicholas presented gifts to charities. George Barathan, from Sri Lanka (later OM Field Leader in Singapore), who was responsible for line-up, saw this visit as 'historic and amazing'.[61]

There were also amazing individuals in OM, among them New Jersey-born Ray Lentzsch. Lane Powell and Debbie Meroff, reporting in 2002, said that Ray had by then visited every country of the world in order to speak about the message of the gospel, often in the open air. He joined OM in 1962 and, for the next thirty years, served in various countries and on the ships. After leaving the *Doulos* in 1992, he settled in Israel, where he had previously been in the 1960s, and began systematically visiting the nations of the world he had not been to before. North Korea was the most difficult of all 214 countries he visited to enter, but in 1995 it waived all visa restrictions for Americans for seven days, during an International Sports and Culture Peace Festival.[62]

George Verwer, writing in 2002, was delighted about the 'tremendous staff of five hundred people on the ships and in the ship ministry'. Familiar themes were still prominent in OM reports at this point, such as the continued ministry of the ships and, linked with that, the role of literature. Two million tracts, donated by the Northern Irish Revival Movement, had been given to pastors and mission workers to distribute in Ghana. But there were also new and significant ventures in view in the new millennium. George had recently been at the EBE (Educational Book Exhibits) Board meeting, which had discussed and agreed on a projected new ship – a replacement for *Logos II*.[63]

In 1997, Bernd Gülker had written to the leadership body of OM Ships about crucial issues for the future: communication, ministry, leaders, staff, vessels, partners, finances and administration. On 'ministry', he set out key goals for the ships: to demonstrate God's love to every visitor and contact; to demonstrate faith practically, by providing good literature and appropriate aid; to communicate with great sensitivity, skill and passion; to follow up and conserve the fruit of every ship visit; and to provide quality management in all ship projects.[64] This letter led to detailed presentations in November 2000 and then in February 2001 – to the OM International Leaders Meeting in Hungary – on the subject 'Purpose Driven Ships'. Bernd noted that the ships were capable of drawing up to a million visitors per year, the same number as attended (in 2000) the 'Pavilion of Hope' at the widely publicised World EXPO in Hanover, Germany. It was clear that OM Ships had a unique ministry, but he argued that in order to make this more effective it was necessary to replace *Logos II* with a more suitable ship.[65]

Those at the core of the new project in its exploratory stage included a handful of experienced leaders from the first *Logos*, such as Lloyd Nicholas, Bernd Gülker, Peter Conlan and Ebbo Buurma. On one occasion in 2001 the project leader, Lloyd Nicholas, sat with Peter Conlan in a café near the OM offices in Atlanta, Georgia, and listed on a paper table napkin the resources available for the new ship project. The list was very short: 'Personnel – two. Money – zero. Ship – none. Strategy – as yet unclear.'[66] However, a further presentation by Bernd Gülker at the 2002 EBE Board meeting, specifically recommending the replacement of *Logos II*, received the affirmation of the Board, and this was followed by the endorsement of the OM International Executive Committee.[67] George Verwer's conviction had deepened that 'Now is the Hour to take bigger steps to make this next ship a reality!!' As with the previous ship projects, there were reasons for holding back, but the ships' teams were committed to advance – and George's call was: 'Let's join with them.'[68]

The initial 'next ship' team was joined by a dynamic group of young, emerging OM leaders, including Christy Schumacher (USA), Graham Jack (UK), Bitten Schriver Ingerslev (Denmark), Su Ling and Han Tek Ng (Singapore), Anthony Pritchett and Ben Wyatt (Australia) and others. Heading up the technical side was former *Doulos* chief engineer, Johannes Thomsen, from Denmark, whose wife Berit was involved with OM Ships' personnel department. David Gillan, then the *Doulos* chief engineer, and his wife Judy, also agreed to serve with the new ship. An attractive leaflet was produced to present the 'Next Ship' project – later named the 'Logos Hope' project. There was increasing recognition of the crucial nature of work with donors and as this new project gained momentum, personal contacts with donors were fostered.[69]

'I want to lift You high'

Although the stress on enterprise was persistent, even more important for George Verwer and for many in OM was energy to live in a way that was Christ-like. George Verwer produced his book *Out of the Comfort Zone* (2000) in order to stress what he had learned from Charles Swindoll's book *Grace Awakening*. To grasp 'grace' was, said George, 'to recognise that individual Christians and groups of Christians, including our group, are free in Christ from legalism, to grow and work as He leads us'. George was disappointed that some churches he knew twenty years ago, born out of a new freedom of the Spirit, were now more rigid in certain ways than the churches they left. He recalled how he went at age nineteen to Mexico, but noted that some churches were now insisting that all directions had to come from 'apostles' and were 'pouring cold water on young people'. As he had done so often before, he pointed to Roy Hession's *Calvary Road*, but against the background of this new legalism, he particularly commended *What's So Amazing about Grace?* by Philip Yancey.[70]

Another familiar theme in George Verwer's thinking in this period, as it had been earlier, was 'balance'. Speaking about the power of the Holy Spirit, his plea was to 'avoid getting into extremes'. He was concerned that extreme ideas about the Spirit had confused many people, and continued:

> We tend to forget that however filled with the Spirit we may be, there is still the human factor. We are ordinary people who struggle, make mistakes and have weaknesses ... When I was a young Christian I had a tendency towards extremism and super-spirituality. If I had not learned to accept the human factor in myself and others, I would have been knocked out of the race very early on.[71]

George Verwer's reflections on how 'down-to-earth' spirituality was to be worked out in mission drew on an eclectic mixture of writers: A.W. Tozer, who spoke about 'reverent scepticism'; C.S. Lewis, writing on pain; Francis Schaeffer and John Stott, who had helped in an understanding of a 'dynamic tension, a balance between life and doctrine'; David Seamands, on healing damaged emotions; and Steve Chalke, on direction in leadership. Breadth contributed to spiritual balance.

This period saw important reflection on OM's history and emphases taking place. Peter Maiden gave an address in which he questioned some of the emphases in William MacDonald's *True Discipleship*.[72] On re-reading this book, he said he had a feeling that what he needed to do was grit his teeth and do his duty. The book did not seem to advocate a discipleship based on gratitude. Peter Maiden also argued that the 'worm theology', as it was increasingly called, failed to take account of humanity made in the image of God. Finally, he suggested that 'forsaking all' had become, for many in OM, associated only with giving up possessions, whereas the call should be to a deeper surrender.[73] George Verwer acknowledged that some had misunderstood the message of brokenness and had developed an unhealthy understanding of themselves and their own personality – a low sense of their self-worth.[74] In a profound analysis, in a chapter in his book *Future Leader* (1999), Viv Thomas dealt with the specific contribution that George Verwer had made to evangelical spirituality, modelling 'strength woven into vulnerability'.[75]

This combination of strength and vulnerability was worked out in many places in OM. In 1992 Pam and Dave Lovett from the USA, who had gone with OM to India in 1983, moved to Tajikistan and set up the Central Asia Development Agency (CADA). In September 2001, after a series of hard experiences and as the OM team was meeting together for fasting and prayer, Pam Lovett had a dream in which she felt something terrible was going to happen.

The dream involved a tall building and the wing of a plane cutting off the top. A few days later, as Debbie Meroff puts it in her account, Pam and Dave were watching television and 'stared in horror as New York's World Trade Center crumbled to dust'. The dream was actually a pointer to new ministry. Tajikistan became crucial to the fight against the Taliban in Afghanistan that followed 9/11. Many Afghans were stranded at the borders without food, clothing or shelter, and as one of the few relief agencies there, partner organisation Operation Mercy gave immediate and then longer-term relief to over five hundred thousand people.[76] Six hundred kilometres of road were built to isolated villages as part of a programme in which villagers were paid desperately needed wheat and oil for time spent helping to build the new road.

As these events in late 2001 were unfolding, a young couple were with OM in Lebanon, trying to learn Arabic. Gary Witherall, from southern England, had gone with OM in 1986 and had spent several years in the ship ministry before going to Moody Bible Institute in 1991. Although George Verwer recommended Bible College training, Gary was perhaps typical of many in OM in thinking that Bible schools exemplified the 'know-it-all, establishment "churchiness" I continually struggled against'. His actual experience at Moody was different, and while there he met Bonnie Penner, from the state of Washington, USA. They married in 1997 and three years later, to their surprise, found themselves considering going to the Arab world. Bonnie wrote in her diary: 'I don't know what God has for us, but I want to be available to go.' By September 2001 they were in Lebanon, with Bonnie working in a prenatal clinic in a Palestinian refugee camp. At this point the words she wrote in her journal were: 'God, I want to surrender all my plans to You today ... I want to lift You high above all else.'[77]

On Monday 18 November 2002, Bonnie and Gary spent the evening with Graham and Linda, local OM leaders. On Wednesday, Bonnie shared her testimony for the first time in Arabic with a women's group, most of them friends of hers and not Christian believers, at the local Christian and Missionary Alliance church. The next day, as she worked at the clinic, she was brutally murdered by a gunman.

As Gary was subsequently 'forced to fall and fall and fall into the abyss of grief', as he put it, as he struggled with his overwhelming pain at the loss of Bonnie, he also experienced the presence of God. On Sunday 24 November, he spoke to hundreds of people who had gathered to pay tribute to Bonnie, including church and political leaders. These are some of the words he said to the large crowd:

> To the President of Lebanon, Prime Minister, and the Speaker of the House.
>
> I'd like to say, I love Lebanon; I love her people and my hometown, Sidon. I'd like to start by thanking the people from Lebanon and from around the world for their e-mails, phone calls, and prayers.
>
> Some people may think that the death of my wife was a waste. Bonnie and I came to Lebanon understanding only a small part of the pain this country has gone through, but we believed that coming with a message of Jesus which gives hope, love, and forgiveness would never be a waste. This is a message for hurting people in a suffering generation. And this message is worth laying down our lives for.

Gary thanked the people of Sidon and southern Lebanon for their love and then spoke of forgiveness: 'I want to let whoever did this crime know that I forgive them. It's a forgiveness that costs me everything that I am, but I can forgive because I know God, through Jesus' blood, has forgiven me. The blood of Jesus was poured out for the sins of the world, and when Bonnie's [blood] poured across the clinic [floor] on Thursday morning, she showed the same love for the women of Sidon.'[78]

Conclusion

In the period 1997–2002 OM became more and more globalised. By the end of the decade, the movement had 2,800 people from eighty different countries serving in ninety countries around the world. This required a great deal of thought about how to engage in partnership. The idea that partnership simply meant the West sending money overseas was questioned. Against the background of the huge investment of OM in work in India over decades,

Joseph D'Souza argued for a continuing full-orbed participation in Indian mission, including prayer, personnel, finances and expertise.[79] Only in this way would there be widespread transformation, not only in India but in many different ways across OM's ministries.

By 2002, the primary leadership of OM internationally was about to be taken up, at George Verwer's initiative, by others. George Verwer had already handed over aspects of his responsibilities to Peter Maiden, there was a strong team of leaders in place across OM's various regions, and in 2002 Joseph D'Souza of India and Francois Vosloo of South Africa, both of whom already had significant experience and standing internationally as well as in their national leadership, were nominated as OM's Associate International Coordinators, to work alongside Peter Maiden. These two nominations were supported at the International Leaders Meeting in Italy in February 2003 and approved by the OM General Council meeting in August 2003 in Keswick, England.

While considerable attention was understandably focused in this period on organisational issues, George Verwer insisted in 1998 that his greatest burden for OM – 'our Fellowship' – had never changed over all the years. He had been reading his old memos and letters that confirmed this. The priority was 'the spiritual life of every person in the work' – their 'communion with God'.[80] A year later, he was happy that 130,000 copies of his book *Out of the Comfort Zone* were in circulation, and he again emphasised: 'Our greatest concern is always our basic spiritual life in Christ.'[81] It was inevitable that, as time went on, the way in which this emphasis was worked out would change. Rodney Hui commented that OM started with the message of 'forsaking all, reaching the world with the gospel, sacrificial lifestyle, resourcefulness while at the same time maintaining some realism, plus humour! – to name a few', and that it was still maintaining that first passion, 'but with a lot more diversity in the interpretation of what is spiritual in different parts of the world'. He saw the impact of the call to spiritual commitment, 'even seen from the relative moderation of today', as being 'still as great as ever, if not greater'.[82]

Chapter 10

On the Cutting Edge

The year 2003 saw the handover of the international leadership of OM from George Verwer, its founder, to Peter Maiden, with Joseph D'Souza and Francois Vosloo as the Associate International Coordinators. This important event, which took place in the Keswick Convention tent on 22 August 2003, with about two thousand OMers and friends present, was further evidence of the way in which George Verwer, as the founder of OM and its leader since the beginning, had been able to delegate responsibility to others.

Peter Maiden was a different personality. George Verwer's summary in 2003 was: 'He's a more quiet, steady person than myself. He's a great Bible teacher. He's a leader in his local church, but he's a great visionary, he's got a great pastor's heart, and he's a leader. We have in OM now 3,500 workers in 90 nations. And his big job will be to work with the leaders and the leaders of the leaders.'[1] Peter Maiden served not only in OM but also elsewhere, for example as chairman of the Keswick Convention.

OM as a movement has continued to develop under the new international leadership in the period from 2003–7, when fifty years of OM's life was celebrated. George Verwer has continued with OM, concentrating on speaking around the world, on relationship-building and overseeing, with a team, a wide range of significant global 'special projects'. At the crucial time of transition in the leadership of OM in 2002–3, Peter Maiden interviewed Drena Verwer about the concerns she had for George, for the movement and for herself. She believed George was going to cope well 'because he's already got so many things on his mind that he wants to do'. Her struggle, she thought, might be 'that inevitably the new leadership won't necessarily do what I think George would have done'. She hoped that OM would stay 'on the cutting edge' and that prayer would remain a priority for the movement.[2] These hopes reflected a desire, after almost fifty years of OM, for both continuity and change.

Emerging mission

In many respects, in the period 2003–7 OM continued to emphasise continuity with the kinds of mission it had promoted in its earliest years, although the language used changed. Reports began to speak of 'emerging mission movements'. Reporting in 2004 on his first full year in his new position, Peter Maiden talked about the 'exciting demographic shift in the Church to the Southern Hemisphere', where it was estimated that two-thirds of all the evangelicals in the world now lived.[3] The shift in the centre of gravity of Christianity as a whole to the 'Global South' is undisputed.[4] It is significant that OM's two new Associate International Coordinators were from the Global South.

In surveying the history of OM, it is clear that in recent decades the growth in personnel has been largely in Asia and in South America. In terms of OM's longer story, India cannot be described as 'emerging', since OM involvement in India has been substantial and consistently growing since the 1960s. But, as will be seen later in this chapter, new developments are emerging in India. East Asia Pacific has, as has been evident in earlier chapters in this book, contributed massively to OM's international work since the 1970s. Latin America has also been important to OM, especially since the 1980s, and in 2005 Peter Maiden wrote: 'We urgently need to see the infrastructure of our ministry in Latin America further develop. This continent has the capacity to make an enormous contribution to world mission.'[5]

In a vast country like Brazil, OM was very aware of needs within as well as beyond the nation. OM was formally organised in Brazil in 1986, and over the subsequent decades, more than 450 Brazilians responded to the call to serve with OM longer-term, all over the globe, with three thousand serving in short-term capacities.[6] Speaking about his time leading OM Brazil, Humberto Aragão commented that OM needed to remain directly involved in serving Brazilians, in partnership with others. For him, 'if you talk about mission and don't talk about poverty, it means nothing'. Ten million children in Brazil – some as young as three – were living on the streets. A quarter of the population of Rio de Janeiro and Sao Paulo were in *favelas* (slums). Humberto argued that, alongside global ministry, there was a need to stress cross-cultural ministry in Brazil. His hope was that OM would be a training and resourcing base. OM's training centre and office was located just outside greater Sao Paulo, a city of over twenty million people.[7] The vision of Humberto Aragão for emerging mission was applied more widely to the countries of Latin America from 2004, as he became OM's Area Coordinator for Latin America.

Much attention was being paid by this time to 'emerging churches' and to 'new ways of being church'. Often the conversation was focused on the West, where the church is generally in decline, and it seems that many of these 'emerging churches' are white and middle-class. However, some who have a more comprehensive missional vision are also looking at emerging church, for example Eddie Gibbs and Ryan Bolger, in *Emerging Churches: Creating Christian Communities in Postmodern Cultures*.[8] OM has engaged with postmodern culture, but OM's 'emerging movements' have involved people from many different cultures becoming committed cross-culturally. Thus the 2006 OM Annual Report described very varied experiences: the commitment to Christ of Lansipe, from Papua New Guinea, and her service with OM in Angola; teams in China helping local believers in their ministries; an Uzbek church planted by Indian OMers in Kyrgyzstan which had already planted a daughter church, and Christians in Algeria meeting daily in homes for prayer. An Arab believer said: 'People in Algeria, especially young people, are thirsty to know God. And whether God uses the internet or satellite TV, dreams or visions or the mention of Jesus in the Koran, His Spirit is reaching out to quench that thirst.'[9]

However, it was difficult for people from Global South nations to join an international movement like OM, because it was basically too expensive. After some thorough research, the decision was made in 2007 to launch an OM initiative, 'Emerging Mission Movements', to make it possible for people to join OM from these nations at a much lower financial support level than applied to those from wealthy economies. The year 2007 saw the launching of pilot teams and Peter Maiden described this as an initiative that many believed could be one of the most significant things done in recent years.[10] As examples of what was happening in OM in 2007 under the heading 'emerging mission', a report from Costa Rica spoke about 317 people involved in OM Central America's Easter outreach in the Atlantic zone, including a fifty-member team of medics, dentists and other workers serving in different communities, and a report from Nepal described a young, growing, enthusiastic church community, with 205 students graduating from OM's three-month evangelism/mission training, funded in large part from a major foundation grant.[11]

Emerging mission was also a feature of the eastern part of Europe, a region that had been a focus for OM from its beginnings. In direct continuity with the early emphasis on ministry in this region and on literature, it was reported in 2006 that the OM Greater Europe literature team had completed forty-four different publishing projects in thirteen languages, publishing a total of 141,000 books.[12] At that point, there were personnel on the ships from several former communist countries. Twenty-two Russians had by then served in different OM fields, including India, Nepal, South Africa and Zimbabwe.[13] There was a particular concern to harness the energy of young people. From its emergence in Germany, TeenStreet became a year-round global mentoring force. Within Europe, the Czech Republic was added as a second TeenStreet venue. Martina and Michal Kocer, at OM's centre in Ceske Budejovice, Czech Republic, were coordinators.[14] In 2005, they committed themselves full time to OM's work.[15] TeenStreet spread from Europe to Brazil, Malaysia, India, South Africa and Uruguay.[16]

Investment in 'Next Generation' or emerging leaders was in tune with OM's beginnings, when a remarkable degree of responsibility was given to people in their late teens or early twenties. In 2003, some who had been leaders in 1963 were still leading. The age profile of OM's leadership had, inevitably, changed markedly. In this context, there was a concern to foster emerging leaders. In an incisive article in 2003, 'Growing Leaders for 2020', Viv Thomas, who had moved on from OM and had become director of Formation, argued that different times and conditions demanded different types of leaders and that 'a trans-cultural organisation' could not function with outdated Western styles. He suggested giving priority to developing 'leaders who have a relationship with God, do their tasks with skill and commitment and have healthy relationships with themselves and others'. He saw leadership formation 'through the lens of spiritual formation', and stated: 'It is just not good enough to take secular models of leadership, baptize them with Christian enthusiasm and vocabulary then let them loose on an unsuspecting church. The result will be disaster.'[17] Taking up the title used by Viv Thomas, *Future Leader* (1999), an OM Future Leaders event (later renamed the Joshua Initiative) was held at Hyderabad, India, with more than two hundred leaders, all forty years of age or younger.[18] Emerging mission required healthy leadership.

Pioneering initiatives

Linked with the idea of emerging mission was another theme that became prominent in OM in this period: 'pioneering initiatives'. One of these was SportsLink, led by Martin Bateman. A report in 2003 described SportsLink's work in Ukraine, along with churches, schools and city officials, in helping to host KidsGames, with over three thousand Ukrainian children participating. KidsGames also proved instrumental in helping the churches involved – mostly Baptist, Pentecostal and Catholic – to build stronger relationships with city and schools officials. This partnership continued, with a monthly local pastors' meeting being held.[19] As part of the Easter 2002 campaign in Central America,

SportsLink organised five days of sports camps. In Chile an adventure team tour included rafting and hiking. In Pakistan, sports ministry included cricket and football tournaments, a KidsGames event and an Adventure Camp.[20]

By 2006, SportsLink was supporting outreach through sports in sixteen nations – through large events, games, coaching of youth, and bringing adults together through sport. Many professionals were involved, including former professional footballers such as Marcel Stoob, who was a member of the Swiss under-21 national team. In Argentina, a Mexican professional trainer was giving sports lessons and running sports days for two hundred children. In Pakistan, 950 young people participated in KidsGames, held in a stadium. A youth seminar for those involved in sports was put on, and several young men and women made commitments to follow Christ. The value of sports was seen in places of conflict. An Israel Challenge team joined a local Arab congregation in offering a sports programme. On the first day, fifty children came, but soon the numbers grew, as did the numbers of people attending the small local church. There was even, as a sign of hope in the midst of great Arab–Israeli tension, two 'reconciliation' soccer camps, bringing together forty-five children and twenty leaders from Christian congregations – Arab and Messianic. The OM Annual Report commented: 'In the conflict and struggle of life in Israel, we witness small miracles of God's uniting love.'[21]

Another 'Link' begun by OM was AIDSLink. Here OM South Africa gave the lead. It was estimated that close to 20 per cent of South Africans were infected with the virus and in 2003 OM South Africa was working with two AIDS orphanages in providing volunteers and resources. They distributed about five hundred videos on AIDS to local churches and a booklet was made available through the *Doulos*. At the time there were very few books on the subject written from an African perspective.[22] Two years later OM South Africa leaders, as they grappled with issues of HIV and AIDS were thinking in terms of an inter-national programme for those interested in ministry to those affected.[23] As a result, they put together a training programme in cooperation with other NGOs. AIDSLink was set up within OM to be proactive in promoting awareness, training and involvement. George Verwer, who was working in partnership on this issue with Patrick Dixon, the author of *AIDS and You* (a book which achieved huge sales, in twenty languages), was involved with OM South Africa in their initiatives.[24]

Ministry to victims of HIV and AIDS also developed within OM India in this period. OM India students, as part of their training experience, spent time at the Freedom Foundation Centre for AIDS-affected children near OM's Hyderabad centre. In 2006, George Verwer again[25] sought to heighten awareness of the needs, and commended a number of books, including *AIDS is real and it's in our church*, by Jean Garland and Mike Blyth.[26] A year later Rosemary Hack, OM's AIDSLink coordinator, highlighted not only the huge challenges but also pioneering initiatives that were being taken. OM India had purchased land, and the vision was to build a small hospital, church, and a school for children affected by or infected with HIV and AIDS.[27]

January 2004 saw a new initiative in OM in New Zealand, with the launching of the TEA (Training, Evangelism, Adventure) programme, the first OM ministry having a focus within that country. Until then, the office had existed only to mobilise, resource and support New Zealanders working with OM overseas. TEA was started by father and daughter, George and Shirley Booth, in response to a need for ministry among backpackers, as well as a desire to help young Christians grow in discipleship and confidence in evangelism. The ten-week programme developed into a popular short-term ministry option for eighteen–thirty year olds from Europe, Asia and America. The leadership team expanded to include Norm and Christy McCarren from the USA, and ten programmes were run over the course of three years, with over fifty young people participating.[28]

Pioneering initiatives have often required partnership, and this has been a constant theme in OM. Under the leadership of Rick Hicks, President of OM USA, there was an emphasis in OM USA on seeking to partner with teams planting churches in pioneer situations. The vision was to expand and enhance the mobilisation

of Americans for greater involvement in missions; effective partnering with churches in the US and internationally, and the training of those who participate in ministry. Together with his wife,
Kathy, the author of *Scaling the Wall*,[29] Rick explored areas such
as understanding generational differences, leadership (his PhD
was a study of leadership on the *Doulos*) and team-building. The
impressive OM USA facilities were expanded so that the aim of
greater mission mobilisation could be achieved. Frank Dietz and
Jack Rendel, serving with OM USA, had important roles as minis-
ters-at-large, especially in connection with work in Latin America. Kathy Hicks' book was on overcoming obstacles to mission
involvement and George Verwer described her approach as
'unique, cutting-edge, and unusual'. In 2006, it was reported that
churches in the USA were forming partnerships with OM ministries in Ireland, Bosnia, the ships, Iraq (Kurds), Russia, Spain and
UK (Turning Point). Groups of churches were partnering with
Near East ministries and with OM in Sudan.[30]

OM had always been a pioneer in the field of literature, especially through STL, and this vision continued. In 2003, OM Lit
became part of the STL Group, in line with STL's global strategy.
Two businesses were acquired: 'Faithworks', offering small publishers a distribution, marketing and sales representation service;
and 'Appalachian Distributors', the second largest wholesale dis-
tributor in the USA, with locations in Johnson City, Tennessee,
and Reno, Nevada. David Passman, who had been chairman of
the OM USA Board, came out of retirement to serve as President/
CEO of what became a $45m operation trading from three loca-
tions – Georgia, Tennessee and Nevada. In the UK, Wesley Owen,
which was the retail arm of STL, had become by 2007 a multi-
channel retailer with over forty shops, a direct-to-consumer catalogue and internet operation, and a large events and conference
division serving British evangelical gatherings like Spring Harvest
and Keswick. STL's publishing division, renamed Authentic, was
one of the UK's leading book and music companies. On 1 March
2007, International Bible Society (IBS), the provider of millions of
Bibles over the course of two centuries, and STL, the global leaders in the distribution of evangelical resources, merged to become

IBS-STL Global.[31] OM's pioneering initiatives in literature had developed in truly remarkable ways.

Relief and development

In the 1990s, a series of pioneering initiatives within OM had to do with relief and development, and this emphasis continued. By 2003, there was an amazing range of involvement. In Europe, education for Roma children was being offered. Further east, in Central and South Central Asia, 2003 saw massive relief for northern Afghanistan, with sixty thousand people fed and other aid delivered. As well as relief, there were development programmes in Central Asia, including micro-enterprises in partnership with local farmers and filters to give villages clean water. In the midst of all this, there were many opportunities to share the Christian faith in meaningful ways. Partner organisation Operation Mercy was able to help victims of earthquakes. A micro-enterprise project for Bedouin women was being explored. In Israel, there was a ministry to the deaf. In Sudan, ministry to street children was continuing. In Zimbabwe, Mike and Linda Van Vuuren were seeking to serve against a desperate backdrop, and Vicky Graham, a nurse, was offering mobile clinics and discipleship classes to the Tonga people in the country. Mercy Teams International was researching opportunities in Myanmar, the Philippines and Cambodia. In Sri Lanka, a partnership had emerged with Community Concern Society.[32]

The ships' involvement in relief ministry continued to develop. During the *Logos II* visit to Guyana, 130 people joined teams providing practical help, including medical services, and repaired homes for children and the aged. Lawrence Tong, from Singapore, the *Logos II* director, stressed the importance of this ministry. Relief was also given in Grenada in 2004, after Hurricane Ivan had roared through Grenada and damaged or destroyed 80–90 per cent of the island's buildings. OM USA was involved in relief work, in partnership with OM Barbados. While *Logos II* was in the Caribbean, teams went from the ship weekly to Grenada to help reconstruct houses. The ship's community raised more than $30,000 to help with relief efforts and supplies. When *Logos II* returned to Grenada in 2006, the government gave a very warm welcome to the ship, with the country's Minister of Education advising the islanders: 'Every Grenadian should come on board and choose at least one good book.'[33]

The terrible tsunami of 26 December 2004 drew a massive response from many agencies, including OM. In India, OM teams, working with others, were involved in tsunami relief from day one. Approximately twelve thousand survivors received some kind of relief, medical care or counselling assistance during the three-month OM programme.[34] BMS World Mission (formerly the Baptist Missionary Society), which began its work in India under William Carey's leadership in the late eighteenth century, partnered with OM in seeking to respond to the tsunami and to other major tragedies. The efforts of OM workers in one village in Tamil Nadu, helped by a BMS grant which was among the largest partnership grants it had ever made, resulted in the redevelopment of the entire village, including the provision of housing and new fishing boats.[35]

One important aspect of this ministry was relationship-building. The OM India teams built relationships with a number of community leaders and were invited to place long-term teams in several areas.[36] In Sri Lanka, six months after the tsunami, Peter Conlan had an interview in Colombo with the country's prime minister and then received a letter from him inviting the *Doulos* to come and help.[37] The *Doulos* went and OMers worked alongside local Sri Lankan churches already engaged in relief construction, trauma counselling and spiritual care. Gary and Sue Dean were very involved in raising funds and assisting with construction of homes. Dr Patrick Railey particularly stressed the important work within OM in this period of counselling people who were 'in many places paralyzed with their grief'.[38]

Against the background of these developments, George Verwer began to address issues which he saw as crucial, using the story of the Good Samaritan and speaking about 'Seven People Lying at the Side of the Road'. He described the 'huge shift [in

OM] in recent years towards the marrying of Gospel proclama-
tion with social action' as something which 'it has been my great
joy to see'. The 'seven' he had listed on the back of his business
card, were: children at risk; abused women; the extreme poor;
HIV/AIDS victims; people with impure water; the unborn –
whose lives needed protection, especially because of widespread
abortion; and the environment. He commended Debbie Meroff's
True Grit, 'the untold story of the suffering women face around
the world *and* how powerfully God is using women to advance
His Kingdom today', which was then OM's best-selling book. On
the environment, he was disappointed that so many evangelical
Christians not only had little concern for the issue but were sometimes known as anti-environmental. He asked: 'How can this be
when our Creator God has asked us to care for his creation?' His
conclusion was typically blunt: 'Not only is our pollution of the
earth totally unacceptable, but this is an issue that our young
people care about; and if we don't connect with them on valid
issues such as preservation of the environment, how can we
expect them to listen to us at all?' The overall appeal was: 'Will
you be a Good Samaritan?'[39]

As an indication that this kind of integral ministry was by now
central to OM's work, the OM Annual Report for 2006 stated:
'Increasingly, God has brought OM ministry face to face with
overwhelming suffering and need, so that He might meet those
needs through us. In doing so, bridges replace barriers in places
formerly hostile to Christian work, as those in need appreciate
faith in action.'[40] Within this, OM recognised its special calling in
India. The 2006 OM Report, under 'resourcing', had this statement: 'That India will be a major defining influence in this century
is beyond question. How Christians respond in the next few years
to the unprecedented spiritual awakening that outstrips India's
impressive economic and technological revival is vital. OM's
focus on economic and social justice, training and church planting recognizes that India must be transformed from within.'[41]

The call for support for those in need in India was taken up at a
Freedom Concert held in Edinburgh, Scotland, on 20 May 2007,
organised by OM and Origin Scotland. As well as music that

emphasised freedom, the audience heard presentations marking the two hundredth anniversary of the abolition of the transatlantic slave trade. Joseph D'Souza then talked about the plight of the Dalit people in India. By this time, there were over fifty Good Shepherd schools catering for eight thousand Dalit children, and their high educational standards were being recognised. Funds were raised at this concert to help cover the cost of constructing a new Education Centre. Many church leaders who attended were shocked by what they heard, and saw the need to become involved in supporting bodies that were taking the Dalit people's struggles seriously.[42]

A real difference

The major ship news in this period was the purchase and the refitting of the new OM ship. By 2004, over thirty-three million people had visited the OM ships – the original *Logos*, the *Doulos*, and later *Logos II*. With the renewed vision to impact the life of every visitor in a fuller way, and to provide more living space on board, plans to replace *Logos II* moved forward. After thorough investigation, the focus of attention became the *Norröna I*, built in Germany in 1973 and operated from 1983 by Smyril Line as a passenger ferry between the Farøe Islands, the Shetland Islands, Norway, Denmark and Iceland. The message about this ship was conveyed to OM worldwide in March 2004: 'After consulting with Peter Maiden and Brian Chilver, the EBE board chairman, Lloyd Nicholas and Bernd Gülker decided to inform Smyril Line that we are ready to match the highest bid.'[43] Peter Maiden wrote in May 2004 about the privilege of being on board the *Norröna I*, along with George Verwer and more than four hundred Christians, mainly from Denmark and the Farøe Islands, for a service of thanksgiving. Crucial roles were played by Lloyd, as ship Project Leader, and Bernd, who was continuing as managing director of the ship ministry.[44]

A great deal of thought had been given before the purchase took place to the question of a name for the new ship. Over 180 names were suggested by OM workers, partners and supporters. A shortlist of the most suitable names was produced and *Logos Hope* won the day. For Bernd Gülker, the name combined 'powerful spiritual significance with our desire to make a real difference in people's lives'.[45] Thought was also being given and action being taken in respect of funding the new ship. Peter Maiden spoke of the need to see a significant increase in giving to the project in order to bring it to completion. By February 2004, $5 million had been raised. This was a result of a great deal of effort by fund-raisers. A further $4.5 million had been pledged. The total cost was estimated at $18 million – financially the largest project ever undertaken by OM. A new multi-media presentation had been developed in order to inform supporters about the project.[46]

Shipyard conversion work on the new ship – the rebuilding phase – took place in Trogir, Croatia. By the middle of 2007, about 80 per cent of the massive project budget for *Logos Hope* had been funded.[47] Mike Hey, the director of *Logos Hope*, was providing training for the emerging ship team. Meanwhile, *Logos II*, although reaching the end of its OM ministry, was still being fully utilised. Later in 2007, the *Logos II* team prepared for the huge step of transfer to the new and considerably larger ship. By the end of 2007, *Logos Hope* had moved from Croatia to Kiel, Germany, for the outfitting phase, which involved finishing cabins, offices and public ministry areas, installing furniture and a range of additional mechanical, electrical and information technology-related work. At the end of December 2007, in Kiel, the *Logos Hope* crew and staff, which comprised a three hundred-strong community, celebrated Christmas together for the first time.[48] A further dream was coming true.

Another new initiative in July was described as 'An OM ship on wheels.' It grew out of a new ministry, 'Transmission', developed as a partnership between OM Finland and OM in the Czech Republic, Hungary and Romania. The idea of this partnership was significant. OM Finland was a long-established part of OM, whereas the other three countries were relative newcomers. Finns first served in OM in 1965. Several thousand Finns served in OM for a summer, a year or longer, and in 2007 over thirty-five Finns were in different fields. Asko Alajoki and Kari Torma helped to shape OM Finland's mission 'to inspire and train Christians to go and to send others into world evangelisation'. BUS4LIFE, as the 'ship on wheels' was called, was being fitted out in Finland, would be based in Hungary and would travel in Central and Eastern Europe, showing movies, operating as a street café and carrying large quantities of literature.[49] The very heavy reliance of OM on vehicles in the early days had been completely overshadowed by the ships: hence the description of this vehicle – unthinkable in the early days of OM – as a 'ship on wheels'.

Although much attention was focused on *Logos Hope* in the period 2003–7, both *Logos II* and the *Doulos* continued to have a significant impact in many ports. In 2007, for example, *Logos II* made a historic visit to Libya, visiting two of the country's ports. In 2004, Daniel Chae from South Korea became *Doulos* director, and a year later the total number of visitors to the ship reached eighteen million. As one example of its impact, the *Doulos* visited Dublin in 2004, as the Evangelical Alliance was launched in the Republic of Ireland. A pre-launch dinner for 150 key leaders was held on board and eight hundred people attended the launch on shore. Mike Mullins, the OM Ireland leader, used this opportunity to encourage evangelicals in Ireland to be united 'and to have a voice to shape this nation'. The ship moved on to Northern Ireland, to the city Catholics call Derry and Protestants call Londonderry. Over thirty thousand visitors came on board, both Catholic and Protestant. John Hume, the 1998 Nobel Peace Prize winner, who was the guest of honour at the opening ceremony, said: 'The very fact that you can have under one roof people from virtually every country in the world is a magnificent symbol to the modern world.'[50]

Breaking down the barriers

In a letter he wrote in October 2006, George Verwer made an appeal to 'get involved in breaking down the barriers and praying for more workers'.[51] The context of the statement was a debate about 'parachurch organisations' and George Verwer saw a danger of new ecclesiastical barriers being erected between those who held different views about the place of such movements in Christian mission. He was responding to allegations that while the church was 'asleep and largely irrelevant' many Christians established these organisations and 'were inclined to desert the local church'.[52] The allegations were not new. In earlier eras and in other parts of the world, this kind of case had been presented. The response by George was robust and compelling. He argued that if such a view were to be adopted, many missional enterprises would be written off 'as second-class or worse', and he offered a long and impressive list of examples of what had been and was being done by such organisations.[53]

It is not surprising that George Verwer, as he looked back on the achievements of OM itself and many other agencies serving the churches – including the involvement of many of these agencies in massive church planting – found the arguments against such missional organisations unconvincing. Many in the mission world and in OM had in any case long questioned whether the division between church and parachurch had any convincing biblical basis. Over the course of fifty years, George and many colleagues in OM had been breaking down these and other unnecessary barriers. There were barriers that prevented young people taking responsibility. OM sought to take down those barriers. There were barriers that prevented people going to certain areas to serve. OM did not recognise those barriers as ultimate. There were racial barriers and those caused by inequality. All, in OM's view, had to go. It is not that OM always achieved freedom for all to serve in the way that they were gifted to do; the most obvious example of limitation had been a reluctance to give leadership to women. However, in many ways OM had been ahead of its time.

The story of OM is a story of change. One of the most significant changes, in the 1980s, was the change in attitude to finance. By the time *Logos Hope* was being bought, fund-raising, and in particular presentations to donors, had reached a level of sophistication that could not have been dreamed of – or, if it had, would have been repudiated – in the early decades. Another significant change was over property. For a long time no property was bought, but by 2006, when it was announced that OM had purchased a fifteen hectare (thirty-seven acre) farm for a conference and training project in Uruguay, few in OM would have known about the earlier rejection of such moves.[54] Another major change was that holistic ministry became much more central. OM also changed its policy over women in senior leadership. At the International Leaders Meeting held in South Africa in February 2006, the ILM (then about 150 senior leaders) voted to invite five women, serving in India, Malaysia, Turkey, Canada and Denmark, to join OM's International Executive Committee. The proposal was accepted, with only one or two dissenting. A few bloggers were upset by the fact that, as one of them put it, 'one more mission agency of evangelical commitments moved into the ranks of evangelical feminism': protest was suggested.[55]

There was little likelihood that protest about such changes would have much impact on OM, since the great strength of the movement was the way in which it had absorbed so many cultures and kept them together. This had been seen in the early days with Westerners and Indians. At a later stage the impact of the East Asians coming into the movement was huge. More recently the presence of Koreans, with Korea now the biggest field in the East Asia Pacific Area, has been very significant. In the period 2005–6, half of those joining OM were from Europe, one quarter from North America and one-sixth from Asia, but in terms of countries, South Korea came third (equal to the UK).[56] In 2007, there were 233 short- and long-term workers from Korea with OM, and many more had been involved short-term. It was recognised that in Korea, as elsewhere, ministry experience with OM had helped to shape international mission leaders.[57] Barriers were being broken down and new workers released.

Alongside the growth of OM outside the Western world, there was a renewed vision within OM for Europe-wide initiatives, especially given the new Europe where communist-constructed barriers between East and West had gone but new challenges were evident. Joop Strietmann, from the Netherlands, then Area

Coordinator for Northern Europe, gave a presentation to OM's International Leaders and Peter Maiden subsequently called the three European Area Coordinators to a meeting at Zaventem, asking each of them to bring at least one other key leader. In 2003 the group – Peter Maiden, Joop Strietman, Paul Stilli, Wim Goudzwaard, Thomas Bucher, Randy Lawler, Philipp Eschbach, Dane Hanson and Frank Hinkelmann – produced the Zaventem Declaration. This important statement, which was produced at a location that was very significant for OM, made a commitment to OM being involved, in partnership with European churches, in a number of areas. These included: 'on the job' training to reach the 'least reached', help plant churches and envision for mission; the creation of platforms enabling specific functions (such as training or ethnic outreach) to be developed; further study of holistic mission in Europe; and appropriate implementation arising from the study. OM's existing European ministries would be evaluated.[58]

The study produced a paper, 'Restoring Hope', which looked forward to what might happen in the period 2007–9. After a brief history of Christianity in Europe and an analysis of the continent's 'current spiritual climate', OM's role in Europe over fifty years was examined. OM now had seven hundred workers in twenty-seven countries in Europe. In most nations, teams were partnering closely with the national Evangelical Alliances and were committed to serving the local churches. The vision for the future was to focus on several major 'ministry streams': caring for the unwanted – those that society has forgotten, i.e. drug/alcohol addicts, prostitutes, Roma, street children, the homeless, orphans; sharing Jesus' love with Muslims; empowering the next generations and challenging the secular and reawakening the religious. This fuller document was signed by Thomas Bucher, Western Europe, Paul Stilli, Central Europe, and Wim Goudzwaard, North East Europe.[59]

With so many different OM initiatives, one important element in holding OM as a movement together was the stress on relationships. As well as close relationships between major leaders, OM's international conferences (from 2006 the name was International Forum), which included the official meeting of the General

Council, brought together the larger OM community on a regular basis. It is possible that in the future these relationships will be harder to maintain. Many early leaders shared experiences in India and on the ships, and this is no longer the case. The ships themselves offered amazing training in living together as a community. However, there are leaders within OM who are skilled in drawing people together, and the recent 'Joshua Initiative', which emphasises the development of younger and future leaders, is a healthy sign for the ministry of OM. A movement that is secure in terms of its past, flexible in its present ministry and open in terms of its future is in a healthy state.

Conclusion

This chapter has outlined the remarkable ministries of OM in the most recent period of the movement's history. There have been many examples of emerging mission, pioneering initiatives and holistic ministry. OM has been operating on a large scale. Under the leadership of Peter Maiden, there has been continuity in terms of OM's core values, coupled with the development of ministries in almost every sphere of OM's work. As has been the case over the past fifty years, there has been a desire to continue to focus on authentic discipleship as the key to spiritual transformation.

In earlier decades, a key element of the required reading list for those joining OM was William MacDonald's book, *True Discipleship*, but by 2007 this was largely unknown to younger OMers. But OM's commitment to 'true discipleship' remains. In 2007, an important book by Peter Maiden, *Discipleship*, was published, in which he argued for the continuing relevance of the 'demands of discipleship'. It is significant that a whole section, comprising seven chapters, examined what he called 'whole life discipleship'. It was this concept of discipleship as involving the totality of life that undergirded OM's stress on holistic mission. Chapters of the book that cover issues of discipleship in the community, spiritual disciplines, discipleship and mission, and 'Jesus: the reason for it all', witness powerfully to the centrality of spirituality in the life of OM's International Director and within the OM community. OM continues to be deeply rooted in the spiritual disciplines. In *Discipleship*, Peter Maiden spoke of a time when, with division threatening OM, he gave himself to a period of fasting, coming away from that time 'with a renewed sense of utter dependence on God for the solution'.[60] What OM leaders believed – in 2007 as in 1957 – was that to remain 'on the cutting edge' of mission was only possible through such dependence.

Epilogue

This Journey of Faith

With the ink still drying on the names of twenty-five students who signed the *Madrid Manifesto* of 1 November 1961, declaring 'the world is our goal ... no matter what the cost', God was taking them at their word. Today, Operation Mobilisation has 4,500 workers from ninety-five nations serving in more than one hundred countries. Once described as the 'best kept secret in missions',[1] a publicity-reticent OM has grown into one of the largest mission agencies in the world.

In the winter of 1963, when the first OM trucks drove across the frozen wastelands of eastern Turkey, Iran and Afghanistan and through the historic Khyber Pass on the overland trail from Brussels to Bombay, there was little idea of all that the Lord would do. As those first young OMers, Western and Indian, reached out with God's love to the poorest of the poor in the slums of Bombay and Calcutta, they could not have known that seeds of one of the greatest spiritual harvests in India's history were being sown. Today, hundreds of thousands of India's outcast Dalits are turning to faith in Christ.

In the 1960s, as clandestine OM gospel-posting teams walked the streets of Istanbul, often keeping just a few minutes ahead of pursuing Turkish police, some must surely have wondered if any fruit could come from this risky outreach. Other teams came alongside the few Turks who were coming to faith in Christ, to encourage and establish them in their new commitment. OM workers were frequently arrested by apologetic Turkish authorities, often unsure themselves of the laws governing the distribution of Christian literature. Few avoided at least brief spells in a Turkish jail. No one could have imagined that these young pioneers were, according to many modern mission analysts, actually laying the foundation for what is today's Turkish evangelical church.

High in the mountains of northern Iraq, on the border of Turkey, in bitter rain and snow, a small OM team brought food and blankets to thousands of homeless Kurdish refugees in March 1991. Families with tiny children and many old people were among those who had fled the terror of Saddam Hussein's army. As the OM team prayed and wept with those who were suffering, and despite the unceasing efforts of the team to provide emergency aid, people continued to die all around them, often from the freezing cold. Longing to do even more, the team could not have foreseen that their efforts would result in the founding of Operation Mercy, which has now grown to include relief work in Sudan, Afghanistan, Azerbaijan, Iraq, Jordan, Kazakhstan, Lebanon, Uzbekistan, Tajikistan and Yemen.[2]

On a grey overcast morning, 26 February 1971, amid doubts raised by some in the Christian press – 'The Gospel Blimp Sails Again!'[3] – MV *Logos* sailed slowly down the river Thames and out to the open sea, beginning her maiden voyage. Among the 130 people on board, there was great excitement and a profound sense of 'being part of something historic that God was doing'.[4] There were also some anxious fears. How many ports would welcome a Christian ship? Would the general public come on board? How long could this new vision last? One church leader grimly commented, 'I'll give the project a year!' Today, thirty-seven years later, as the much larger *Logos Hope* begins her maiden voyage, there are again some anxious fears. But there are also prayers of thanksgiving for the 37 million people who have now been on board the OM Ships in more than 140 nations, and for the tens of thousands who have come to faith in Christ.

Is there an echo of OM's original heartbeat still heard today as frontline teams, including the ships, seek to bring help and hope to a hurting world? Back in January 1959, in a report of a Christmas outreach to slum communities on the vast rubbish tip outside

Mexico City, George Verwer wrote: 'Praise God for the decisions that were made for Christ by the people who live on the garbage dump. What a blessed ministry we had out there.'[5] Almost fifty years later, in January 2007, a *Doulos* international concert was held near the infamous 'Smokey Mountain' garbage dump outside Manila in the Philippines. The ship journalist wrote: 'Before the show began crew-members played games with hundreds of children clamouring for their attention. Then as the daylight faded people crowded around the outdoor stage.' At the end of what must have been one of the ship's more unusual concerts, with a stinking rubbish tip as the backdrop, 'the Good News of Jesus Christ was then preached to one thousand people'.[6]

None of OM's front line activity is possible without armies of unsung heroes. Staff and volunteers throughout the movement's history have burned the midnight oil in OM offices around the world to keep the ministry advancing. The strategic vision of 'home offices' in places such as South Africa, South East Asia, Korea, Australasia, South America, Europe and North America, has multiplied the effectiveness of the work. Leadership from OM's national Boards of Directors has also played a significant role in guiding OM's growth and development. However, Peter Maiden, OM's International Director, says that 'ultimately, it is the sending churches, prayer partners, supporters and friends around the world who have walked this journey of faith with OM, from the earliest days, that has made all the difference'.[7]

Yet as the young and enthusiastic George Verwer, Dale Rhoton and Walter Borchard first handed out Gospels during the summer of 1957, they could little have dreamed that 120,000 young people from more than a hundred nations would eventually follow in their footsteps to become involved in mission training with OM. Using their college vacation for that first outreach, they could not have realised that missiologists would later describe this as a pioneering step in the birth of short-term missions. Nor could they have known that this would ultimately lead to more than one hundred million people being touched by the gospel through OM's ministry and to one of the largest Christian literature distribution programmes in history.

But there was no great scheme for the future when the three would-be missionaries and an old Dodge truck loaded with Gospels left Chicago, virtually unnoticed, fifty years ago. There was no thought of building a global mission agency, no idea of ships, and no strategy to mobilise tens of thousands into global missions. But clearly God had a wider design from the start and it is his sovereign purpose which has become OM's ongoing story.

OM is continually changing as new challenges and opportunities sometimes demand even greater steps of faith. What remains unchanged is an unshakable commitment to the gospel and to the sharing of God's love creatively and compassionately in some of the most unreached regions of the world. What has also not changed, from those early sleeping-on-the-floor OM conferences, is the core message of total commitment, 'living the life', and absolute dependence upon God's love, his grace and his leading. There still remains a strong sense that it is 'Not by might nor by power, but by my Spirit, says the Lord . . .'[8]

So, with today's OMers, many still in their teens, coming from every part of the world, and adding their signatures to the 'manifesto' of global mission, OM's extraordinary journey of faith and 'spiritual revolution' moves forward.

Peter Conlan
December 2007

Some Ministries Founded by Former OMers

Virgil Amos (USA) *Ambassadors Fellowship*
Federico & Marta Aparisi (Spain) *Camps*
Dave Armstrong (UK) *STV Videos*
Frank & Leena Arthur (Sweden) *Media Serve*
Terry Ascott (Cyprus) *SAT-7*
In-Sook Baek (Korea) *MK Nest*
Stephen Banna (India, Karnataka) *Hope Ministries*
Pepe & Judith Barrios (Mexico) *Radio, church planting*
George Baxter (UK) *Interaction*
Ron & Annabeth Beard (USA) *Alpha*
Yodhistir Behra (India, West Bengal) *First Generation Christians*
Federico Bertuzzi (Argentina) *Misiones Mundiales*
Ben Bester (South Africa) *Global Careers*
Narayan Bhagat (Nepal) *Handicapped Prayer Ministry*
Matthias Boerhoop (Netherlands) *Ministries Argentinas*
George & Alison Burch (Bulgaria) *Silk Road Institute*
Ken Burnett (UK) *Prayer for Israel*
David & Margaret Burt (Spain) *Grupos Biblicos Universitarios*
Pablo Carrillo (Spain) *PM International*
Steve Cassidy (USA) *Orphan's Hope*
Joseph Chacko (India, Goa) *Source of Life Ministries*
Sung-Chul Cho (Korea) *Coach Mission Fellowship*
Paul Choi (Korea) *Korea Harbor Evangelism*
Mike Evans (France) *Farel Publishing*
John Ferwerda (USA) *Middle East Media*

Ron George (UK) *People International* and *World in Need*
Jonathan Gilmore (Italy) *Fellowship of Evangelical Missionaries (FEMI)*
John Gladstone & Priscilla Gladstone (India, Mumbai) *Friendship Centre India*
Daniel Gonzalez (Spain) *Cursos Biblicos* and *Alturas*
Gopu (India, Chennai) *Elshadi*
Arunn Kumar Gundami (India, Karnataka) *Prayer Mobilisation*
Lars-Göran Gustafson (Sweden) *Business Aid* and *Knowledge for Life*
Nathan H. (India, West Bengal) *New Light*
Nick Hall (UK) *Kerygma Video Trust*
Sue Halstead (UK) *Love in Action*
Dave Hicks (USA) *AlongSideAsia*
Bob Hitching (UK) *Spear World In Need*
Mark Hopkins (UK & Nigeria) *Grace and Light*
Ed Hoyer (Canada) *Magazine*
D.B. Hrudaya (India, Orissa) *Orissa follow-up*
John & Pauline Hymus (UK) *Lingua Link*
B.D. Immanuel (India) *Karnataka Subhasamachara Mandali*
Kurt Jost (Italy) *Fellowship of Evangelical Missionaries (FEMI)*
C.M. Joy (India, Manipur) *The Harvest Team*
David Chul-Hwan Jun (Korea) *Friends of All Nations*
Vinod Kalpal (India, Karnataka) *Hungipanki Tribal Ministries*
Steve Kaptain (Nepal) *Christian Youth Connection Nepal*
George Khalil (Israel) *Bookshop*
Mobin Khan (USA) *International Outreach*
Jay & Jean Krause (USA) *MultiLanguage Media*
Greg Livingstone (USA, UK) *Frontiers*
Roger Malstead (UK) *Firm Foundation Trust*
Thomas Mathai (India, Kerala) *New Life Ministries/New Life Pubs*
Bob McCleod (Canada) *Media Matters*
Mike McKinley (USA) *Retreat and Training Center*
Mel & Sharon Middleton (Canada) *Freedom Quest*
George Miley (USA) *Antioch Network*
Stuart & Maureen Moreton (France) *Auto-Mission*

Bennie Mostert (South Africa) *Jericho Walls International*
Marsh Moyle (Slovakia) *Central European Mission Fellowship (CEMF)*
P. Mukherjee (India, Bhubaneshwar) *Care & Share*
Ric & Darlene Munro (Canada) *Aslan Video*
D. Naik (India, Orissa) *Gospel and Social Action Ministries*
Doug Nichols (USA) *Action International*
P.R Paricha (India, Kuttak) *Indian Evangelical Association*
Barnabas Soo-Jin Park (Korea) *Hannah International Mobilization*
Stuart & Verna Park (Spain) *Grupos Bíblicos Universitarios*
Patabpani (India, Bhubaneshwar) *Bisjyothi Ministries*
S. Patro (India) *Love Orissa*
Arul Paul (India, UP) *Medical Ambassadors*
Joseph Paul (India, Tamil Nadu) *Orphanage*
Trevor Penrose (UK) *Translation Trust*
Resham Raj Poudel (Nepal) *Nepal Gospel Outreach* and *Nepal Mission Society*
Norman & Debbie Przybylski (USA) *Elijah Company, Inc.*
Durai Raj and Muthan (India, Ootty) *Badga for Christ*
Graham & Frieda Roberts (Australia) *Equip & Encourage International*
Harley Rollins (USA) *Rollins Associates*
Bill Roop (Spain) *Doorway To Spain*
Sukrit Roy (India, Calcutta) *Christ Mission Ashram*
Mauricio Salazar (Belgium) *Coffee shop ministry*
Librado Salgado (Albania) *Church planting*
Thomas Samuel (India) *Quiet Corner Ministries*
Danny Smith (UK) *Jubilee Action and Jubilee Campaign*
Tiny Snell (Netherlands) *Stichting Hand*
A. Stephan (India) *Cornerstone World Challenge*
Heinz Strupler (Switzerland) *New Life International*
Viv Thomas (UK) *Formation*
Clive Thorne (UK) *Southampton Asian Christian Outreach*
Vijayakumar (India, Salem) *Salem Orphanage*
Bill & Tami Sue Webster (Canada) *Precision Media*
Chris Williams (India) *Love Maharashtra*

K.P. Yohannan (USA) *Gospel for Asia*
Paul Young (UK) *Off the Fence*
Hae-Seok Yu (Korea) *Fellowship for International Mission*

Notes

Pam Wilson and David Greenlee developed this list with help from many other OMers including Jonathan McRostie, Gary Sloan, Nora Norrish, Sue Priestley, Keith and Rita Haywood, and others from OM India and OM Ships.

A Selection of English Language Books about OM and/or Written by OMers

Arlene Adams, *Go East Young Man* (OM Greater Europe Team, 1998)

Richard Briggs, *Global Action: Personal Discipleship Manual for the World Christian* (Carlisle: Authentic Lifestyle, 1997)

Bill Drake, *Wear the Crown: Inspiring Stories of the Persecuted Church* (Bartlesville, OK: Genesis Publishing Group, 2006)

Joseph D'Souza, *Dalit Freedom* (Centennial, CO: Dalit Freedom Network, 2004)

Joseph D'Souza and Benedict Rogers, *On the Side of the Angels: Justice, Human Rights and Kingdom Mission is a New Call for Justice from the Christian Church* (Centennial, CO: Dalit Freedom Network, 2007)

David Greenlee, ed., *From the Straight Path to the Narrow Way: Journeys of Faith* (Waynesboro, GA: Authentic Media and Secunderabad, India: OM Books India, 2006)

David Greenlee, ed., *Global Passion* (Carlisle: Authentic Lifestyle and Secunderabad, India: OM Books, 2003)

David Greenlee, *One Cross, One Way, Many Journeys* (Atlanta, London, Hyderabad: Authentic Publishing, 2007)

David Hicks, *Globalizing Missions: The Operation Mobilization Experience* (Miami: Editorial Unilit, 1994)

Kathy Hicks, *Scaling the Wall* (Waynesboro, GA: Gabriel Publishing, 2003)

Rick and Kathy Hicks, *Boomers, Xers and Other Strangers: Understanding the Generational Differences that Divide Us* (Colorado Springs: Focus on the Family, 1999)

Rodney Hui, *Been There, Done That* (Carlisle: OM Publishing, 2000)

Rodney Hui, *Keep Going* (Milton Keynes: Authentic Media, 2004)

Lenna Lidstone, *You Will See Hoopoes* (Carlisle: Authentic Lifestyle, 2003)

David Lundy, *We are the World: Globalisation and the Changing Face of Mission* (Carlisle: OM Publishing, 1999)

William MacDonald, *True Discipleship* (Bromley: Send the Light, 1963)

Peter Maiden, *Discipleship* (Milton Keynes, Colorado Springs, Hyderabad: Authentic, 2007)

Peter Maiden, *Take my Plastic* (Carlisle: OM Publishing, 2003)

Deborah Meroff, *Riding the Storm* (London: Hodder & Stoughton, 1996)

Deborah Meroff, *The Touch of the Master* (Waynesboro, GA: OM Literature, 1998)

Deboroh Meroff, *True Grit: Women Taking on the World, for God's Sake* (Milton Keynes: Authentic Media, 2004)

George Miley, *Loving the Church ... Blessing the Nations* (Waynesboro, GA: Gabriel Publishing, 2003)

Elaine Rhoton, *The Logos Story* (Waynesboro, GA: OM LIT, 1992 [1988])

Elaine Rhoton, *The Doulos Story* (Milton Keynes: Authentic, 1997)

Brenda Ridpath, *From Little Acorns: A Tribute to Alf Ridpath* (privately published, 2007)

Chacko Thomas, *Heaven is Richer by Ten Lions* (London: OM, 2006)

Viv Thomas, *Future Leader* (Carlisle: Paternoster, 1999)

Viv Thomas, *Paper Boys* (Milton Keynes: Authentic Media, 2004)

Viv Thomas, *Second Choice* (Carlisle: Paternoster Press, 2000)

George Verwer, *The George Verwer Collection* (comprising *The Revolution of Love*, *No Turning Back* and *Hunger for Reality*) (Milton Keynes: Authentic Media, 1998)

George Verwer *Literature Evangelism* (Chicago: Moody Bible Institute, 1963)

George Verwer, *Out of the Comfort Zone* (Carlisle: OM Publishing, 2000)

George Verwer, *Revolution of Love and Balance* (Bromley: STL, 1980)

Michael Wakely, *Can it be True? A Personal Pilgrimage through Faith and Doubt* (Kregel Publications, 2004)

Michael Wakely, *Generosity: Big-heartedness as a Way of Life* (Leicester: Inter-Varsity Press, 2004)

Gary Witherall, *Total Abandon* (Carol Stream, IL: Tyndale House, 2005)

K.P. Yohannan, *Revolution in World Missions* (Carollton, TX: GFA books, 1986)

Notes

Preface

1 George Verwer, *Out of the Comfort Zone* (Carlisle: OM Publishing, 2000).
2 Scott Moreau, Harold Netland and Charles van Engen, *Evangelical Dictionary of World Missions* (Grand Rapids, Mich.: Baker Books, 2000).

Chapter One – Reckless Abandonment

1 The later version was: 'Let a thousand flowers bloom.'
2 William MacDonald, letter to the Board of Emmaus Bible School, not dated but 1960–1.
3 George Verwer, *Send the Light* (New Jersey: STL, 1960).
4 George Verwer has often pointed out that many reports wrongly state that this was a Billy Graham Crusade.
5 The letter enclosing the Gospel of John was from Daniel Clapp, dated 15 July 1953.
6 See J. A. Carpenter, ed., *The Youth for Christ Movement and its Pioneers* (New York: Garland, 1988).
7 I am indebted here to an interview with Walter Borchard on 28 February 2007.
8 Verwer, *Send the Light*, p. 1.
9 Dale Rhoton, foreword to George Verwer, *Out of the Comfort Zone* (Carlisle: OM Publishing, 2000), p. ix.
10 Rhoton, foreword to *Out of the Comfort Zone*, p. x.

11 Elisabeth Elliot, *Shadow of the Almighty* (San Francisco: HarperCollins, 1989 edition), pp. 43–6.
12 Loren Cunningham, *Is that Really You God?* (Seattle: YWAM, 1984), pp. 26, 38.
13 E. Elliot, *Through Gates of Splendor* (New York: Harper & Brothers, 1957).
14 William Martin, *The Billy Graham Story* (London: Hutchinson, 1992), p. 231.
15 *The Living Bible*, trans. Kenneth N. Taylor (Wheaton, Ill.: Tyndale House Publishers, 1971).
16 Verwer, *Send the Light*, p. 1.
17 Verwer, *Send the Light*, p. 1.
18 *Relay*, Vol. 2, No. 3 (1997), p. 6.
19 Interview with Walter Borchard.
20 G.M. Marsden, *Fundamentalism and American Culture: The Shaping of Twentieth-Century Evangelicalism, 1870-1925* (New York: OUP, 1980), especially pp. 176–195.
21 M. Silk, 'The Rise of the "New Evangelicalism": Shock and Adjustment', in W.R. Hutchison, ed., *Between the Times: The Travail of the Protestant Establishment, 1900-1960* (Cambridge: CUP, 1989), p. 280.
22 Oswald J Smith, *Passion for Souls* (London: Marshall, Morgan & Scott, 1950).
23 The Waorani were often referred to as the Auca – which in Quechua means savage.
24 Elizabeth Jean Snavely Holt, *From Chicago to the Ends of the Earth* (Farnborough: privately published, 2006/07), p. 33.
25 Letter to STL prayer partners, summer 1958.
26 Report in Jean (Hall) Davey files. I am indebted to Jean Davey for these files and for an interview held on 12 March 2007.
27 Verwer, *Send the Light*, p. 2.
28 George Verwer, 'Ten ingredients of Operation Mobilisation', video of message at Hollybush Christian Fellowship, 5 May 1996.
29 Letter to STL prayer partners, summer 1958.
30 I am grateful to Vera Zabramski for these tapes. Most of the messages are by George Verwer. One is by Billy Graham.
31 William MacDonald to the Board of Emmaus Bible School.
32 Notes from Jean (Hall) Davey.
33 Notes from Peter Conlan's OM conference notebook – summer 1965.

34 Jean Hall, December 1958.
35 Letter to STL prayer partners, summer 1958.
36 I am grateful to Greg Livingstone, e-mail, 9 July 2007.
37 Richard Griffin, in D. Greenlee, ed., *Global Passion* (Carlisle: Authentic Lifestyle, 2003), p. 202.
38 Verwer, *Send the Light*, p. 3.
39 Jean Hall, 'Diary of my first trip to Mexico', 20 December 1958.
40 Holt, 'From Chicago', p. 34.
41 William MacDonald to the Board of Emmaus Bible School. Nikita Krushchev was then the President of the USSR.
42 Stephen Neill, *A History of Christian Missions* (New York: Penguin, 1987), pp. 510–58.
43 Martin Robinson, *To Win the West* (Crowborough: Monarch, 1996), pp. 58–74.
44 John Miles, 'An Assessment of Short-Term Missions', MA, Birmingham Bible Institute. From the website of SEEDBED (http://www.seedbed.info/): published there by permission of the author ©2000 John Miles.
45 David Hicks, *Globalizing Missions: The Operation Mobilization Experience* (Miami: Editorial Unilit, 1994), p. 10.
46 *The Christian Herald*, 22 February 1964, p. 150.
47 George Verwer, *George Verwer's International Update* (Carlisle: Operation Mobilisation, 2003).
48 Verwer, *Send the Light*, p. 4.
49 William MacDonald to the Board of Emmaus Bible School.
50 Dale Rhoton, foreword to *Out of the Comfort Zone*, pp. x–xi.
51 Bertil Engqvist, 'Revolution of Love Discovered', in Greenlee, ed., *Global Passion*, pp. 136–7.
52 William MacDonald to the Board of Emmaus Bible School.
53 Verwer, *Send the Light*, p. 4.
54 Tim Grass, *Gathering to His Name* (Carlisle: Paternoster Press, 2006), p. 118.
55 Grass, *Gathering to His Name*, p. 214.
56 William MacDonald to the Board of Emmaus Bible School.
57 For more on the 'faith principle' see H.H. Rowdon, 'The Concept of "Living by Faith"', in A. Billington, A.N. Lane and M. Turner, eds, *Mission and Meaning: Essays presented to Peter Cotterell* (Carlisle: Paternoster, 1995), pp. 339–56; T. Larsen, '"Living by Faith": A short history of Brethren practice', *Brethren Archivists and Historians Network Review*, Vol. 1, No. 2 (1998), pp. 67–102.

58 N. Summerton, 'George Müller and the Financing of the Scriptural Knowledge Institution', in N.T.R. Dickson and T. Grass, eds, *The Growth of the Brethren Movement* (Carlisle: Paternoster, 2006), pp. 49–79.

59 T.A. Shaw and D.A. Clough, eds, *Amazing Faith* (Chicago: Moody Publishers, 2003), p. 139.

60 See interview with Drena Verwer, 27 September 2002, in Greenlee, ed., *Global Passion*, pp. xv–xviii.

61 Rhoton, foreword to *Out of the Comfort Zone*, p. x.

62 Prayer letters from the team in Monterrey, 6 June 1959 and 9 July 1959.

63 Interview with Walter Borchard. When Walter Borchard committed himself to social work, he encountered evangelicals who took the view that social ministry was a product of liberal theology.

64 Verwer, *Send the Light*, p. 4.

65 *Moody Memo*, 18 March 1960.

66 Interview with Jean Davey, 12 March 2007.

67 Billy Graham, *The Secret of Happiness* (New York: Doubleday, 1955).

68 STL prayer letters in 1959, particularly 9 July 1959.

69 *Uplook*, November–December 2005, p. 18.

70 Richard Tiplady, *World of Difference* (Carlisle: Paternoster, 2003), p. 110.

71 Ian Randall, 'A Missional Spirituality: Moravian Brethren and eighteenth-century English evangelicalism', *Transformation*, Vol. 23, No. 2 (2006), pp. 204–14.

72 See K. Fiedler, *The Story of Faith Missions* (Oxford: Regnum Books, 1994).

73 Tiplady, *World of Difference*, p. 110.

74 Dana Robert, *Occupy Until I Come* (Grand Rapids, Mich.: Eerdmans, 2003).

75 William MacDonald to the Board of Emmaus Bible School.

Chapter Two – A Revolution of Love

1 'What is Operation Mobilization?', published winter 1963–4.

2 George Verwer's *Literature Evangelism* (Chicago: Moody Bible Institute, 1963) is a unique manual.

3 *A Dios por La Ciencia* (Barcelona: Lumen, 1941).

4   Confidential report by George Verwer included in a letter of 19 November 1960 from Jean Hall.

5   Elizabeth Jean Snavely Holt, 'From Chicago to the Ends of the Earth' (Farnborough, 2006/07), p. 41.

6   George Verwer, *Miracles in Spain* (STL, 1961); Thomas Samuel, *Operation Mobilisation* (Bombay: PAC Printers, 1965).

7   Interview with Jean (Hall) Davey on 12 March 2007.

8   George Verwer to Prayer Partners, 12 November 1960.

9   Jean Hall to Prayer Partners, 19 November 1960.

10 George Verwer report, 25 August 1961; George Verwer to Prayer Partners, 13 September 1961.

11 Billy Graham, *Peace with God* (New York, Doubleday, 1953).

12 George Verwer to Prayer Partners, 25 October 1961. Christa Fischer married Ray Eicher.

13 Interview with Jean Davey.

14 Letter from Mike McKinley, 1 June 1998.

15 Holt, 'From Chicago', pp. 43–5; information from Jean Davey.

16 Papers of Mary Lee and Albert Edward Bobby – Billy Graham Center, Wheaton College, Ill., USA. Collection 171.

17 George Verwer report, 25 August 1961.

18 George Verwer to Prayer Partners, 19 November 1960.

19 George Verwer, 'Report of my short trip to Europe', January 1967.

20 I am greatly indebted here and elsewhere to an interview with George Verwer, 29 June 2007.

21 T.A. Shaw and D.A. Clough, eds, *Amazing Faith* (Chicago: Moody Publishers, 2003), p. 139.

22 George Verwer, Letter to Prayer Partners, 2 August 1961.

23 George Verwer to Prayer Partners, 1 September 1961.

24 Shaw and Clough, eds, *Amazing Faith*, p. 141.

25 George Verwer to Prayer Partners, 1 September 1961.

26 Roger Malstead, interviewed by Paul Ericksen in 1986. Billy Graham Center, Wheaton. Collection 337.

27 *International Herald Tribune*, 22 November 1961.

28 Roger Malstead, interviewed by Paul Ericksen in 1986.

29 Interview with George Verwer, 29 June 2007.

30 Mike McKinley, 'Laborers into His Harvest' (unpublished paper, 1989).

31 'The Madrid Manifesto', 1 November 1961.

32 *The Christian*, 29 June 1962, p. 5.

33 *The Christian*, 2 March 1962, p. 1.

34 George Verwer, Letter to Prayer Partners, 1 January 1962.

35 George Verwer, Letter to Prayer Partners, 2 March 1962.

36 For information in this paragraph I am indebted to the interview with George Verwer, 29 June 2007.

37 See Roger Shuff, *Searching for the True Church: Brethren and Evangelicals in Mid-Twentieth-Century England* (Carlisle: Paternoster, 2005), p. 217.

38 Interview with George Verwer, 29 June 2007.

39 Alec Bracket did this work for forty years.

40 *A Short History of Operation Mobilisation* (Send the Light, 1984), p. 5.

41 George Verwer, 'Leaders' Letter', c. early 1963.

42 *A Short History of Operation Mobilisation* (1984), p. 6.

43 George Verwer, 'Leaders' Letter', c. early 1963.

44 See, for example, *Specific Preparation Pamphlet for Summer Crusades* (c. 1960), p. 1.

45 'Europe Mobilises', in *A Brief History of Operation Mobilisation* (1984).

46 *Christian Life*, August 1963, p. 18.

47 'What is Operation Mobilization?', 1963–4.

48 Greg Livingstone, e-mail, 9 July 2007.

49 Interview with George Verwer, 29 June 2007.

50 Howard Norrish, in 'History of OM – Middle East and North Africa'. I am grateful to Peter Ferguson for this.

51 George Verwer, Letter to Prayer Partners, Winter 1963.

52 'What is Operation Mobilization?', 1963–4.

53 *Operation Mobilisation in the Muslim Middle East* (Zaventem: OM, 1968), pp. 16–17.

54 Interview with Jean (Hall) Davey.

55 Jean Walker, Diary of a summer in Spain.

56 Some of her diary was published: Jean Walker, 'Excerpts from a Pioneer's Diary', 4 July to 27 August 1963, in *Keswick '07*, p. 52.

57 I am indebted to Peter Conlan for this observation.

58 'What is Operation Mobilization?', 1963–4.

59 I am indebted to Birgitta Conlan for this section: e-mail 9 August 2007.

60 Gerry and Jean Davey to Prayer Partners, September 1965.

61 Howard Norrish, 'The Development of a Tentmaking Ethos in Operation Mobilisation', in D. Greenlee, ed., *Global Passion* (Carlisle: Authentic Lifestyle, 2003), pp. 124–35.

62 John Watts, Prayer Letter, December 1966.
63 Stephen C. Hart, 'The Early History of S.T.L.' (1993).
64 Keith Beckwith, Prayer Letter, 14 December 1966.
65 Jonathan McRostie, 'Suffering and Missions', in Greenlee, ed., *Global Passion*, p. 60.
66 George Verwer, 'Report of my short trip to Europe', January 1967.
67 *Moorlands Message*, Spring 1967.
68 Interview with Gerry Davey on 12 March 2007.
69 Jonathan McRostie to Prayer Partners, report on 1966–7.
70 George Verwer, 'Special letter to all Americans', 13 August 1964.
71 Greg Livingstone, 'Does it Work?', in *Stepping Out, A Guide to Short-Term Missions* (Seattle: YWAM Publishing, 1992), p. 24.
72 Jonathan McRostie to Prayer Partners, report on 1966–7.
73 McRostie, 'Suffering and Missions', in Greenlee, ed., *Global Passion*, pp. 66–7.
74 Peter Conlan, 'Incurable Fanatic – Unshakeable Friend', in Greenlee, ed., *Global Passion*, pp. 193–4.
75 William MacDonald, *True Discipleship* (Bromley: Send the Light, 1963), p. 7.
76 'Operation Mobilisation Strategy for the Summer of 1964' (Winter 1963).
77 'A Glance Back – A Leap Forward' (OM: 1967), pp. 13–14.
78 P. Hocken, *Streams of Renewal: The Origins and Early Development of the Charismatic Movement in Britain* (Carlisle: Paternoster Press, 1997), p. 108.
79 George Verwer, *Extremism* (Bombay: Thomas Samuel [1964]), p. 1; interview with Gerge Verwer, 17 July 2007.
80 Verwer, *Extremism*, pp. 2–5.
81 Verwer, *Extremism*, pp. 5–11.
82 'Discipleship Manual' (OM: 1963, many printings), pp. 32–3.
83 Verwer, *Extremism*, pp. 11–25.
84 George Verwer, Letter, mid-1960s.
85 Foreword, William MacDonald, *True Discipleship*.
86 George Verwer, Letter to OMers, 'Fellow nobodies', 24 August 1964.
87 Roy Hession, *The Calvary Road* (Fort Washington, Pa.: Christian Literature Crusade, 1950).
88 I am indebted to Peter Maiden for this point, one that he would take up later in OM's story.
89 Verwer, *Extremism*, p. 25.

90 George Verwer, 'More questions answered concerning Operation Mobilisation' (1963), p. 20.

Chapter Three – Go East

1 O.M. *India News*, December–January, 1993–4, p. 8. (This was the 30th Anniversary issue and it was republished in England in 1993).

2 David Lundy, *We are the World* (Carlisle: OM Publishing, 1999), p. 72.

3 Regina Alexander, *The OM India Story* (Lucknow, 1989), p. 3. I am indebted to Ray Eicher for this history, which he edited.

4 It was publicised in India in an article 'Miracles in Europe', *Information Bulletin*, No. 33, 1963, pp. 1–5. The *Bulletin* is issued quarterly by Bharat Khristya Sahitya Sangh, Evangelical Literature Fellowship India.

5 Thomas Samuel, 'Preparing for Ministry', in *A Vision worth Living For* (1975), pp. 40–1.

6 Alexander, *The OM India Story*, p. 3.

7 Thomas Samuel, 'I Saw God at Work', *Information Bulletin*, No. 35, December 1963, p. 3.

8 I am indebted to Frank Dietz, a member of the first team that went to India, for help with this section: e-mail, 10 February 2007.

9 I am indebted to Marcus Chacko, 'A Study of the Paradigm Shifts of Operation Mobilisation, India, 1964–1994', Union Biblical Seminary, Bibvewadi, Pune, Maharashtra, MDiv (1997). See pp. 18–19.

10 Alexander, *The OM India Story*, p. 4.

11 Frank Dietz, e-mail, 10 February 2007.

12 Alexander, *The OM India Story*, p. 5.

13 Lundy, *We are the World*, p. 72.

14 Frank Dietz, e-mail, 10 February 2007.

15 Alexander, *The OM India Story*, pp. 5–6.

16 O.M. *India News*, December–January, 1993–4, p.8.

17 George Verwer, 'Leaders Memo', Bombay (1964); 'George Verwer, Personal Confidential Observations', 3 April 1964. I am grateful to Mike Wiltshire for this material.

18 For Bakht Singh see T.E. Koshy, *Brother Bakht Singh of India* (Secunderabad: OM Books, 2003).

19 For Norman Grubb see N. Grubb, *Once Caught, No Escape* (London; Lutterworth Press, 1969); cf. Ian Randall, *Entire Devotion to*

God (Ilkeston: Wesley Fellowship, 1998). WEC at that time stood for Worldwide Evangelisation Crusade.

20 Koshy, *Brother Bakht Singh*, p. 502: citing interview with George Verwer, 1991.

21 Thomas Samuel, 'Pioneering Operation Mobilisation in India', in *A Vision worth Living For* (1975), p. 45.

22 Alexander, *The OM India Story*, pp. 6–7.

23 I am indebted for these observations to Peterson Anand, who served with OM until 1989.

24 Ray Eicher, e-mail, 21 November 2007.

25 Alexander, *The OM India Story*, pp. 10–15.

26 Chacko, 'A Study of the Paradigm Shifts of Operation Mobilisation, India, 1964–1994', p. 19.

27 Alexander, *The OM India Story*, pp. 8–9.

28 *OM News*, Spring 1977, p. 1; For the history of Christianity in India see Cyril Bruce Firth, *An Introduction to Indian Church History* (Delhi: ISPCK, 2005, rev. ed.); Mark T.B. Laing, ed., *The Indian Church in Context: Her Emergence, Growth and Mission* (Delhi: CMS/ISPCK, 2003).

29 Interview with George Verwer, 29 June 2007.

30 Chacko, 'A Study of the Paradigm Shifts of Operation Mobilisation, India, 1964–1994', p. 45. The name of the OMer is not given.

31 Thomas Samuel, 'Pioneering Operation Mobilisation in India', in *A Vision worth Living For* (1975), pp. 46–8.

32 *Spiritual Revolution* [hereafter *SR*], No. 12 (1966).

33 *SR*, No. 15 (1967).

34 *SR*, No. 25 (1968).

35 *SR*, No. 26 (1968).

36 Alfy Franks, *Brief History of Operation Mobilisation India* (2002).

37 *SR*, No. 26 (1969). Italics as in the original.

38 *Hebron Messenger*, 25 April 1965, cited in Koshy, *Bakht Singh*, p. 503.

39 *SR*, No. 26 (1969).

40 Koshy, *Bakht Singh*, pp. 503–8, citing interview with George Verwer, 1991.

41 Koshy, *Bakht Singh*, p. 510.

42 *SR*, No. 26 (1969).

43 Franks, *Brief History of Operation Mobilisation India* (2002).

44 Greg Livingstone, in D. Greenlee, ed., *Global Passion* (Carlisle: Authentic Lifestyle, 2003), pp. 204–5.

45 Thomas Samuel, 'Pioneering Operation Mobilisation in India', in *A Vision worth Living For* (1975), p. 48.

46 K.P. Yohannan, *Revolution in World Missions* (Corrollton, TX: gfa books, 1986), p. 27; dedication.

47 Frank Dietz, e-mail, 10 May 2007.

48 I am grateful to Mike Wiltshire for this information: interview on 3 July 2007.

49 George Verwer, Letter of December 1966 'O.M.'s recent problem with the Customs Office in Bombay'.

50 'Send the Light', 13 December 1966.

51 Gorge Verwer, Letter dated March 1967.

52 Alexander, *The OM India Story*, pp. 29–30.

53 Alexander, *The OM India Story*, p. 31.

54 Interview with George Verwer and Peter Conlan, 29 June 2007.

55 Franks, *Brief History of Operation Mobilisation India* (2002).

56 M. Wakely, 'Shadows of Doubt', *Evangelical Missions Quarterly*, Vol. 39, No. 4 (October 2003), p. 468.

57 Franks, *Brief History of Operation Mobilisation India* (2002).

58 Alexander, *The OM India Story*, pp. 21, 24.

59 Alfy Franks, e-mail, 10 May 2007.

60 Alexander, *The OM India Story*, pp. 30–1.

61 Yohannan, *Revolution in World Missions*, p. 26.

62 Chacko, 'A Study of the Paradigm Shifts of Operation Mobilisation, India, 1964–1994', pp. 25–6.

63 Yohannan, *Revolution in World Missions*, p. 29.

64 Lundy, *We are the World*, pp. xi–xiii; Alexander, 'The OM India Story', pp. 22–3. The details vary a little in the two accounts.

65 Alexander, *The OM India Story*, pp. 34–6.

66 This was reported by Mr Ghulam Rasool Bhatt, whom Marcus Chacko visited in 1983.

67 Chacko, 'A Study of the Paradigm Shifts of Operation Mobilisation, India, 1964–1994', p. 27.

68 Lundy, *We are the World*, pp. xiii–xiv.

69 *A Closer Look at OM India* (OM India, 1992), p. 5.

Chapter Four – A Lot of Ship

1 *MV Logos: The Miracle Ship* (Bombay: OM, not dated), p. 2.

2 Elaine Rhoton, *The Logos Story* (Waynesboro, GA: OM LIT, 1992 [1988]), p. 14.

3   Frank Dietz, e-mail, 10 May 2007.
4   See Brenda Ridpath, *From Little Acorns: A Tribute to Alf Ridpath* (privately published, 2007).
5   Rhoton, *The Logos Story*, p. 15.
6   George Miley, *OM Ships - History* (Mosbach, Germany: OM Ships, 1982), p. 1.
7   Graham Scott and George Verwer, *The Need for an Ocean Going Ship for World Evangelism* (Bolton: OM, 1966).
8   Rhoton, *The Logos Story*, pp. 19–22.
9   Miley, *OM Ships - History*, p. 2.
10 Rhoton, *The Logos Story*, pp. 22–3.
11 Alfy Franks, *Brief History of Operation Mobilisation India* (2002).
12 Rhoton, *The Logos Story*, p. 23.
13 Rhoton, *The Logos Story*, pp. 24–6.
14 *MV Logos: The Miracle Ship*, p. 3.
15 *MV Logos: The Miracle Ship*, p. 3.
16 Rhoton, *The Logos Story*, pp. 28–30 and chapter 4.
17 Rhoton, *The Logos Story*, pp. 49–50.
18 Taking cameras on trips, as if OMers were tourists, was forbidden under OM rules at the time.
19 George Verwer to OM leaders, 3 June 1969 (from Bromley, Kent).
20 Rhoton, *The Logos Story*, chapter 5.
21 Scott and Verwer, *The Need for an Ocean Going Ship*, p. 1.
22 George Verwer, 'Life on the "Logos"' (OM, 1971), p. 1.
23 *MV Logos: The Miracle Ship*, pp. 5–10.
24 Rhoton, *The Logos Story*, pp. 63–70.
25 Miley, *OM Ships - History*, p. 3.
26 Regina Alexander, 'The OM India Story' (Lucknow, 1989), p. 38.
27 Mike Wiltshire, 'The Educational Ship Logos in Bombay', 10 October 1971.
28 Rhoton, *The Logos Story*, pp. 79–82.
29 Miley, *OM Ships - History*, p. 4.
30 George Verwer, 'The Visit of M/V Logos to Indonesia' (Bolton: OM, 1972).
31 Rhoton, *The Logos Story*, pp. 84–6.
32 Peter Conlan had returned to the ship from completing an Outward Bound course in the USA. George Verwer immediately saw the possibilities for a parallel spiritual course.
33 Frank Dietz, e-mail, 22 May 2007.

34   George Verwer, 'A Second Ship?', written in 1973 and included in a newsletter of April 1975.
35   Rhoton, *The Logos Story*, pp. 37–8.
36   Miley, *OM Ships - History*, p. 5.
37   Rhoton, *The Logos Story*, pp. 100–4.
38   Verwer, 'Life on the "Logos"', p. 3.
39   Miley, *OM Ships - History*, pp. 5, 6.
40   Verwer, 'Life on the "Logos"', pp. 3–4.
41   Rhoton, *The Logos Story*, p. 105.
42   George Verwer, 'The Visit of M/V Logos to Indonesia', pp. 3–5.
43   I am indebted to an e-mail from Kamal Fahmi, 4 February 2007.
44   I am grateful to Mike Stachura and John Lewis for this information. For subsequent developments see chapter 10 below.
45   Verwer, 'A Second Ship?', pp. 3–4.
46   'International Ship Letter', 25 November 1972.
47   *The Ship 'Logos' – Break-throughs in Bombay* (January–February, 1973).
48   'International Ship Report', 13 March 1973.
49   *Ethiopian Herald*, 26 October 1973.
50   Rhoton, *The Logos Story*, p. 131.
51   *OM News*, spring 1977, p. 1.
52   'Freetown Report', February 1977.
53   'Ship Ministry Weekly Report', 1 March 1977.
54   Allan Adams, 'Can Hurting People be Fruitful Missionaries', in D. Greenlee, ed., *Global Passion* (Carlisle: Authentic Lifestyle, 2003), p. 50.
55   See David Hicks, *Globalizing Missions: The Operation Mobilization Experience* (Miami: Editorial Unilit, 1994).
56   See Rodney Hui, *Been There, Done That* (Carlisle: OM Publishing, 2000).
57   I am grateful to Rodney Hui, e-mail, 16 March 2007.
58   Scott and Verwer, *The Need for an Ocean Going Ship for World Evangelism*.
59   Rhoton, *The Logos Story*, p. 105.
60   Rhoton, *The Logos Story*, chapters 11 and 13.
61   Patrick Johnstone and Jason Mandryk, *Operation World* (Carlisle: Paternoster Lifestyle, 2001), pp. x–xi.
62   Miley, *OM Ships - History*, pp. 21–2.
63   Elaine Rhoton, *The Doulos Story* (Milton Keynes: Authentic, 1997), pp. 4–6.

64   Verwer, 'A Second Ship?' (April 1975), pp. 1–3.
65   Miley, *OM Ships - History*, pp. 12–13.
66   Rhoton, *The Doulos Story*, pp. 7–8.
67   Verwer, 'A Second Ship?' (April 1975), pp. 3–7.
68   http://www.freewebz.com/iasmm/newsletter.html, accessed 17 July
     2007; Peter Conlan, e-mail, 9 August 2007.
69   Verwer, 'A Second Ship?' (April 1975), pp. 7–8.
70   Miley, *OM Ships - History*, pp. 18–19.
71   Rhoton, *The Logos Story*, 'Facts and Figures'.
72   *A Brief History of Operation Mobilisation* (Send the Light, 1984),
     p.14.
73   Rhoton, *The Logos Story* - sub title.

Chapter Five – Spirit-Controlled Expansion

1   Letter from George Verwer, 25 April 1971.
2   Letter from George Verwer, 'Third Decade Memo', March 1975.
3   Regina Alexander, *The OM India Story* (Lucknow, 1989), p. 39.
4   Thomas Samuel, 'Pioneering Operation Mobilisation in India', in
     A Vision worth Living For (1975), pp. 40–1.
5   Alexander, *The OM India Story*, p. 39.
6   Marcus 'A Study of the Paradigm Shifts of Operation Mobilisation,
     India, 1964–1994', Union Biblical Seminary, Bibvewadi, Pune,
     Maharashtra, MDiv (1997), p. 31.
7   George Verwer, 'Some informal reflections on the urgency of our sit-
     uation in India' (c.1969).
8   Thomas Samuel, 'Pioneering Operation Mobilisation in India', in
     A Vision worth Living For (1975), pp. 48–55.
9   Alfy Franks, e-mail, 14 May 2007.
10   All of this is drawn from Alfy Franks, *Brief History of Operation
     Mobilisation India* (2002).
11   *Spiritual Revolution*, January 1975, pp. 2–5.
12   I am grateful to K.P. for information in an e-mail of 1 August 2007
     and a subsequent telephone conversation.
13   Letter from George Verwer, 'Third Decade Memo', March 1975.
14   Alexander, *The OM India Story*, pp. 33–4.
15   David Lundy, *We are the World* (Carlisle: OM Publishing, 1999), p.
     68. David Lundy suggested that OM's statement about this involved
     a judging of nationals as less spiritually mature.

16 Conversation with George Verwer, 17 July 2007.

17 Alexander, *The OM India Story*, pp. 40–1.

18 Lundy, *We are the World*, p. 75.

19 Chacko, 'A Study of the Paradigm Shifts of Operation Mobilisation, India, 1964–1994', p. 31.

20 Alexander, *The OM India Story*, pp. 43–4.

21 Alexander, *The OM India Story*, pp. 28–9.

22 Letter from George Verwer, 25 April 1971.

23 *A Short History of Operation Mobilisation* (Send the Light, 1984), p. 10.

24 Letter from George Verwer, 25 April 1971.

25 I am indebted to Jonathan McRostie for this information.

26 Minutes of 'Bolton '72', 4 May 1972.

27 D. Johnson, *Contending for the Faith* (Leicester: , 1979), p. 245.

28 Tim Robson and Nigel Lee, Letter to Prayer Partners, April 1972.

29 Letter to OM prayer partners, 'Operation Impossible', April 1972.

30 'British Monthly Report (OM)', January 1973.

31 'International Monthly Report (OM)', January 1973; 'Matters for Prayer', 1974–1975.

32 'News from Europe', 18 January 1977.

33 Interview: Peter and Win Maiden and Peter and Birgitta Conlan, 9 March 2007.

34 William Farel was a leading sixteenth-century Reformer who worked with John Calvin in Geneva.

35 Interview with Gerry Davey on 12 March 2007; *OM News*, Spring 1977, p. 4.

36 Richard Wurmbrand to Peter Conlan, 29 June 1983. Richard Wurmbrand told his story in *Tortured for Christ* (1967).

37 I am grateful to Dale and John Hymus for their help regarding these developments.

38 Arlene Adams, *Go East Young Man* (OM Greater Europe Team, 1998), chapters 1–4 and pp. 32–4; John , e-mail, 26 June 2007.

39 This story is told in Pentti Heinilä, *Streng Vertraulich* (2003). One of the problems was how to replace the weight of the literature that was removed so that the truck would have the same weight on departure from the country.

40 Adams, *Go East Young Man*, pp. 28–9. Another mission attempted this and twenty Romanians working with them were caught and put in prison.

41 Adams, *Go East Young Man*, pp. 30–2.

42   *A Short History of Operation Mobilisation* (STL, 1984), pp. 12–13.
43   Letter from George Verwer, 25 April 1971.
44   Their names have been changed.
45   'History of OM – Middle East and North Africa'.
46   Greg Livingstone, e-mail, 9 July 2007.
47   I am grateful to Terry and to Mark Vanderhoven for the material which they sent me.
48   'Matters for Prayer', 1974–1975.
49   *A Short History of Operation Mobilisation*, p. 8.
50   'The Call of Iran' (Zaventem: OM, 1974).
51   I am grateful to Julyan Lidstone, e-mail, 22 August 2007.
52   Regina Alexander, *The OM India Story* (Lucknow, 1989).
53   I am indebted to Mike for his help: e-mail, 23 July 2007; *ServingTogether*, June 2005, pp. 4–5.
54   The Leadership Manual (OM, 1975), pp. 9–10.
55   The Leadership Manual, p. 43.
56   George Verwer, 'Special Memo for all Offices', reprint, September 1975. This memo covered many aspects of OM administration.
57   George Verwer, 'Thoughts on why we should not get involved in buying property' (1975), pp. 3–4.
58   Interview with George Verwer, 29 June 2007.
59   George Verwer, 'Thoughts on why we should not get involved in buying property', p. 6.
60   Greg Livingstone, e-mail, 9 July 2007. 'Frontiers' grew to be a mission with over a thousand long-term missionaries serving among Muslims in many countries.
61   'Introducing Peter Maiden', Operation Mobilisation information sheet (2003).
62   Notes of London Bible College Faculty Meeting, 9 December 1964. London Bible College is now the London School of Theology.
63   See, for example, Bill Musk, *Kissing Cousins? Christians and Muslims Face to Face* (Oxford: Monarch Books, 2005).
64   Ian Randall, *Educating Evangelicalism: The Origins, Development and Impact of London Bible College* (Carlisle: Paternoster Press, 2000), pp. 184–5.
65   See T. Chester, *Awakening to a World of Need* (Leicester: Inter-Varsity Press, 1993), p. 23.
66   *Christianity Today*, 15 March 1974, pp. 12–16.
67   *The Leadership Manual*, p. 29.

68 Peter Conlan, 'Potential Dangers in the OM set up' (Kathmandu, Nepal, 1968).

69 'Finances', September 1975.

70 *Witness*, October 1966, p. 372.

71 Tim Grass, *Gathering to his Name* (Carlisle: Paternoster, 2006), p. 494.

72 *The Leadership Manual*, p. 50.

73 Charles Price and Ian Randall, *Transforming Keswick* (Carlisle: Paternoster/OM, 2000), chapter 6.

74 Patrick Johnstone, *Operation World*, the 1978 edition had been produced (Milton Keynes: Authentic, 2001).

75 Dale Rhoton, *The Logic of Faith* (STL, 1978).

76 Ralph Shallis, *From Now On* (STL, 1979).

77 Letter from George Verwer to OM workers, 11 November 1978.

78 Conversation with George Verwer, 17 July 2007. Martyn Lloyd-Jones was opposed to tapes of his sermons being distributed but made an exception in this case. Tony Sargent was minister of the Worthing Tabernacle in the south of England and then Principal of the International Christian College, Glasgow. He wrote *The Sacred Anointing: The Preaching of Dr Martyn Lloyd-Jones* (London: Hodder & Stoughton, 1994).

79 Letter from George Verwer to OM workers, 11 November 1978.

80 George Verwer, *Revolution of Love and Balance* (Bromley: STL, 1980), was published later.

81 All of this is in George Verwer, 'Third Decade Memo', March 1975.

82 I am indebted to Peter Conlan for this thought.

Chapter Six – The Enormous Value of Teamwork

1 George Miley, *OM Ships – History* (Mosbach, Germany: OM Ships, 1982), p. 19.

2 Elaine Rhoton, *The Doulos Story* (Milton Keynes: Authentic, 1997), pp. 10, 20.

3 Miley, *OM Ships – History*, pp. 19–20.

4 Rhoton, *The Doulos Story*, pp. 14–17.

5 Miley, *OM Ships – History*, pp. 19–21.

6 For this story see David Martin, *Tongues of Fire: The Explosion of Protestantism in Latin America* (Oxford: Blackwell, 1993).

7 Rhoton, *The Doulos Story*, pp. 33–4, 41; Miley, *OM Ships – History*, pp. 21–3.
8 I am grateful to David Greenlee for information in this section.
9 David Greenlee, 'Cookbooks, Firemen, Jazz Musicians and Dairy Farmers', in D. Greenlee, ed., *Global Passion* (Carlisle: Authentic Lifestyle, 2003), p. 163.
10 Rhoton, *The Doulos Story*, pp. 46–54; Frank Dietz, e-mail, 12 July 2007. Norman Lewis, author of *Priority One* (1988), told Frank Dietz that Protestant missionaries in Argentina had not moved the Latin American Church one iota towards missions.
11 Rhoton, *The Doulos Story*, chapters 6 and 7.
12 Miley, *OM Ships – History*, pp. 25–6.
13 Rhoton, *The Doulos Story*, p. 98.
14 See Kyung Hwan (Barnabas) Kim, 'The MV Doulos Training: An Alternative Model for Ministry Preparation', Columbia International University, DMin (2004), pp. 27–9.
15 Rhoton, *The Doulos Story*, chapter 8; Allan Adams, e-mail, 7 June 2007.
16 Chacko Thomas, *Heaven is Richer by Ten Lions* (London: OM, 2006), pp. 58–9.
17 David Greenlee, in Rhoton, *The Doulos Story*, chapter 8.
18 Miley, *OM Ships – History*, p. 22.
19 Decio de Carvalho was the nephew of the Decio de Carvalho who was on the *Logos*.
20 I am grateful to Frank Dietz for details; see T.M. Johnson and S.S. Kim, 'Describing the Worldwide Christian Phenomenon', *International Bulletin of Missionary Research*, Vol. 24, No. 2 (2005), pp. 80–4.
21 Miley, *OM Ships – History*, p. 23.
22 For Love Europe and TeenStreet see chapters 7 and 9 below.
23 I am indebted to Bernd Gülker for this section. Mosbach is near Heidelberg.
24 Miley, *OM Ships – History*, p. 24–7.
25 Peter Conlan, 'China Report', 13 March 1980.
26 Peter Conlan, 'Confidential Report', March 1980. Wong Ming Dao is also known as Wang Mingdao.
27 Peter Conlan, 'Glimpses from China', *Gateway*, summer 1981, p. 5.
28 Go Teg Chin and Peter Conlan, 'China Report', 2 February 1981.
29 *Gateway*, summer 1981, pp. 2–3.
30 *Crusade*, December 1981, p. 39.

31 *Gateway*, summer 1981, p. 5.
32 Elaine Rhoton, *The Logos Story* (Waynesboro, GA: OM LIT, 1992 [1988]), p. 151.
33 Allan Adams, 'Logos Port Report', 12 May 1982.
34 Rhoton, *The Logos Story*, pp. 155–6.
35 Rhoton, *The Logos Story*, chapter 15; Conversation with Lloyd Nicholas, 30 June 2007.
36 *Crusade*, December 1981, p. 39; Notes on Special China Mini-Consultation, 29 October 1982.
37 See D. Aikman, *Jesus in Beijing: How Christianity is Transforming China and Changing the Global Balance of Power* (Washington, DC: Regnery Publishing, 2003). David Aikman, a former senior foreign correspondent for *Time* magazine who has covered China for over thirty years, predicts huge growth in China's Christian population.
38 Miley, *OM Ships – History*, p. 23.
39 Rhoton, *The Doulos Story*, p. 157.
40 David Greenlee, 'International Update', May 2007.
41 Rhoton, *The Doulos Story*, pp. 162–5.
42 Dale Rhoton, 'God's Faithfulness', in Greenlee, ed., *Global Passion*, p. 43.
43 Peter Conlan, e-mail 18 July 2007.
44 I am indebted to David Greenlee for his help with this section.
45 Rhoton, *The Doulos Story*, pp. 165–7.
46 *Stories from Italy* (1986).
47 Frank Dietz, 'Latin America', 22 April 2005.
48 Humberto Aragão, 'Leading under Risk of Failure', in Greenlee, ed., *Global Passion*, p. 79.
49 Frank Dietz, 'Latin America', 22 April 2005.
50 I am grateful to Vera Zambramski for supplying me with this tape.
51 George Verwer, *Out of the Comfort Zone* (Carlisle: OM Publishing, 2000), pp. 114–15, 127.
52 T.A. Shaw and D.A. Clough, eds, *Amazing Faith* (Chicago: Moody Publishers, 2003), pp. 144–5.
53 Allan Adams, e-mail, 8 June 2007.
54 Interview with George Verwer, 29 June 2007.
55 Rhoton, *The Doulos Story*, pp. 169–72.
56 Rhoton, *The Doulos Story*, chapter 10.
57 Greenlee, 'Cookbooks, Firemen, Jazz Musicians and Dairy Farmers', p. 166; David Greenlee, *One Cross, One Way, Many*

Journeys (Atlanta, London, Hyderabad: Authentic Publishing, 2007), pp. 15–16

58 Rhoton, *The Doulos Story*, pp. 178–80.

59 Rhoton, *The Doulos Story*, chapter 11.

60 The Leadership Manual, p. 20.

61 Interview with George Verwer, 29 June 2007.

62 George Miley, 'Mobilizing Churches for Frontier Missions', *International Journal of Frontier Missions*, Vol. 11, No. 3 (1994), p. 157.

63 For more see George Miley, *Loving the Church...Blessing the Nations* (Waynesboro, GA: Gabriel Publishing, 2003).

64 David Greenlee, e-mail, 2 January 2007.

65 *South Africa Dry Dock*, November 1986; Rhoton, *The Doulos Story*, p. 190.

66 See Peter Tarantal, 'The Place of Networks in World Evangelization', in Greenlee, ed., *Global Passion*.

67 *Doulos & Logos: 1987 at a Glance*, p. 2.

68 Allan Adams, e-mail, 8 June 2007; Rhoton, *The Doulos Story*, pp. 240–7.

69 *Doulos & Logos: 1987 at a Glance*, p. 5.

70 Rhoton, *The Doulos Story*, pp. 247–54.

71 Rodney Hui, *Been There, Done That* (Carlisle: OM Publishing, 2000), p. 100.

72 The Princess had recently completed a doctoral degree in Development Education.

73 Rhoton, *The Doulos Story*, pp. 254–9.

74 Rhoton, *The Doulos Story*, pp. 302–4.

75 Rhoton, *The Logos Story*, chapter 16.

76 'Ship Data' (*Antonio Lázaro*), 1968.

Chapter Seven – Trusted and Appreciated

1 Nigel Lee, 'European Summer Campaigns', 27 August 1986.

2 George Verwer, 'Communist Lands', March 1981.

3 Nigel Lee, 'European Summer Campaigns', 27 August 1986.

4 For the beginnings of the movement in Britain see Peter Hocken, *Streams of Renewal* (Carlisle: Paternoster Press, 1997).

5 Nigel Lee, 'European Summer Campaigns', 27 August 1986.

6 Ian Randall and David Hilborn, *One Body in Christ: The History and Significance of the Evangelical Alliance* (Carlisle: Paternoster Press, 2001), chapter 12.

7 *Idea*, summer 1985, p. 3.

8 Ian Randall, *The English Baptists of the Twentieth Century* (Didcot: Baptist Historical Society, 2005), chapter 10.

9 Nigel Lee, 'European Summer Campaigns', 27 August 1986.

10 Frank Fortunato, 'Worship and Mission', in D. Greenlee, ed., *Global Passion* (Carlisle: Authentic Lifestyle, 2003), pp. 20–9. See also Frank Fortunato, Paul Neeley, and Carol Brinneman, *All the World is Singing: Glorifying God through the Worship Music of the Nations* (Atlanta, GA: Authentic, 2006).

11 Nigel Lee, 'European Summer Campaigns', 27 August 1986.

12 Peter Conlan, 'Love Europe', September 1986.

13 Peter Conlan, 'Love Europe Distinctives', paper for Field Leaders' meetings, 1986.

14 For the development of Frontiers see www.frontiers.org

15 Peter Conlan, 'Love Europe Distinctives', paper for Field Leaders' meetings, 1986.

16 Peter Maiden, restricted memo, 18 September 1987.

17 Stuart McAllister, 'Love Europe', autumn 1987.

18 George Verwer, 'Our greatest step of faith since launching the MV Doulos', undated; *Love Europe News*, October 1989.

19 George Verwer, 'Middle East Report', March 1981.

20 Lenna Lidstone, *You Will See Hoopoes* (Carlisle: Authentic Lifestyle, 2003), chapters 8 and 9.

21 Lidstone, *You Will See Hoopoes*, pp. 59–60.

22 Julyan Lidstone, e-mail, 8 August 2007.

23 George Verwer, 'Middle East Report', March 1981.

24 Grace Ferguson, 'Keeping on for the long haul', in Greenlee, ed., *Global Passion*, pp. 3–10.

25 Kamal Fahmi, e-mail, 17 March 2007.

26 David Greenlee, e-mail, 2 January 2007.

27 Howard Norrish, 'The Development of a Tentmaking Ethos in Operation Mobilisation', in Greenlee, ed., *Global Passion*, pp. 126–9, 134.

28 J. Christy Wilson, *Today's Tentmakers* (Wheaton Ill.: Tyndale, 1979).

29 Norrish, 'The Development of a Tentmaking Ethos in Operation Mobilisation', pp. 133–4; I am grateful to Roger Malstead and Gordon Magney for help with the details.

30 Arlene Adams, *Go East Young Man* (OM Greater Europe Team, 1998), pp. 35–9.

31 Rodney Hui, e-mail, 28 March 2007. For Rodney Hui see his *Been There Done That* (Carlisle: OM Publishing, 2000).

32 *Love Europe News*, October 1989.

33 Alfy Franks, *Brief History of Operation Mobilisation India* (2002).

34 Regina Alexander, *The OM India Story* (Lucknow, 1989), p. 39.

35 Alfy Franks, *Brief History of Operation Mobilisation India* (2002).

36 David Lundy, *We are the World* (Carlisle: OM Publishing, 1999), pp. 75–6.

37 Joseph D'Souza, 'A flaw in recruiting strategy?', *Evangelical Missions Quarterly*, Vol. 36, No. 2 (2000), p. 156.

38 Lundy, *We are the World*, pp. 78–9.

39 David Lundy, *Servant Leadership for Slow Learners* (Carlisle: Authentic Lifestyle: 2002), pp. 67–8.

40 See Juliet Thomas, 'Intercession' in Greenlee, ed., *Global Passion*, pp. 30–7.

41 David Hicks, *Globalizing Missions: The Operation Mobilization Experience* (Miami: Editorial Unilit, 1994), pp. 25, 29.

42 Alfy Franks, *Brief History of Operation Mobilisation India* (2002).

43 Lundy, *We are the World*, pp. 1–2, from *OM News India*, summer 1996, p. 4.

44 I am grateful to Gerry Davey for this information. $4m was (at that time) £2,300,000.

45 Dave Brown, 'STL: Report for 1980', April 1981.

46 George Verwer, 'Special Communication to all OM Leaders', 28 April 1981.

47 Papers regarding the Leadership Conferences are held by Peter Conlan.

48 George Verwer, 'How the work of Operation Mobilisation is coordinated', May 1984.

49 Jonathan McRostie, 'Suffering and Mission', in Greenlee, ed., *Global Passion*, pp. 61–8.

50 *Operation Mobilisation Policy Manual* (1985).

51 'Introducing Peter Maiden', OM, 2002.

52 Interview: Peter and Win Maiden and Peter and Birgitta Conlan, 9 March 2007.

53 For his thinking see Viv Thomas, *Future Leader* (Carlisle: Paternoster, 1999).
54 David Greenlee, e-mail, 22 August 2007.
55 Hicks, *Globalizing Missions*, pp. 24–9.
56 George Verwer, *No Turning Back* (Carlisle: OM Publishing, 1983), pp. 20–1.
57 See Ian Randall, *What a Friend we have in Jesus* (London: DLT, 2005), chapter 7.
58 Richard Foster, *Celebration of Discipline* (San Francisco: Harper and Row, 1978).
59 Verwer, *No Turning Back*, chapters 6 and 10.
60 George Verwer, 'Special Communication to all OM Leaders', 28 April 1981.
61 Lundy, *Servant Leadership for Slow Learners*, p. 43.
62 George Verwer, 'How the work of Operation Mobilisation is coordinated', May 1984.
63 Allan Adams, e-mail, 8 June 2007. See his essay, 'Pastoral care issue for short-termers in mission', (1997), accessed 8 June 2007.
64 Charismatic Working Group, Report, 1988.
65 George Verwer, 'The Lordship of Christ', in Greenlee, ed., *Global Passion*, pp. xxi–xxix.
66 Verwer, *No Turning Back*, Dedication.
67 David Greenlee, e-mail, 23 November 2006.
68 J.E. Plueddemann, 'Theological Implications of Globalizing Missions', in C. Ott and H.A. Netland, eds, *Globalizing Theology: Belief and Practice in an Era of World Christianity* (Grand Rapids, Mich.: Baker, 2006), p. 253.
69 *Love Europe News*, October 1989.
70 Hicks, *Globalizing Missions*, p. 32.
71 George Verwer, 'The Lordship of Christ', in Greenlee, ed., *Global Passion*, p. Xxix.

Chapter Eight – A Thoroughly Global Organisation

1 David Hicks, *Globalizing Missions: The Operation Mobilization Experience* (Miami: Editorial Unilit, 1994), pp. 6–7.
2 David Lundy, *We are the World* (Carlisle: OM Publishing, 1999), pp. 142–3.

3   See for example Larry D. Pate and Lawrence E. Keyes, 'Emerging Missions in a Global Church', *International Bulletin of Missionary Research* (October 1986), pp. 156–61.

4   Samuel Escobar, 'The elements of style in crafting new international mission leaders', *Evangelical Missions Quarterly*, Vol. 28 (January 1992), pp. 6–15.

5   Hicks, *Globalizing Missions*, pp. 15–19.

6   Minutes of the OM Field Leaders' Meetings, Hyderabad, India, 25–31 January 1993.

7   Hicks, *Globalizing Missions*, p. 19.

8   Lundy, *We are the World*, pp. 142–3.

9   Hicks, *Globalizing Missions*, pp. 20–2.

10 George Verwer, 'Leaders' Letter', 9 May 1994.

11 Peter Maiden, 15 November 1994, cited in Lundy, *We are the World*, p. 169.

12 Hicks, *Globalizing Missions*, pp. 24–5.

13 David Greenlee, e-mail, 15 June 2007.

14 Lundy, *We are the World*, pp. 131–2.

15 Bernd Gülker, e-mail, 17 July 2007.

16 Hicks, *Globalizing Missions*, p. 27.

17 Interview with Peter Conlan and Mike Lyth, 3 July 2007.

18 'Forward to 2001: A Plan for the Future of OM' (1994), pp. 1–14.

19 George Verwer, 'Leaders' Letter', Autumn 1995.

20 'Ship Ministry News', August 1991; Elaine Rhoton, *The Doulos Story* (Milton Keynes: Authentic, 1997), chapters 19–21.

21 Rhoton, *The Doulos Story*, pp. 376–7.

22 Bernard Lewis, 'The Roots of Muslim Rage', *The Atlantic Monthly*, September 1990.

23 Samuel P. Huntington, 'The Clash of Civilisations', *Foreign Affairs*, Summer 1993.

24 Samuel P. Huntington, *The Clash of Civilizations and the Remaking of World Order* (London: Simon and Schuster, 1996).

25 George Verwer, 'Leaders' Letter', 9 May 1994.

26 I am grateful to Carol Ann Poynor at Mosbach for this report and other documents.

27 David Greenlee, 'Setting the Sails for the New Millenium: A Study of the Impact of the Ministries of OM Ships' (Carlisle: OM, 1999), p. 84.

28 George Verwer, 'Urgent communication to OM leaders worldwide', May 1996.

29 Rodney Hui, *Been There, Done That* (Carlisle: OM Publishing, 2000), p. 7.
30 Marlieske Smilde, 'Port Report', Shanghai, China, 24–30 July 1996.
31 Sarah Schafer, 'Onward Christian Soldiers', *Newsweek*, 10 May 2007, citing a volume edited by Daniel Bays, of Calvin College, Michigan, USA, *Christianity in China: From the Eighteenth Century to the Present* (1996).
32 'Port Report', Shanghai, China, 24–30 July 1996.
33 Arlene Adams, *Go East Young Man* (OM Greater Europe Team, 1998), chapters 8–11.
34 Mike Stachura, 'Seven Principles for Highly Effective Short-Term Missions', *East-West Church & Ministry Report* published through Samford University & Beeson School of Divinity in Birmingham, Alabama. For more see www.samford.edu/groups/global/index.html.
35 Debbie Meroff, '*Logos II* Port Report', 1990; Ronnie Lappin, e-mail, 7 July 2007.
36 Deanna Ricketts, '*Doulos* Port Report', 1992; Elaine Rhoton, *The Doulos Story* (Milton Keynes: Authentic, 1997), chapter 18.
37 Lenna Lidstone, *You Will See Hoopoes* (Carlisle: OM Publishing, 2000), pp. 95–105.
38 I am indebted to Julyan Lidstone for information in this section, e-mail, 22 August 2007.
39 Lidstone, *You Will See Hoopoes*, pp. 135–41.
40 I am indebted to Julyan Lidstone for information in this section, e-mail, 22 August 2007.
41 Debbie Meroff, *Riding the Storm* (London: Hodder & Stoughton, 1996), pp. 103–5.
42 Edith Carter, 'Port Report', Riga, Latvia, 24–30 May 1995.
43 I am indebted to Gerry Davey for an interview on 12 March 2007 and to information from EELAC.
44 Keith Danby, 'The STL Story, 1987–2007' (2007).
45 Lidstone, *You Will See Hoopoes*, chapter 12.
46 He was later to become International Director of Arab World Ministries.
47 Lundy, *We are the World*, p. 61.
48 Alfy Franks, *Brief History of Operation Mobilisation India* (2002); Lundy, *We are the World*, p. 76.
49 Lundy, *We are the World*, pp. 79–80.
50 Greenlee, 'Setting the Sails for the New Millenium', p. 27.

51 I am grateful to Carol Ann Poynor at Mosbach for this report.

52 Marlieske Smilde, 'Port Report', Toamasina, Madagascar, 29 November–5 December 1995.

53 See, for example, Kelly O'Donnell, *Missionary Care: Counting the Cost for World Evangelization* (Pasadena: William Carey Library, 1992).

54 One contribution was by David Greenlee and Yong Joong Cho, 'The Potential and Pitfalls of Multicultural Mission Teams', *International Journal of Frontier Missions*, Vol. 12 (1995), pp. 179–83.

55 See Allan Adams' essay, 'Pastoral care issues for short-termers in mission' (1997), accessed 8 June 2007, www.eihc.org/pastoral .pdf.

56 Greenlee, 'Setting the Sails for the New Millenium', p. 109.

57 George Verwer, 'International Leaders' Letter', mid-February 1995. See Charles Swindoll, *The Grace Awakening* (Dallas: Word Publishing, 1990).

58 George Verwer, 'Leaders' Letter', 9 May 1994.

59 'Forward to 2001', p. 62.

60 George Verwer, 'International Leaders' Letter', mid-February 1995.

61 See Lundy, *We are the World*, p. 21.

62 See http://www.briercrest.ca/, accessed 15 January 2007.

63 Alfy Franks, *Brief History of Operation Mobilisation India* (2002)

64 http://www.usa.om.org/omindia/partnership.htm, accessed 20 June 2007.

65 Vivian Thomas, 'Growing Leaders for 2020', in D. Greenlee, ed., *Global Passion* (Carlisle: Authentic Lifestyle, 2003), pp. 84–5.

66 George Verwer, 'End of Year Leaders' Letter', 20 December 1994.

67 Peter Maiden, 'OM in the 1990s' (undated).

68 In some cases cultural sensitivities were in operation. But in India, for example, the nation was willing to accept female political leadership.

69 George Verwer, 'International Leaders' Letter', mid-February 1995.

70 See Keith Jones, 'The European Baptist Federation: A Case Study in Baptist Interdependency, 1950–2006', University of Wales PhD thesis (2007).

71 For a fuller list see the Appendix.

72 Hicks, *Globalizing Missions*, pp. 32–3.

73 George Verwer, 'Spring Leaders' Letter', April 1996.

74 Peter Maiden, 'OM in the 1990s' (undated).

75 George Verwer, 'New Year Leaders' Letter', January 1994.

76 Lundy, *We are the World*, pp. 103–4.

77 David Greenlee, e-mail, 23 November 2006.

Chapter Nine – Transforming Lives and Communities

1   Information from Global Action literature. The categories of Global Service and Global Challenge (very short term) followed.
2   George Verwer, 'International Leaders' Letter', March 1997.
3   George Verwer, 'End of Year Leaders' Letter', December 1997.
4   For the DFN see www.dalitnetwork.org.
5   Benedict Rogers, 'The "Untouchables": The Human Face of India's Caste System', *Crisis*, 7 May 2007.
6   For theological reflection on transformation, see David Greenlee, *One Cross, One Way, Many Journeys* (Atlanta, London, Hyderabad: Authentic Publishing, 2007), chapter 9, and footnotes to the chapter.
7   For an introduction, see Joseph D'Souza, *Dalit Freedom* (Centennial, CO: Dalit Freedom Network, 2004), chapter 33. See also Joseph D'Souza and Benedict Rogers, *On the Side of the Angels: Justice, Human Rights and Kingdom Mission* (Centennial, CO: Dalit Freedom Network, 2007).
8   See the AICC: http://www.aiccindia.org, accessed 4 July 2007.
9   See *New York Times*, 29 January 1999.
10   AICC documents: http://www.aiccindia.org/newsite/0804061910/aboutus.asp, accessed 4 July 2007.
11   Rogers, 'The "Untouchables": The Human Face of India's Caste System', 7 May 2007.
12   Joseph D'Souza, 'Foreword', Udit Raj, *Dalit and Religious Freedom* (New Delhi: Justice Publications, 2005).
13   Rogers, 'The "Untouchables": The Human Face of India's Caste System', 7 May 2007.
14   D'Souza, *Dalit Freedom*, pp. 70–1.
15   Rogers, 'The "Untouchables": The Human Face of India's Caste System', 7 May 2007.
16   *Christian Century*, 5 December 2001.
17   Rogers, 'The "Untouchables": The Human Face of India's Caste System', 7 May 2007.
18   *Mission Frontiers*, 4 March 1999.
19   Alfy Franks, e-mail, 8 January 2007.
20   For this section I am indebted to Joseph D'Souza, 'Good Shepherd Community Church Movement' (2004).
21   K. Lajja, e-mail, 2 September 2007.
22   I am grateful to Alfy Franks for this information.

23 'OM Annual Report', 2003.
24 See http://www.dalitchild.com/php/faqslist.php, accessed 4 July 2007.
25 Rebecca Barnhart, 'Albania and the Balkans' (OM Report, 2005); Dane Hanson, e-mail, 17 July 2007.
26 Rebecca Barnhart, 'Bosnia-Hercegovina' (OM Report, 2006). Field Leader – Annelea Blignaut.
27 Rebecca Barnhart, 'Kosovo' (OM Report, 2005).
28 Rebecca Barnhart, 'Moldova' (OM Report, 2005).
29 Jonathan McRostie, e-mail, 7 August 2007.
30 Lisa Howard, 'Ukraine' (OM Report, 2007).
31 Kamal Fahmi, e-mails, 19 January and 4 February 2007.
32 Port Report, 'Bahrain and the Yemen', May 1998.
33 Julyan Lidstone, e-mail, 9 August 2007.
34 George Verwer, *Out of the Comfort Zone* (Carlisle: OM Publishing, 2000), chapter 5.
35 Rodney Hui, e-mail, 16 March 2007.
36 Peter Tarantal, 'The Place of Networks in World Evangelization: A Southern African Perspective', in D. Greenlee, ed., *Global Passion* (Carlisle: Authentic Lifestyle, 2003).
37 Jonathan McRostie, e-mail, 7 August 2007.
38 'OM Southern Africa Report', Autumn 2002.
39 George Verwer, 'End of Year Leaders' Letter', December 1997.
40 David Lundy, *We are the World*, p. 5.
41 George Verwer, *Out of the Comfort Zone*, chapter 5.
42 George Verwer, 'End of Year Leaders' Letter', December 1998.
43 George Verwer, 'End of Year Leaders' Letter', December 1997.
44 George Verwer, 'End of Year Leaders' Letter', December 1998.
45 Lloyd Nicholas, 'The Greening of OM Ships' (OM, 1997).
46 George Verwer, 'Spring Leaders' Letter', 19 May 1999.
47 George Verwer, 'International Leaders' Letter', September 1999.
48 George Verwer, 'Leaders' Letter', September 1998.
49 For Bill Drake see www.billdrake.com/meetbill.htm.
50 George Verwer, 'Leaders' Letter', 16 July 2002.
51 Martin Bateman, e-mail, 19 July 2007.
52 George Verwer, 'Leaders' Letter', 16 July 2002.
53 See http://www.starfishasia.com/who.htm, accessed 9 July 2007.
54 '*Logos II* Port Report', Acapulco, Mexico, 15 October–11 November 1997.

55 David Greenlee, 'Setting the Sails for the New Millenium: A Study of the Impact of the Ministries of OM Ships' (Carlisle: OM, 1999), p. 26.

56 Steve Browne, '*Doulos* Port Report', Yangon, Myanmar, 11–16 December 1998.

57 Bernd Gülker, 'Ship Report', 1999, De Bron.

58 Laura Luce, '*Doulos* Port Report', Bougainville Island, Papua New Guinea, 16–21 September 1999.

59 Marlieske Smilde, '*Doulos* Port Report', Nanjing, China, 19–24 October 2000.

60 Megan Jones, '*Logos II* Port Report', Monrovia, Liberia, 25 February–2 March 2000.

61 Paul Beck, '*Doulos* Port Report', Ho Chi Minh City, Vietnam, 22 February–2 March, 2001.

62 Lane Powell and Debbie Meroff, 'Ray Lentzsch: God's Gospel Globetrotter', *Lausanne World Pulse*, 7 June 2002.

63 George Verwer 'Leaders' Letter', 16 July 2002.

64 Bernd Gülker, 'Leadership Letter', November 1997.

65 Bernd Gülker, 'Anticipating the Future for OM SHIPS: Purpose Driven Ships' (2000); 'Into the future with Purpose Driven Ships' (2001).

66 I am indebted to Lloyd Nicholas for this information: conversation, 9 July 2007.

67 Bernd Gülker, 'The Next Ship', *Relay*, July 2002.

68 George Verwer 'Leaders' Letter', 16 July 2002.

69 David Greenlee, 'Setting the Sails', pp. 87–8. This section of the study was limited to looking at fund donors.

70 George Verwer, *Out of the Comfort Zone* (Carlisle: OM Publishing, 2000), chapter 1, referring to Charles Swindoll, *The Grace Awakening* (Dallas: Word Publishing, 1990), Roy Hession, *The Calvary Road* (Fort Washington, Pa.: Christian Literature Crusade, 1950), and Philip Yancey, *What's So Amazing about Grace?* (Grand Rapids: Zondervan, 1997).

71 Verwer, *Out of the Comfort Zone*, pp. 24–6.

72 William MacDonald, *True Discipleship* (Bromley: Send the Light, 1963).

73 I am grateful to Peter Maiden for a summary of this address.

74 Verwer, *Out of the Comfort Zone*, p. 55.

75 Viv Thomas, *Future Leader* (Carlisle: Paternoster Press, 1999), chapter 16.

76 Deborah Meroff, *True Grit: Women Taking on the World, for God's Sake* (Milton Keynes: Authentic Media, 2004), chapter 4.
77 Gary Witherall, *Total Abandon* (Carol Stream, ILL: Tyndale House, 2005), chapters 4–8.
78 Witherall, *Total Abandon*, p. 107.
79 *Mission Frontiers*, November–December 1994.
80 George Verwer, 'End of Year Leaders' Letter', December 1998.
81 George Verwer, 'End of Year Leaders' Letter', 22 December 1999.
82 Rodney Hui, e-mail, 16 March 2007.

Chapter Ten – On the Cutting Edge

1 *Mission Network News*, 12 August 2003.
2 Drena Verwer, in D. Greenlee, ed., *Global Passion* (Carlisle: Authentic Lifestyle, 2003), p. xviii.
3 Peter Maiden, 'A remarkable year' (2004).
4 See Dana L. Robert, 'Shifting Southward: Global Christianity since 1945', *International Bulletin of Missionary Research*, Vol. 24, No. 2 (2000), pp. 50–8.
5 Peter Maiden, 'Introduction to OM Annual Report, 2005'.
6 Julio Moromisato, OM Brazil Field Leader, e-mail, 26 July 2007.
7 Debbie Meroff, 'Giant Steps for Brazil', 2003.
8 Eddie Gibbs and Ryan Bolger, in *Emerging Churches: Creating Christian communities in Postmodern Cultures* (London: SPCK, 2006).
9 'Transforming lives and communities', OM Annual Report, 2006.
10 Peter Maiden, 'OM International Update', July 2007.
11 Peter Maiden, 'OM International Updates', June and July 2007; David Greenlee, e-mail, 11 July 2007.
12 'Transforming lives and communities' – 'Europe'.
13 Peter Maiden, 'OM International Update', October 2006.
14 In 2000 Michal and Martina, who were then working for the Klet Observatory in Czech Republic, discovered a minor planet in the asteroid belt between Mars and Jupiter. Their request to name it 'Jerusalem' was approved by the International Astronomical Union. See http://www.klet.org/?stranka=discoveries&menu_id=7& uroven=2, accessed 10 July 2007.
15 Rebecca Barnhart, 'TeenStreet Central Europe Breaking Ground' (2005).
16 See http://www1.teenstreet.om.org, accessed 7 July 2007.

17 Viv Thomas, 'Growing Leaders for 2020', in Greenlee, ed., *Global Passion*, pp. 84–91. For Viv Thomas on spirituality and spiritual formation, see his *Paper Boys* (Milton Keynes: Authentic Media, 2004).

18 Peter Maiden, 'OM International Update', March 2005.

19 Rebecca Barnhart, OM Report, 'KidsGames' (2003).

20 'OM Annual Report', 2003.

21 'Transforming lives and communities' – Pioneering Initiatives.

22 'OM Annual Report', 2003.

23 Peter Maiden, 'International Update', March 2005.

24 'OM Ministry Focus: HIV/AIDS', May 2005; P. Dixon, *AIDS and You* (Eastbourne: Kingsway, 1989).

25 George , 'Seven People Lying at the Side of the Road' (2006): http://www.georgeverwer.com/sevenPeople.php, accessed 7 July 2007.

26 Jean Garland, and Mike Blyth, *AIDS is real and it's in our church* (Nigeria: Africa Christian Textbooks, 2003, republished 2005).

27 Rosemary Hack, 'Help and Hope in India', *STL Missions News*, February 2007.

28 Shirley Booth, e-mail, 4 July 2007.

29 Kathy Hicks, *Scaling the Wall* (Waynesboro, GA: Gabriel Publishing, 2003).

30 'Transforming lives and communities' – 'Resourcing'.

31 Keith Danby, 'The STL Story, 1987–2007' (unpublished paper, 2007).

32 'OM Annual Report', 2003.

33 Peter Maiden, 'OM International Update', September 2006.

34 Peter Maiden, 'OM International Update', May 2005.

35 David Kerrigan, Director for Mission, BMS World Mission, e-mail, 20 August 2007.

36 Peter Maiden, 'OM International Update', May 2005.

37 Letter to Peter Conlan from Prime Minister Mahinda Rajapaksa, 10 June 2005.

38 *Mission Network News*, 16 February 2005.

39 George Verwer, 'Seven People Lying at the Side of the Road' (2006): http://www.georgeverwer.com/sevenPeople.php, accessed 7 July 2007.

40 'Transforming Lives and Communities' – 'Relief and Development'.

41 'Transforming Lives and Communities' – 'Resourcing'.

42 Peter Maiden, 'OM International Update', July 2007.

43 Bernd Gülker, 'Charting the Course', Prayer Day, 28 March 2004.

44 Peter Maiden, 'OM International Update', May 2004.

45 *Mission Network News*, 6 February 2004.
46 *Mission Network News*, 28 March 2003.
47 Peter Maiden, 'OM International Update', June 2007.
48 http://www.logoshope.org/, accessed 1 January 2008.
49 Peter Maiden, 'OM International Update', July 2007.
50 I am grateful to Carol Ann Poynor for this report.
51 George Verwer, 'Denominations or Denominationalism?', *Mission Mobilisation Network*, October 2006.
52 *Newfrontiers*, Vol. 2 Issue 14 (2006), pp. 3–11.
53 George Verwer, 'Denominations or Denominationalism?', *Mission Mobilisation Network*, October 2006.
54 Peter Maiden, 'OM International Update', July 2007.
55 See http://www.tbayly.wordpress.com, accessed 8 July 2007.
56 David Greenlee, 'Why Did I Join OM? Influential Recruiting Tools, Personal Motives to Join and Hopes of New OM Workers', 7 April 2006.
57 I am indebted to Steve Moon, Director, Korea Research Institute for Missions, for his comments: e-mail, 1 July 2007. At the end of 2006 the statistics held by the Research Institute recorded 166 Koreans serving long-term with OM. I am also indebted to Jihan Paik, e-mail, 14 August 2007.
58 'Zaventem Declaration', 16 April 2003.
59 'Restoring Hope'. I am indebted to Goudzwaard for this paper: e-mail, 15 July 2007.
60 Peter Maiden, *Discipleship* (Milton Keynes, Colorado Springs, Hyderabad: Authentic, 2007), p. 142.

Epilogue – This Journey of Faith

1 Rev Dr Stuart Briscoe, Pastor Emeritus, Elmbrook Church, Brookfield, USA, has often used this phrase.
2 Julyan Lidstone, June 2007.
3 David Winter, *Crusade* magazine, August 1970. David later graciously published a revised opinion after visiting the ship.
4 Interview with Mike Wiltshire, 10 July 2007.
5 George , 'Report from New Jersey', January 1959.
6 I am indebted to Ken Miller at the Ships HQ for locating the *Doulos* reports for January 2007.
7 Interview with Peter Maiden, 4 July 2007
8 Zechariah 4:6

Index